In Pursuit of Utopia

IN PURSUIT OF UTOPIA

*Los Angeles
in the Great Depression*

ERROL WAYNE STEVENS

UNIVERSITY OF OKLAHOMA PRESS : NORMAN

Library of Congress Cataloging-in-Publication Data

Names: Stevens, Errol Wayne, author.
Title: In pursuit of Utopia : Los Angeles in the Great Depression / Errol Wayne Stevens.
Description: Norman : University of Oklahoma Press, [2021] | Includes bibliographical references and index. | Summary: "A history of popular radical movements in Southern California during the Great Depression and an examination of voter support based on the promise of immediate relief despite the programs being unworkable, and in some cases even danger-ous"—Provided by publisher.
Identifiers: LCCN 2020053112 | ISBN 978-0-8061-6924-8 (hardcover) ISBN 978-0-8061-9226-0 (paper) Subjects: LCSH: Socialism—California—Los Angeles Region—History—20th
century. | Depressions—1929—California—Los Angeles Region. | Los Angeles Region (Calif.)—Social conditions—20th century. Classification: LCC F869.L857 S74 2021 | DDC 979.494—dc23
LC record available at https://lccn.loc.gov/2020053112

The paper in this book meets the guidelines for permanence and durability of the Committee on Production Guidelines for Book Longevity of the Council on Library Resources, Inc. ∞

Copyright © 2021 by the University of Oklahoma Press, Norman, Publishing Division of the University. Paperback published 2023. Manufactured in the U.S.A.

All rights reserved. No part of this publication may be reproduced, stored in a retrieval system, or transmitted, in any form or by any means, electronic, mechanical, photocopying, recording, or otherwise—except as permitted under Section 107 or 108 of the United States Copyright Act—without the prior written permission of the University of Oklahoma Press. To request permission to reproduce selections from this book, write to Permissions, University of Oklahoma Press, 2800 Venture Drive, Norman OK 73069, or email rights.oupress@ou.edu.

*For Ellen Mitsu Stevens,
the better part of Team Stevens*

Contents

Preface, by Ellen Stevens		ix
Acknowledgments, by Errol Wayne Stevens		xi
Introduction	Los Angeles, Cradle of Utopias	1
One	Gopher Prairie, U.S.A.	8
Two	The Crash	25
Three	The Downward Spiral	38
Four	Self-Help	54
Five	The God That Failed	73
Six	Salvation from the Left	92
Seven	The Utopian Society	111
Eight	The Townsend Plan	128
Nine	End Poverty in California	151
Ten	Ham and Eggs	174
Conclusion	The Politics of Fear	197
Notes		201
Suggested Readings		223
Index		227

Preface

Errol Stevens and I had been married for fifty-one years in January 2019 when he was diagnosed with terminal brain cancer. After we moved here in 1984, he fell in love with Southern California and its history. He was hired by the Natural History Museum of Los Angeles County as head of the new Seaver Center for Western History Research. In 1994, Errol left the museum to become head of the Special Collections Department of the Charles Von der Ahe Library at Loyola Marymount University. During these years he wrote numerous articles on Southern California and the book *Radical L.A.: From Coxey's Army to the Watts Riots, 1894–1965*, published by the University of Oklahoma Press in 2009.

Errol spent the last year of his life struggling to complete this book between rounds of radiation and chemotherapy treatments. He managed to submit *In Pursuit of Utopia* for publication before his passing in January 2020. Without the help of his longtime friend from the Natural History Museum of Los Angeles County, Curator Emeritus Tom Sitton, this book would have never been published. Errol considered Tom an encyclopedia of knowledge about Southern California. Tom was literally at Errol's bedside when he passed and selflessly put aside his own research and writing to help bring Errol's work to fruition.

I am so grateful for the patience and kindness of the following people who helped me obtain the photos for this book: Erika Dowell, Associate Director and Curator of Modern Books and Manuscripts, Lilly Library, Indiana University; Molly Haigh, Library Special Collections, Charles E. Young Research Library, University of California at Los Angeles; Christina Rice, Senior Librarian, Photo Collection, Los Angeles Public Library; and Kristen Wilkens, Digitalization Assistant, Lilly Library, Indiana University.

I was so lucky to have my two daughters support me throughout this process. Miyo Stevens-Gandara guided me through the many technical problems I encountered and took the photograph of the author to be used for promotional purposes. Emiko Condeso prepared the Los Angeles County map with Tom Sitton.

Special thanks also to James Kent Calder, Senior Acquisitions Editor of University of Oklahoma Press, for taking on the difficult task of posthumous publication and for his kindness and help. Copyeditor John Thomas and managing editor Steven B. Baker were instrumental in bringing the book to fruition. We are also deeply grateful to Errol's former professor at Indiana University, Walter Nugent, now Professor Emeritus, University of Notre Dame; Charles Rankin, former Editor-in-Chief, University of Oklahoma Press; William Deverell, Professor, University of Southern California; and Maurice Isserman, Professor, Hamilton College, for their friendship, generosity, and support during this difficult time for our family.

Ellen Stevens

Acknowledgments

One of the pleasures of writing this book was the opportunity to meet many knowledgeable people who helped me along the way. At the top of this list is Tom Sitton, the preeminent historian of Los Angeles and the county of which it is a part. There seems to be no fact about Southern California that Tom does not know. In countless conversations over the years, he has pointed me to sources that I might otherwise have overlooked. He has also loaned or given me materials from his own collections. My debt to him is beyond measure. Also very helpful to me was Clay Stalls, who, as I was writing this book, was curator in special collections at the Hannon Library at Loyola Marymount University and also curator of California collections at the Huntington Library. At both institutions, he guided me to valuable materials. At the Huntington, Peter Blodgett located materials that I otherwise would never have discovered. His profound knowledge of the Huntington's collections is unparalleled and irreplaceable.

Special thanks go to Loren Gatch of the University of Central Oklahoma, who I have never met. In a selfless act of kindness, he sent me, unsolicited, a photocopy of Clark Kerr's nine-hundred-page dissertation on the self-help cooperatives. This became the primary source for the chapter on that subject. Professor Gatch's kind gesture gives substance to the term "community of scholars."

Special thanks to Breon Mitchell, former director of the Lilly Library at Indiana University, for arranging a travel grant that enabled me to spend a week in Bloomington to use the library's Upton Sinclair collection.

Thanks to John Cahoon and Betty Uyeda for their help and hospitality while I used the collections of the Seaver Center at the Natural History Museum of Los Angeles County. Thank you also to Carrie Marsh of the Honnold Library's special collections department for her assistance with the Jerry Voorhis collection. There are many other librarians at various institutions throughout Southern Californian whose names I never learned but from whom I benefited immensely. These institutions include the Southern California Library for Social Studies and Research, the USC special collections department, UCLA special collections, the Los Angeles Public Library, and the Los Angeles County Public Library, particularly the California History Resource Center in Norwalk.

I am grateful for the support of my family: my wife, Ellen, to whom this book is dedicated; my daughters, Miyo and Emiko; my granddaughters, Rie and Aya; and my grandsons, Jhonen and Lukas. They all gave me the support I needed to finish this project during some very tough times.

Errol Wayne Stevens

INTRODUCTION

Los Angeles, Cradle of Utopias

> In this land of tropical sunshine and little rain, schemes for the improvement of the genus homo, physically, mentally, morally, spiritually, economically, socially, politically and whatnot, spring up overnight and mount the skies like Jack's beanstalk.
>
> *Los Angeles Times,* October 8, 1938

In his classic work *Southern California: An Island on the Land,* Carey McWilliams observed that the "abuse of Southern California has become a national pastime" and that nothing attracted more attention in this regard than the region's utopian politics—its "flair for the new and the untried." Although this fascination with fads and social nostrums of all kinds goes back to the nineteenth century, in this instance McWilliams referred to the mass movements that burst onto the scene during the Great Depression. "Nothing quite like them developed elsewhere," McWilliams wrote. "They could have originated only where and when they did, in Southern California in the 1930s." Articles in the national press left the impression that "about 1934, Southern California became politically insane."[1]

Why did these movements take on such importance in Southern California? Why did they attract such large followings from a conservative population? The most common explanation at the time was not the strictly economic circumstances but the character of Southern Californians. Members of the intellectual elite of the 1920s delighted in portraying Los Angeles as a materialistic place inhabited by people of limited intelligence and lowbrow cultural tastes. The region seemed to be the distillation of everything in America that repelled these intellectuals. H. L. Mencken, editor of the influential magazines *Smart Set* and *American Mercury*, wrote that Los Angeles had "more morons in it than the whole State of Mississippi." The literary critic Edmund Wilson echoed his sentiments. His highest praise was that Los Angeles had "more lovely girls serving peach-freezes and appetizing sandwich specials with little pieces of sweet pickle on the side than any other city in the world."[2]

Morrow Mayo, an acerbic commentator on the Los Angeles scene, thought that its inhabitants suffered from nothing more than simple boredom. He believed that, as soon as recent migrants from points east thawed out from the winter cold of their native states, they slipped into a state of ennui. For relief they turned to fads and social movements of various sorts. Mayo wrote that any "geomancer, soothsayer, holy jumper, herb-doctor, whirling dervish, snake-charmer, medicaster, table turner, or Evil Eye, practicing any form of black magic, demonology, joint-jerking, witchcraft, thaumaturgy, spirit-rapping, back-rubbing, physical torture, or dietical novelty" would find a willing audience. He concluded that Southern Californians were gullible types who, out of sheer boredom, would follow anyone who promised them spiritual or economic salvation.[3]

One of the best-known books about Southern California during the period is Nathanael West's 1939 novel *The Day of the Locust*. West drew on his experiences as screenwriter when he lived and worked in Hollywood for about a decade during the 1930s. Like Mayo, West saw Southern Californians as a people who suffered from a serious case of boredom. He wrote that all "their lives they had slaved at some kind of dull, heavy labor, behind desks and counters, in the fields and at tedious machines of all sorts, saving their pennies and dreaming of the leisure that would be theirs. . . . Where else should they go but California, the land of sunshine and oranges?" Yet these unimaginative midwesterners soon discovered that sunshine and oranges were not enough. They became deeply dissatisfied and felt that their lives were empty and without meaning. They had slaved for nothing and were somehow cheated. "They didn't know what to do with their time," West wrote. Presumably, if these migrants had stayed in Iowa or some such place and spent their winters shoveling snow they would have been happy or at least not bored. In *The Day of the Locust* this general dissatisfaction with life turned dull, upstanding midwesterners into angry mobs.[4]

These writers are entertaining but should not be accepted at face value. Oddly enough, some historians have done exactly this. It may be that seeing Southern California as the butt of a joke is simply too good to resist. Arthur M. Schlesinger Jr., the quintessential eastern establishment historian, wrote that during the Depression Angelenos "turned to social prophets with the same credulous faith so many of them had but recently expended on Aimee Semple McPherson." He apparently agreed with Mayo and West that Southern Californians were simpleminded people who were likely to follow anyone with a prescription for spiritual or economic salvation. Schlesinger does not say if he believed that they did this out of boredom, but it is clear that he thought the inhabitants of the region pursued their utopian politics because of some basic character flaw.[5]

David M. Kennedy, in *Freedom from Fear: The American People in Depression and War*, repeated Schlesinger in describing Southern Californians as all too willing to follow prophets selling unrealistic panaceas. Kennedy does not trace this gullibility to the character of transplanted midwesterners. Instead, he blames it on the polyglot character of the population. Kennedy saw Southern Californians as "rootless, restless souls, including sun-seekers from the Midwest, refugees from the Dust Bowl, immigrants from Mexico and the far shores of the Pacific, and drifters of every purpose and credo." Kennedy is especially harsh on Upton Sinclair, who he dismisses as an "addict of causes, romantic and eccentric champion of the underdog, a man who subsisted largely on a diet of brown rice, fruit, and celery, a conscience-driven sentimentalist." If Kennedy had done his homework, he would have known that Sinclair was not a vegetarian in the 1930s. In any case, one might also ask why that diet is evidence of a character flaw, or, for that matter, what exactly is wrong with being a champion of the underdog or having a conscience.[6]

Jackson K. Putnam, in *Old Age Politics in California*, describes the region as "utterly devoid of charm" and its inhabitants a commonplace people running commonplace businesses. "There seemed to be," he wrote, "an enveloping aimlessness, emptiness, and banality about southern California life that was only partly masked by the strident hucksterism of the state's promoters." Putnam also saw boredom as the main flaw in the character of the population, without offering an explanation for this boredom, but labeled Southern Californians a "diverse and disorganized people" who were not interested in just finding solutions to immediate problems "but of immediately solving all human problems and achieving perfection."[7]

Another distinguished historian, Robert M. Fogelson, the author of *The Fragmented Metropolis*, believed that Los Angeles was a vast sprawl, a fragmented metropolis with no common identity or sense of community. The "interminable lines of streets and the monotonous rows of houses blurred boundaries between sections of the region, and the widespread use of private automobiles inhibited casual contacts that formerly stimulated personal relationships in Los Angeles." Fogelson feels on solid ground when he cites *The Day of the Locust*, a work of fiction, as support for his arguments, and concludes that "ennui," the emptiness at the core of life in the region, "encouraged eccentric thought and erratic action, an inclination to tinker with ideas and to tamper with institutions."[8]

A few writers chose not to try to explain the political behavior of Southern Californians in terms of the character of the population. McWilliams, while thinking the region unlike any other place in the world, hinted that the behavior of Southern Californians might be best explained in economic terms. "The real crackpots of Los Angeles in the thirties," he wrote, "were the individuals who ordered tons of oranges and vegetables dumped in the bed of the Los Angeles River, while thousands of people were unemployed, hungry, and homeless." Leonard Leader, in *Los Angeles and the Great Depression*, agreed that Los Angeles was "a crucible for many bizarre movements during the depression" but did not think that Southern Californians lived empty lives, suffered from boredom, or possessed any other character flaws that might account for their actions. Instead, he pointed to the failure of the business approach to recovery and to the "many vacuums" that blocked traditional responses to economic distress. Los Angeles was a "city where normal political aspirations were systematically suppressed, where politics itself was a mixture of vagueness and subject to ebbs and flows of cross filing, recall, referendum and initiative, where such structures of strength as the eastern political machine and a strong trade union movement were missing." In the absence of traditional political outlets, Angelenos explored new political solutions and forms of action.[9]

The purpose of this book is to examine in detail several of the movements that emerged in Southern California during the Great Depression. They include the Utopian Society, the Townsend Plan, End Poverty in California, Ham and Eggs, and the self-help cooperatives. I have added the communists and the free-market capitalists to the list. They are quite different from the others, and from each other, but both were quasi-religious movements that demanded unquestioning devotion from their followers. With the exception of the self-help cooperatives, all of these movements (including the communists and capitalists), claimed to have the One Big Answer that would not only end the Depression but eradicate all poverty and misery—in other words, transform the very nature of human existence.

In 1930 almost a third of the people living in Los Angeles were born in one of the states of the East North Central or West North Central census divisions. About 20 percent of them came from Illinois, Missouri, Ohio, Iowa, and Kansas. Suburban cities in Los Angeles County also had large percentages of midwesterners in their populations. Forty-six percent of the population of Long Beach, the second-largest city in Los Angeles County and sometimes called "Iowa by the Sea," hailed from a midwestern state. The large number of midwesterners in the population of Los Angeles and surrounding communities left a lasting imprint on the region. Even today, tree-lined streets of many neighborhoods in Los Angeles and its suburbs, if one ignores the occasional palm and orange tree, are reminiscent of midwestern towns. State societies kept old connections alive. Society banquets and picnics were a prominent feature of Southern California social life. In the 1920s, each year over 150,000 people attended the Iowa Society picnic at Bixby Park in Long Beach.[10]

As a group, these midwesterners tended to be conservative both politically and socially. Religion was an important part of their lives. Catholics made up the single largest denomination in the mid-1920s, but taken together the congregations of Protestant churches—led by Methodists, Baptists, Presbyterians, Disciples of Christ, and Congregationalists—slightly outnumbered them. Los Angeles had the reputation of a town that went to bed early—the kind of place where waiters piled chairs on tables around diners who tarried too long over their evening coffee. The bon vivant Willard Huntington Wright complained that Los Angeles "pleasure resorts are as unexciting as a church bazaar."[11]

Many of these midwesterners came from a category of migrant called the "tenth tourists," which Freeman Tilden described in an article in *World's Work* in 1931: "They are the ones-in-tens who never went home—or who went home to sell out and return." Many of these "one-in-tens" were retired or about to retire. In 1930, 6.3 percent of the population of the city of Los Angeles were sixty-five years of age or older. The national average was 5.4 percent. Of the five largest cities in the United States, Los Angeles had the highest percentage of residents in this age group. For Los Angeles County as a whole, the figure was 6.8 percent. Many of the towns in the county also had large percentages of older residents. Over 12 percent of the population of Pasadena (originally called the Indiana Colony) were sixty-five or older. For Monrovia the figure was 11 percent, Pomona almost 10 percent, Long Beach and Santa Monica around 9 percent, and Alhambra 8 percent.[12] Other cities on the West Coast had large percentages of older people in their populations—Portland 6.6 percent, San Diego 9.1 percent—but in absolute numbers Los Angeles had a much larger population of old people than anywhere else in the West. Its population of residents sixty-five years or older was 77,523. In Los Angeles County the figure was 149,028. The county's number of the aged was larger than the entire population of the city of San Diego and almost a quarter (23.5 percent) of the population of San Francisco County.[13]

In the first half of the twenty-first century, we no longer think of someone who is sixty-five as very old. Life spans have increased and people are staying active longer than in 1930. In 2014 the life expectancy of a new-born American male was 76.5 years and females 81.3. In 1930 the life expectancy of a man was only 58.1 years. A woman could expect to live 61.6 years. During the Depression decade, the senior years started much earlier. A worker who lost his or her job at age forty could not expect to work again. Lowering the age that defined an "old" person to forty-five years greatly increases the pool of the elderly. The 1930 census showed 345,415 people living in Los Angeles who were forty-five years or older. In Los Angeles County the figure was 613,960.[14]

In the early years of the Great Depression, older people were especially vulnerable to economic crises. The safety nets that Americans have become accustomed to did not exist in 1930. Few people had pensions. The federal Social Security Act signed into law in 1935 did not begin to provide small monthly benefits until 1940. Mutual aid societies provided limited support to those fortunate enough to belong to one. The retired and those who had lost their jobs and were too old to find another depended on savings, help from relatives, the generosity of their neighbors, churches and other charitable organizations, and the county relief system. In the winter of 1933/34, the Great Depression was entering its fifth year; retirees and the older unemployed had reached the limit of their resources.

The geographic coverage of this book is Los Angeles and the metropolitan region of which it is a part. For my purposes this metropolis coincides with Los Angeles County. It is almost impossible to discuss meaningfully the Great Depression in Los Angeles without including the county. California law placed the responsibility for relief programs on the counties, not the municipalities.

This book does not attempt a defense of the various utopian solutions to the economic crisis. That would be futile in any case. Most were provably unworkable. It became apparent during the research for this book that Los Angeles during the Depression had an abundance of unemployed salespeople, stock dealers, and real estate brokers who had made their livings persuading people to buy something. They were very skilled in the art of the sale and had extraordinary organizing skills. They make up a colorful cast of true believers, opportunists, hustlers, con artists, grifters, and devoted followers. As McWilliams might have written, such a collection of characters could not have existed anywhere else in America except in Southern California.

1

GOPHER PRAIRIE, U.S.A.

> Los Angeles has been referred to as a city, but it actually is only a huge, exaggerated village; an Iowa or Kansas small town suddenly multiplied by five hundred. . . . It has taken its general aspect—the sickly, wan complexion; the tendency to depress the heart and stultify the mind—from Gopher Prairie.
>
> Louis Adamic, *The Truth about Los Angeles*

In the fall of 1922, Louis Adamic, a young Slovenian émigré, arrived at Los Angeles Harbor on an oil tanker. His first impressions of Southern California were far from positive. Instead of being greeted by the region's celebrated sunny skies and balmy temperatures, he disembarked in the midst of a rainstorm that turned the streets of the harbor town of San Pedro into muddy rivers. He jumped on board a Pacific Electric train and rode it twenty-five miles north to downtown Los Angeles. Within hours of his arrival, two men cornered him in a restaurant's basement restroom and robbed him of most of his possessions. Wandering into the city's old Plaza with nothing but a bruise on his head and a few coins in his pocket, he met an aging prostitute who took pity on him, bought him dinner, and gave him a place to sleep.[1]

When Adamic had recovered sufficiently to continue his explorations, he found a city of transplanted midwesterners. "Folks from the East and the Corn Belt . . . retired farmers and crossroad grocers and small-town dry-goods and hardware merchants" had moved to Southern California "to live in bungalow courts and eat in cafeterias." These "Christian peasants and shopkeepers" brought with them certain beliefs and habits of mind that gave the city its essential character. Adamic could not walk down the street without someone handing him a religious tract promising salvation or inviting him to a revival. In Pershing Square and in the Plaza, Adamic listened to soapboxers who regularly held forth on a wide range of topics. Most of them, he recalled, were "professional atheists, or 'Christ-killers,' full of sound and fury, as fanatical in their way as the religionists were in theirs." Adamic considered Angelenos, regardless of the message they preached or followed, to be a simple people. "The Folks," he called them. They were "easily swayed by the smooth-tongued rogues and quacks who appeal for their support in the name of 'the principles for which our good old Abe Lincoln stood,' in the name of decency and horse sense, in the name of Jesus Christ and the Old-fashioned Religion." As he came to know the city, Adamic overcame his original disdain and realized that for a young man with literary ambitions—such as he was— there was no better place than Los Angeles to learn about America. "I would have to travel all over the United States to witness things that I can see here almost any day," he wrote. "Droll, sad, pathetic, sacred, profane things."[2]

John Clinton Porter was the perfect mayor for this kind of city. He took office on July 1, 1929, a successful businessman, conservative in his political and cultural views, a believer in the Christian Protestant God, and virulently anti-alcohol. Like many of the voters who elected him, he was a native of the Midwest, arriving with his Iowan parents when he was thirteen years old. At age fifty-eight he was tall and imposing in stature, with an athletic build and a mane of gray hair. Superficially he looked like a leader. The *Los Angeles Times* political reporter Kyle D. Palmer suggested that there was less to the mayor than his appearance suggested. He observed that Porter was the kind of a man whose "thought processes" were "slow, painstakingly careful, cautious, almost hesitant." Once arriving at a conclusion, he held to it dogmatically, seldom abandoning or modifying his position. Such stubbornness might be considered evidence of deeply held convictions or a sign of a rigid mind.[3]

The mayor's religious views were so conservative that opponents worried he might institute blue laws closing businesses and shutting down public events on Sunday. These fears proved unwarranted, but Porter showed little tolerance for those who did not share his religious views. He hired his own group of investigators to root out enemies, who happened to be mostly Catholics and Jews. The head of this unit, the rabidly reactionary preacher Martin Luther Thomas, became widely known as the "super-snooper of city hall." Porter was determined to see that Prohibition remained the law in Los Angeles in practice as well as in theory. Whatever the occasion, he never hesitated to make his position clear when it came to the subject of drink. While touring France with a contingent of American mayors, Porter made a spectacle of himself by walking out of a banquet rather than raising a glass of wine in a toast. His uncompromising views on issues such as drink may have repelled some, but they earned plaudits from others. As a candidate, Porter won the endorsements of several religious leaders and clergy, including that of the fundamentalist pastor of Trinity Methodist Church, Robert "Fighting Bob" Shuler. He also won the support of the Ku Klux Klan. Porter disingenuously claimed to have sought the support of neither.[4]

Porter campaigned on not only his Christian moral values but also his experience as a successful businessman. He was a graduate of Los Angeles Business College and the owner of an automobile parts and salvage company. At the time of his election, his only experience in city affairs was as a member of the 1928 Los Angeles County grand jury. He saw this lack of background in politics as positive rather than negative, claiming that his brief service as a grand juror was more than enough to educate him about the problems the city faced. Campaigning on a platform of public integrity, he promised to tackle government corruption and inefficiency with a combination of Christian morality, common sense, and business expertise. He held firm to the belief that it was businessmen, not politicians, who knew what was "best for the entire city."[5]

Stanley Rogers, writing in the *National Municipal Review*, felt that Los Angeles deserved the man they elected. As "dumb as Mayor Porter is, he is not an unfitting representative of the majority of the voters of Los Angeles." At least as far as religion was concerned,

Rogers was correct. Many voters shared the mayor's profound commitment to conservative Protestant beliefs. To borrow a term from a later time, in the 1920s Southern California was the land of the megachurch. Several charismatic preachers presided over congregations numbering in the thousands. The brand of Christianity delivered in these sanctuaries was usually conservative, frequently fundamentalist, and emphasized old-fashioned and very midwestern values. Dancing, any kind of gambling, immodesty in women, and, most certainly, alcohol consumption were not tolerated. Church leaders boasted of the size of their congregations and the physical dimensions of their buildings. Indiana-born James Whitcomb Brougher led Temple Baptist Church, the largest in the Northern Baptist Convention. One writer called Temple Baptist "a regular religious department store." The Reverend Herbert Booth Smith, pastor of the Immanuel Presbyterian Church, headed the second-largest Presbyterian Church in the United States. Dr. Gustav A. Briegleb led the wealthy and conservative congregation of the Westlake Presbyterian Church.[6]

During this period no other Los Angeles clergy matched the fame of Robert P. Shuler and Aimee Semple McPherson. Shuler, born and raised in a cabin in the Blue Ridge Mountains of Virginia, found his calling as a preacher while still in his teens. His combative style and ambition often put him at odds with friend and foe alike. In 1920 he was serving as the pastor of a church in Paris, Texas, when his bishop, to be rid of him, arranged his transfer to the Trinity Methodist Church in Los Angeles. Shuler's fiery sermons soon revived the moribund congregation. Each Sunday he easily filled the three-thousand-seat sanctuary, and by 1926 Trinity Methodist was the second-largest congregation in the city. Reverend Shuler saw it as his mission to expose immorality everywhere—in city government, in local cultural institutions, and in the lives of ordinary people. He spread the word not only from the pulpit but in *Bob Shuler's Magazine* and on the air with his own radio station, KGEF.[7]

Edmund Wilson, dropping in to hear one of Shuler's sermons, thought the clergyman's appeal was perfect for the retired farmers sitting in the pews who "were glad to get an intimate peek into the debauched goings-on of their neighbors, and at the same time be made to feel their own superior righteousness." Shuler believed that Jews, Catholics, and foreigners were behind the rising immorality he thought infected Los Angeles. The "Jew-owned" motion picture industry and the immoral lives of its stars were prime targets. He also attacked elected officials' toleration of gambling, prostitution, and illegal liquor. Mayor George Cryer, the political boss Kent Parrot, and Chief of Police James E. Davis were special targets of the preacher's righteous invective. Shuler supported the Ku Klux Klan because he believed that in its attacks on Jews, Catholics, and illegal alcohol the secret society championed the principles of true Christianity. In 1928 he vigorously opposed the candidacy of Catholic presidential candidate Al Smith, who he believed was a puppet of the papacy. Wilson, revealing his own brand of bigotry, thought that the preacher's message had a special appeal for "those dowdy and dry-faced women, those dowdy and pasty girls, those old men with thin necks and sparse hairs, drooping forward their small bald foreheads, drawing in their recessive chins."[8]

"Sister" Aimee Semple McPherson, ten years younger than Shuler, was born Aimée Elizabeth Kennedy in Ontario, Canada, in 1890. While still in her teens, she fell in love with and married Robert Semple, an itinerant Pentecostal preacher. The couple signed up to be missionaries in China, but shortly after arriving there Semple died and left his young wife alone and pregnant with a baby girl. She managed to return to the United States and found her way to New York, where the young widow married businessman Harold McPherson and gave birth to a boy. The marriage did not work out, and she became seriously ill. According to her own account, as she lay on the verge of death God spoke to her and offered her a choice to serve him or join him in heaven. She chose the former, and when she recovered her health she abandoned her husband and returned to Ontario with her two children.

Aimee Semple McPherson answered God's call by becoming an itinerant evangelist. The young woman and her children, along with her mother, toured the country in an automobile called the "Gospel Car." A sign on its side asked the question, "Where will you spend eternity?" McPherson drove across the United States, holding tent revivals along the way. At the end of 1918, she arrived in Los Angeles and decided to settle there. The young evangelist bought a plot of land in Echo Park, a neighborhood north of

Aimee Semple McPherson performs religious services in her Angelus Temple in 1930. Herald Examiner Collection, courtesy of the Los Angeles Public Library.

downtown Los Angeles, and built a church with the proceeds of a nationwide revival tour. On January 1, 1923, the $300,000 building opened. It was topped with an unsupported dome 110 feet high and 107 feet across. She had the ceiling painted blue with white clouds, giving the interior the feeling of an outdoor meeting place. The sanctuary seated more than five thousand people.[9]

Dressed in a white flowing gown, McPherson presided over services that resembled theater productions. Her Pentecostal services emphasized a more emotional approach to religion than those practiced in fundamentalist churches such as Shuler's Trinity Methodist. Her path to salvation rested on four pillars called the Foursquare Gospel: salvation through Jesus Christ, speaking in tongues, faith healing, and the premillennial return of Christ. The church claimed to have twenty thousand members and was not affiliated with any of the major Protestant denominations. Like Shuler, McPherson opposed modernist ideas such as Darwinism and critical approaches to the Bible. She defended traditional values and attacked dancing, going to the movies, smoking, drinking, and other "immoral" activities. She sought the support of the Ku Klux Klan when it suited her purposes but sometimes criticized the racist organization. Like Shuler, she exploited the new medium of radio to reach an audience beyond the auditorium of her church. Two 250-foot radio towers flanked the domed structure. KFSG (Four Square Gospel) went on the air in February 1924.[10]

Shuler did not approve of McPherson, believing that she was a charlatan who cared too much for money. He attacked her from the pulpit of his church and wrote books criticizing her ministry and questioning her personal morality—a charge that was not without substance. In May 1926, McPherson disappeared while swimming near Santa Monica. Searches for her body found nothing and it seemed that she must have drowned, but five weeks later she appeared in Mexico, claiming that she had been kidnapped. This proved to be a weak cover story. She apparently had run off with her lover, the station's radio operator. This titillating scandal increased her notoriety but did not undermine her popularity.[11]

• • • •

Louis Adamic's description of Los Angeles as an overgrown midwestern town is not entirely inaccurate, but there is more to the story. Some 30 percent of the American-born population of Los Angeles in 1930 were born in a midwestern state, about 20 percent were native Californians (including the children of midwestern migrants), and 50 percent were born in other states, with no region predominating. In addition to these non-midwestern immigrants, about 21 percent of Los Angeles's population were foreign-born—a decidedly un–Gopher Prairie characteristic. They came from a large number of European countries. Not surprisingly, the largest single foreign-born group was from Mexico—about 4 percent of the total population. Another 3.7 percent identified themselves in the U.S. census as being of Mexican ancestry but born in the United States. Furthermore, of the white American-born population almost 9 percent had at least one parent of foreign birth. In 1930 the nonwhite population of Los Angeles was still very small. African Americans made up 3.1 percent of the population and Asians 2.2 percent. Although Los Angeles was not yet the ethnically diverse city that it became at the end of the century, its population was not homogenous even in the 1920s.[12]

Despite the fact that the average age of its population was greater than the nation as a whole, Los Angeles was hardly a nursing home for the aged—as Adamic suggested when he called it a city of "the sickly, wan complexion." On the contrary, during the 1920s Los Angeles was one of the fastest-growing cities in the United States. It was, in fact, a boomtown, probably closer in resemblance to the rowdy San Francisco of the Gold Rush era than to a sleepy midwestern Gopher Prairie. In the entire country only Miami and St. Petersburg, Florida, grew faster than Los Angeles during the twenties. During that decade, the population of Los Angeles more than doubled—from 576,673 residents in 1920 to 1,238,048 in 1930—rising from the tenth- to the fifth-largest city in the country. To put this growth in perspective, the population increase during the 1920s (661,375) was greater than the entire population of San Francisco in 1930 (634,394). The county of Los Angeles experienced a population increase of almost 136 percent during this period. Compton, a small town of 1,478 in 1920, acquired 11,038 new residents—an increase of more than 700 percent. Inglewood grew by almost 500 percent, Glendale by more than 363 percent, Alhambra by 224 percent. Long Beach's growth rate of 155 percent in the 1920s was actually lower than the 212 percent recorded in the previous decade.[13]

Real estate and oil were two engines that powered this tremendous growth. Housing construction and the frenzied buying and selling of property created a speculative bubble during the first years of the decade. Between 1921 and 1923, the valuation of buildings in the city of Los Angeles increased from about $82 million to over $200 million. Southern California's voracious appetite for building materials denuded entire forests in the Pacific Northwest. A busy coastal trade brought lumber south to be unloaded at San Pedro and stacked in huge lumberyards employing hundreds of men. This was the golden age of the subdivider. Entire communities sprouted up like mushrooms all over the Los Angeles Basin and in the San Gabriel and San Fernando valleys. Those who had enough money purchased homes in subdivisions with paved streets and sidewalks. Those with modest incomes bought empty lots with no improvements other than a crudely graded road that connected them to the rest of Southern California. They pitched a tent or lived in a shack

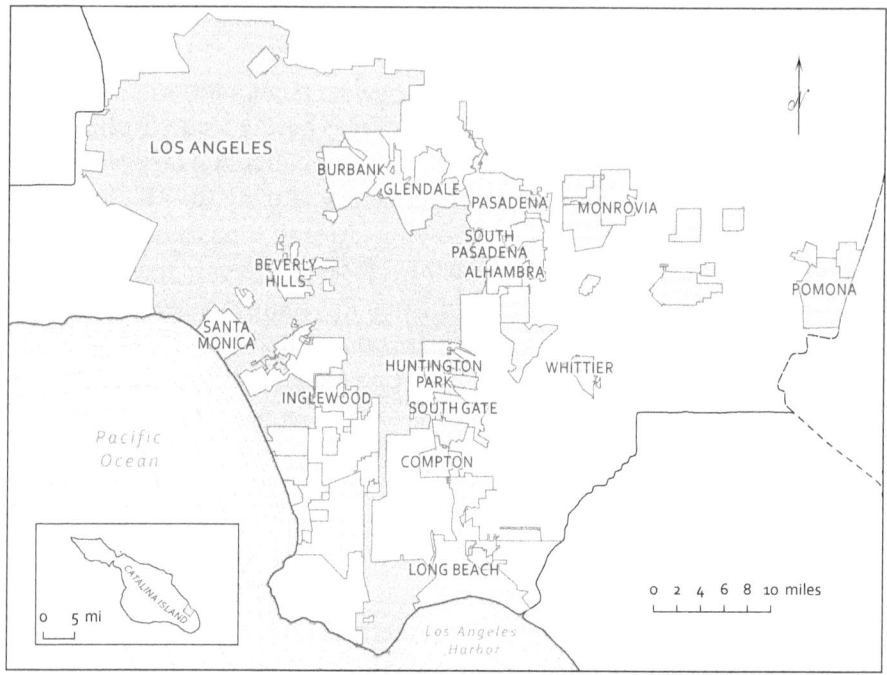

The southern portion of Los Angeles County and its cities in the 1930s. The more populous cities based on the 1930 U.S. Census are labeled. Courtesy of T. Emiko Condeso.

while they built their homes. These "suburban homesteaders," as the historian Becky Nicolaides called them, raised chickens and planted gardens and carved out a life of self-sufficiency under the Southern California sun.[14]

The prospect of fortunes to be made in real estate was so enticing that many workers abandoned good jobs to get a piece of the action. In 1923, at the height of the boom, an estimated 12,000 salespeople, about a third of the state's total, sold real estate in Southern California. In 1923 a syndicate that included Harry Chandler of the *Los Angeles Times* paid $21,000 to erect a sign in the Hollywood Hills to advertise a new subdivision. Illuminated by four thousand lightbulbs and visible for miles across the Los Angeles Basin, it spelled out the word HOLLYWOODLAND. Later shortened to simply HOLLYWOOD, the iconic sign that is a symbol for the glamor and glitz of the movie industry became one of the most famous tourist attractions in the world.[15]

Other techniques subdividers used to attract customers were not as dramatic but still effective: free lunches, lectures, group excursions, and, of course, high-pressure sales talks. Agents walked the streets in downtown Los Angeles passing out free tickets for bus tours of new properties. After a tour with commentary from the guide, lunch, and lecture came a chance to sign on the dotted line in one of the "closing" offices—temporary huts set up on the property—where an agent and typist awaited. The real estate firm of Dickinson & Gillespie had a fleet of World War I surplus biplanes with the company's name spelled out in bold letters on the sides. Fritz Burns, one of the company's agents and a future Los Angeles real estate mogul, flew one of the planes for more than a hundred miles alongside a passenger train headed for Los Angeles. The passengers had the name Dickinson & Gillespie firmly implanted in their brains on arrival. Yet not all prospective buyers were welcome. Virtually all subdivisions were for whites only. The "Summary of Building Restrictions" for Windsor Hills, a Dickinson & Gillespie property, assured purchasers that "racial restrictions are perpetual and binding forever." The boom peaked in 1923 but, unlike the boom of the 1880s that crashed hard, there was no bust. Los Angeles continued to grow, at a slower but steady rate. Real estate remained a profitable business.[16]

The discovery of oil fed the Southern California boom. During this decade Los Angeles County became one of the world's leading producers of oil. Locals had long known that deposits of petroleum existed in Southern California. They often used seepage in the form of tar, called *brea*, for fuel and other purposes. In 1893, Edward L. Doheny found oil just west of downtown in what was then a residential neighborhood. He developed a huge field there that reached its maximum output in 1901. In 1917 the Standard Oil Company discovered oil in Montebello, a suburban community east of Los Angeles. In 1920 prospectors found the black gold at Huntington Beach, a small community in Orange County, near the Los Angeles County border, and a few months later Shell Oil Company discovered an oil deposit at Signal Hill in Long Beach. The most dramatic strike was in Santa Fe Springs, a small Los Angeles County town a few miles to the southeast of the city of Los Angeles. On the night of October 30, 1921, workers struck a gusher on the property of Alphonzo Bell, a former tennis champion. The following February another well on Bell's property struck oil and exploded with such force that it blew a crater in the ground and ignited a huge fireball. The fire raged for days, attracting sightseers from all over the region.[17]

Unlike the discovery of other major oil fields in the United States and elsewhere, those in Southern California did not take place in remote or rural areas but in places that had already been subdivided and settled. Oil companies scrambled to negotiate leases with individual landowners. Legally, landowners owned all mineral resources under their property, but the "rule of capture" meant that the first to pump the oil out of the ground owned the oil. Dense groves of oil wells sprouted up in areas like Signal Hill and Santa Fe Springs. Normally, five acres of land accommodated one oil well, but in the most productive parts of Los Angeles County there was often one well per acre of land. In a very short time Los Angeles Harbor became one of the world's great oil seaports. The traffic was so great that the number of tankers passing through the Panama Canal on the way to Los Angeles helped make the canal a paying proposition.[18]

The oil boom led to intense competition among oil companies to pressure residents to sign leases at potentially productive sites. Promoters made money by selling shares in these leases, borrowing some of the techniques of real estate agents to attract investors such as organizing excursions to the oil fields and enticing potential investors with free lunches and band concerts. Buying shares in a well was never a sure thing because it was never certain that a well would hit oil or, if it did, pay enough to meet expenses. For the promoters, even dry wells could be profitable if the money sold in shares exceeded the cost of drilling operations. Investors got their money only after all expenses had been paid, including commissions, advertising costs, drilling costs, office expenses, and so on, but the salespeople got their money first. The most notorious of the oil promoters was C. C. Julian, whose brilliant advertising campaigns persuaded thousands of ordinary people to invest in oil stocks. The secret of his success was his ability to raise money by convincing his investors that he was a straight shooter. His newspaper ads began with the bold headline, "Julian Refuses to Accept Your Money Unless You Can Afford to Lose! Widows and Orphans, This Is No Investment for You!" Like the speeches of his contemporaries in the clergy, such as Shuler and McPherson, a Julian speech could draw huge audiences. In 1924 he called a stockholders meeting that filled the Hollywood Bowl with 30,000 people.[19]

In addition to real estate and oil, the Los Angeles Stock Exchange, founded in 1899 as the Los Angeles Oil Exchange, attracted the dollars of investors large and small. Investments there were theoretically safer, but the exchange suffered from many of the same weaknesses as the one on Wall Street. Margin sales were common, allowing buyers to purchase stock with up to 50 percent of the value in borrowed money. The California Corporations Department strictly regulated the sale of securities, but the volume of business swamped the office. Most reputable stockbrokers belonged to the Exchange, but many small operators ran unregulated "bucket shops" that sold securities as well. These loosely supervised operations often sold stocks on the installment plan, making it easier for small investors to get into the market—and over their heads. "Switchers" often persuaded new arrivals to trade their out-of-state securities for local and often fraudulent paper to avoid taxes on out-of-state securities. Loan sharks charged high interest for loans to buy securities. Critics like H. L. Mencken believed that the tendency of midwesterners to follow anyone with a prescription for salvation, good health, or earthly wealth made the region a haven for unscrupulous promoters. But as the historian Jules Tygiel pointed out, there was no reason to believe that Southern Californian retirees, from the Midwest or elsewhere, were any more likely to invest their money foolishly than anyone else. The boom psychology infected everyone, even the elite of the region's business and financial community, who often got in over their heads.[20]

During the 1920s, Los Angeles County became an important industrial center. At the beginning of the century, San Francisco led in industrial production, but this soon changed. During the decade, Los Angeles County rose from the twenty-eighth largest industrial center in the United States to the ninth. The number of manufacturing establishments in the county tripled and the wage earners who worked in them increased from about 60,000 to about 115,000. By the end of the decade, the value of manufactured goods produced in Los Angeles County was more than double that of San Francisco. The industrial department of the Los Angeles Chamber of Commerce played an important part in attracting industry. Much in the same way that the All Year Club promoted tourism, the department issued reports on the advantages of Southern California for industry and advertised the virtues of the region for business.[21]

During the 1920s, several national corporations established branch plants in the area. Given its growing importance in the life of Southern California, it is not surprising that many of these industries involved the automobile. Goodyear Tire and Rubber Company, B. F. Goodrich, and Firestone Tire and Rubber Company built plants in Los Angeles County. In 1929 the Samson Tire and Rubber Company constructed a factory in the style of an ancient Assyrian palace in what became the City of Commerce. The building still stands and has since become a factory outlet. In 1928 Willys-Overland opened an automobile assembly plant; two years later the Ford Motor Company opened a factory in Long Beach that turned out 80,000 vehicles in its first year. Numerous oil refineries, a natural industry for a place that had abundant petroleum and plenty of automobiles, sprang up in the region. Standard Oil built its second West Coast refinery near what is now Los Angeles International Airport. The town that grew up around the refinery took the name El Segundo, "the second" in Spanish. The aircraft industry, which became a major employer in years leading up to World War II, got its start in the 1920s. The good weather and the clear skies made the region particularly suitable for building airplanes. Glenn Martin established the first aircraft plant in Los Angeles before World War I. With the help of a $15,000 loan that Harry Chandler helped to arrange, Donald Douglas got his start by building three torpedo planes for the U.S. Navy. Lockheed Aircraft opened a plant in Hollywood in 1926 and later moved to Burbank.[22]

The region's best-known industry, a far more glamorous one than turning crude oil into gasoline or rubber into tires, was motion pictures. In 1908, William N. Selig made the outdoor scenes for his fourteen-minute film *The Count of Monte Cristo* in Southern California. This was the first storytelling movie made in Southern California. D. W. Griffith filmed his paean to white supremacy, *The Birth of a Nation*, in the region in 1914. That film has the dubious distinction of being both a landmark in the history of moviemaking as well as a monument to racism. During the decade, studios such as Metro-Goldwyn-Mayer, Paramount Pictures, United Artists,

Warner Brothers, R.K.O., and Fox Studios became important employers in Los Angeles County. According to the U.S. census, in 1929 the industry employed more than eight thousand wage earners and more than seven thousand salaried employees.

In addition to its marvelous climate and access to a large and expanding market, Southern California had one other thing that appealed to potential employers—a largely nonunion workforce. During the 1920s, Los Angeles earned a well-deserved reputation as the city of the open shop. A powerful business coalition that included the Los Angeles Chamber of Commerce, the Merchants and Manufacturers Association, and the ultra-conservative Better America Federation enforced the nonunion policy. For the business community, the Open Shop was more than just a principle of labor relations. It was enshrined in businesspeoples' minds as holy writ. They considered it the highest expression of patriotism, true religion, and the American way. Harry Chandler's ambition was to make Los Angeles the "white spot" of America. By this he meant a place free of the scourge that haunted other large American cities—organized labor.

Boomtown Los Angeles does not quite fit the image of the tired city of "Christian peasants and shopkeepers" that Adamic saw when he disembarked at San Pedro. Los Angeles County was part of a dynamic and increasingly diverse community. It included the wealthy communities of Beverly Hills, South Pasadena, and San Marino and the ethnically diverse neighborhood of Boyle Heights on the east side of Los Angeles, where Japanese Americans, Jews, and Mexican Americans lived together. It also included the working-class towns such as South Gate, Compton, and Huntington Park in the vast area that stretched south from the city of Los Angeles to the harbor.

Literary critics such as H. L. Mencken or Edmund Wilson surely enjoyed the spectacles to be found in Shuler's or McPherson's churches, but it is unlikely that they visited, or even knew of, G. Bromley Oxnam's Church of All Nations. Oxnam was born in Los Angeles in 1891 of a conservative Republican family. The *G* in his name was for Garfield, the Republican president assassinated in 1881. He was the son of Thomas Henry Oxnam, a Cornish tin miner who immigrated to the United States in the mid-nineteenth century and followed an itinerant life as an engineer in the mining camps of the American West. The senior Oxnam was a devout Methodist who liked to describe himself as a "preacher first; engineer second." He had no sympathy for organized labor and no interest in modernist trends in religion, such as the "Social Creed of Methodism," adopted in 1908, which expressed sympathy and concern for the plight of the poor.[23]

As a young man, Bromley Oxnam worshipped his father and shared his views, but as often happens his opinions began to change when he went to college. At the University of Southern California, he fell under the influence of the sociologist Emory Bogardus, whose classes included fieldwork in the slums of the city. Bogardus introduced the young man to Walter Rauschenbusch and his book *Christianity and the Social Crisis*. Rauschenbusch was a leader of the Social Gospel movement, which emphasized a concern for the condition of the poor in this life rather than on salvation for the next one. Although Oxnam's views shifted decidedly to the liberal side of the political spectrum, he never lost his devotion to his father and his commitment to Christian service. For Oxnam, who remained active in the Methodist Episcopal Church throughout his college years, the ministry was a natural choice of career.

After he graduated from USC, Oxnam went on to Boston University, where he received a divinity degree. He studied with the social activist Harry F. Ward, head of the Department of Social Service. Upon his return to Los Angeles in 1918, it was natural that his interests should lead him to ask Methodist church leaders for permission to begin a new ministry among the city's poor and immigrant populations. At that time, E. P. Ryland, a pacifist who would soon lose his position because of his anti-war views, appointed the young minister pastor of Newman Methodist Episcopal Church on the east side of downtown Los Angeles. Church parishioners had moved out of the area, once an affluent neighborhood, as it became more industrial and attracted poor immigrants.

Oxnam's new parish consisted of 213 city blocks that housed 60,000 people. Forty-two nationalities made their homes there—whites, blacks, Mexicans, Chinese, Japanese, Spanish, Italians, Greeks, all living in close proximity. The neighborhood was a grim collection of run-down buildings, shanties, factories, packinghouses, saloons, pool halls, and cheap hotels. The air was foul and everything was covered in soot. Crime, juvenile delinquency, disease, prostitution, and vice were part of everyday life. In 1921, Oxnam sold the Newman Church and purchased two old three-story apartment buildings that included sufficient space for a playground. This would be the home of the Church of All Nations. Oxnam conducted traditional services, but they were not his main focus. By the mid-1920s, the official church membership was only 111—a far cry from that of the megachurch, but it was less of a church than a Christian social center. All Nations operated a free clinic that served thousands. Nurses were on duty around the clock and made home visits. Oxnam offered many services that local residents needed: a milk station, a daycare center for single mothers, and a lunchroom where women workers could get a meal for twenty cents. All Nations sold donated clothing at low prices. It also provided educational lectures for working women. One of Oxnam's innovations was a movie night that offered films more wholesome than the entertainments available to young people in the neighborhood. It was immensely popular.

Oxnam did not want to operate a rescue mission such as Midnight Mission, located only a few blocks away. He made no attempt to proselytize or to exclude anyone because of their religion or race. Catholics, Protestants, Jews, and Buddhists participated in All Nations programs. Blacks, whites, and Asians mixed together in youth programs, such as the All Nations camp located in the Southern California mountains. Songfests were conducted in Spanish and Yiddish. Unlike other clergy, Oxnam supported organized labor. He opened the Newman Church and All Nations to union meetings and often lectured at the Labor Temple. He invited the socialist Upton Sinclair to speak at his church and presided over a free-speech meeting after Sinclair's arrest for reading the U.S. Constitution during a strike in San Pedro in 1923. Despite the miniscule size of his congregation, Oxnam reached a huge audience through his public speaking. In an Armistice Day address in 1921, he spoke to 20,000 people in Lincoln Park on the east side of Los Angeles. In 1924 his audiences totaled at least 120,000 people.[24]

In 1923, Oxnam decided to run for the Los Angeles school board. His opponents, especially Col. Leroy Smith, a Methodist lay preacher and spokesman for the Better America Federation, labeled Oxnam a radical Bolshevik. Oxnam was actually a moderate Christian socialist committed to helping the poor, but in the conservative atmosphere of Los Angeles in the 1920s this charge had some traction. Accurate or not, being branded a Bolshevik made it difficult for Oxnam to continue his work in Los Angeles. He left the Church of All Nations in 1927 to become president of DePauw University in Indiana. Robert A. McKibben, a gifted administrator, continued the church's work during the Great Depression years.[25]

• • • •

The boom psychology affected everyone—from the leaders of the business community to small-time investors. Eager to increase the size of their nest eggs, the midwesterners and others who moved to Southern California to enjoy their golden years invested their money in real estate, oil securities, and the stock market. This was not a local phenomenon. John Kenneth Galbraith observed that Americans in general during the 1920s displayed "an inordinate desire to get rich quickly with a minimum of physical effort." The boom years in Los Angeles produced a large population of talented individuals skilled at selling things. When the stock market crashed in 1929, they were suddenly out of work, but they were trained to keep an eye out for the main chance. They looked for other things to sell—things that offered hope to those who had given up hope. Where there is misery, there is money.[26]

2

The Crash

> The "spirit" of capitalism is that of the salesman who exudes confidence. When . . . most participants are searching for new (and, if possible, easy) ways to make money, panics, crises, and meltdowns become inevitable.
>
> Joyce Appleby, *The Relentless Revolution*

On the afternoon of October 21, 1929, a group of dignitaries including Mayor John Porter, Lieutenant Governor H. L. Carnahan, and Commissioner of Corporations Arthur H. Garland presided over the groundbreaking of the new home of the Los Angeles Stock Exchange. The proposed eleven-story headquarters on Spring Street was to be constructed of granite and gray limestone and contain the largest trading floor west of Wall Street. It included offices, spectators' galleries, telegraphic services, a ticker transmitter room, two auditoriums, and various other facilities. Miss Inez Vermillion, who was there because she was the longest-serving employee of the exchange and the only woman among the dignitaries, broke a bottle of water decorated with red and white ribbons on the jaws of a steam shovel filled with dirt. Prohibition dictated the use of water rather than the customary champagne. In any case, had an alcoholic beverage been used, the teetotaling mayor would have boycotted the ceremony. The participants in the dedication saw the construction of the new exchange as evidence that Los Angeles had come into its own as the leading financial center of the West Coast. Although optimism about the future was the order of the day, the timing of the event was ironic. Three days later, on October 24, the New York Stock Exchange crashed.[1]

October 24, Black Thursday, traditionally marks the beginning of the Great Depression. As the day progressed, the fall in stock prices accelerated and, in much the same way that a few spooked cattle can start a general stampede, the panic spread rapidly. Sellers, eager to unload their holdings, were hard pressed to find willing buyers. The volume of transactions was so great that the ticker could not keep up with trading. On the West Coast, transcontinental communications fell so far behind that no one knew what was going on. In retrospect, this was not necessarily a bad thing. If investors in Southern California had been fully aware of the extent of the rout in New York, the losses in the Los Angeles market might have been greater. As it was, the damage was severe. Margin traders, speculators who bought stock with borrowed money, were badly hurt. Lenders called in their loans because, in most cases, borrowers had used the very stock that was rapidly losing value as collateral. Investors who otherwise might have tried to weather the storm had no choice but to sell. The *Los Angeles Times* reported that "hardly a margin trader escaped without serious damage or utter ruin. It was a stern lesson for the speculator of small means to take, and hundreds were forced to bow in submission to a stock market gone mad."[2]

In the afternoon of this unsettling day, Thomas W. Lamont of the house of Morgan in New York organized a group of bankers who brought in a considerable amount of money to support prices in the New York exchange. This took the steam out of the panic, but the market still closed with a loss. Friday, October 25, was quiet, and it seemed to many that what had happened was one of those frightening, but not uncommon, "corrections." President Herbert Hoover reassured everyone that the nation's "fundamental business" was "sound and prosperous." The *Los Angeles Times* agreed, assuring its readers that the collapse in stock prices had nothing to do with the value of American businesses. "There is no connection between this correction or overindulgence in speculation and the state of general business." The paper quoted Los Angeles real estate magnate Joe Toplitzky, who believed that the market had bottomed out:

"In my opinion it is time for those who have surplus funds to purchase the leading stocks," he said.³

Reassuring frightened investors was the correct thing to do. After all, this was not the first time that the market had gone through a breathtaking decline. As unnerving as they were, these "breaks" seemed to be part of the very nature of the system. On June 11, 1928, a collapse in the value of bank stocks, the so-called Giannini break (for A. P. Giannini, founder of the Bank of America), had sent the Los Angeles market into a spin and left brokers and traders dazed and dumfounded. The *Los Angeles Times* considered it "the most exciting and tumultuous day in the exchange's history." The market took another dive in December and yet another in March 1929. All of these events followed a similar pattern. The financial community called them corrections and drew a distinction between the paper economy of the stock exchange and the real economy of factories, businesses, and workers. Those who survived these frightening disruptions saw a moral lesson. These losses, they felt, were the deserved punishment for those who had gambled recklessly and needed to be brought down to earth. Such corrections were not only inherent in the system but also fair, because they punished those who had sinned. The fact that the market rebounded with renewed vigor after each of these breaks seemed proof enough that they served the useful purpose of bringing the market back to a rational relationship to the real economy.⁴

The break that occurred the week of the dedication of the new Los Angeles Stock Exchange building did not follow the pattern of the past. Black Thursday was followed by Black Monday. When it opened that day, after a nervous weekend, the market resumed its downward plunge. Lamont and his banking pool withdrew, admitting that they did not have the resources to stop the massive selloff. Black Tuesday followed Black Monday. Over sixteen million shares changed hands on that day, a record-breaking volume. At the closing bell, the Dow Jones Industrial Average stood at 261—down from the record September high of 382 points. In Los Angeles, F. H. Kraft, a retired grocer and small-time investor in the market, died of a heart attack while watching the returns in his broker's office.⁵

Los Angeles's financial leaders did not give up easily on the view that the latest market panic was just another correction. On Thursday, October 31, a *Los Angeles Times* editorial looked back over the events of the past few days. The chief danger in the recent troubles, the paper said, was "largely psychological." After all, "no real money" had been lost in the disaster. It was just a matter of one group of speculators losing and another group winning. "What one group has lost another has gained." The important thing was that the "production of commodities and their sale go on; pay rolls are met; bills are discounted; crops are raised; human wants continue and must be satisfied—all without any relation whatever to what may happen at the corner of Wall and Broad streets." The editorial writer emphasized the useful moral lessons of the crash. "Incidentally it probably will make a good many amateur speculators, taken away from useful pursuits by the lure of easy money, go back to work." The market experienced a brief rally on Wednesday, the day before the editorial appeared, but this was more of a last gasp than a sign of recovery. For the rest of the year, the market continued its bumpy ride downward. In ten short weeks, the value of stocks in the market had fallen by 50 percent.[6]

The disaster felt on Wall Street and Spring Street quickly sent ripples through the economy. Industrial production in the nation fell by more than 9 percent from October to the end of the year. In the year following the crash, factory employment in Los Angeles dropped by more than 23 percent. On November 23, President Hoover telegraphed the nation's governors and the mayors of large cities and encouraged them to increase spending for public improvements. Mayor Porter proudly pointed to the construction of the Colorado River aqueduct and improvements in city parks, schools, and playgrounds. He estimated that the future costs of these programs would amount to over $100 million. In a telegram to the president, Porter promised that "in so far as it is physically possible" every dollar would go for "actual labor and materials." Middlemen and contractors who normally siphoned off 25 percent of the money appropriated would be eliminated. "In the emergency before us, I feel that every unnecessary profit should be eliminated, and thus bring about lasting prosperity."[7]

In early December, community leaders in Los Angeles arranged a day-long conference at city hall on the unemployment problem. Called under the auspices of the Church Federation, attendees included representatives of several important businesses and community groups. Mayor Porter addressed the gathering. Attendees assumed that the crisis would not last long and that extraordinary measures—especially those that required a greater expenditure of tax money for relief—would not be necessary. The conference drew up a tentative program for dealing with the Depression that business and political leaders would follow for the next three years despite its inadequacies. The plan recommended that a "coordinating executive" be appointed as manager. It asked that the city and county speed up construction and improvement projects and promise their employees employment for the next six months. The conference requested that the city council and the Los Angeles County board of supervisors cooperate in clearing up the Los Angeles River bottom and county and city parks and use labor that might otherwise end up on relief. It encouraged government departments and private employers to patronize local industries and businesses. The group prioritized aid to residents by asking for two jobless registries, one for local unemployed and another for nonresidents. For transients who refused employment, the conference asked that the city and county create a work farm where law enforcement officials could send them. The worry that outsiders might take advantage of the generosity of Southern Californians was a recurring theme throughout the Great Depression.[8]

There were others in the community who believed that the situation called for more direct government involvement. One such group was the International Unemployed Conference, with headquarters in the impoverished industrial district on the Los Angeles eastside, located only a few feet away from the Church of All Nations. The leading figure in the organization was a somewhat odd character, James Eads How, a deeply religious man who had devoted his life to helping the unemployed and the homeless. Born into a wealthy St. Louis family, How sported a long beard, wore old clothes, and traveled around the country living the life of a hobo. He spent much of his inherited wealth helping the homeless and soon acquired the nickname "millionaire hobo." As a young man he founded the International Brotherhood Welfare Association and established hobo colleges in the poor sections of cities across the nation. These "colleges" provided lodgings and educational and cultural activities for men who were homeless and unemployed. In the mid-1920s, How married and settled in Los Angeles and, probably to please his new wife, commissioned Rudolph M. Schindler to design a home in the

Silver Lake neighborhood of Los Angeles. He asked the architect to include extra rooms with a separate entrance to accommodate travelers in need of shelter. His wife, Mrs. Ingeborg How, soon divorced her husband, claiming that he "preferred the companionship of the Knights of the road" and had a bad habit of bathing only infrequently.[9]

How appeared before the Los Angeles City Council in late January and asked for an appropriation of $100,000 for unemployment relief. This call for direct government action was in contrast to Hoover's call for private and voluntary assistance. The *Los Angeles Times* sarcastically described How's request as "an opportunity" for the council "to enshrine itself in the hoboes' Hall of Fame." Councilman E. Snapper Ingram raised the specter of an army of unemployed arriving in the city should the council appropriate the funds. Councilman Evan Lewis characterized it as a "demand to turn over $100,000 of the taxpayers' money to a small, irresponsible group to divide among themselves." How approached the board of supervisors with a similar request, but both the city and the county denied his petitions. How's fight to help the unemployed in Los Angeles ended soon afterward when he collapsed and died while on a trip to the headquarters of his International Brotherhood Welfare Association in Cincinnati.[10]

Despite the growing unemployment lines, the *Los Angeles Times*, the foremost mouthpiece of the capitalist system in the city, continued its optimistic predictions that the economic downturn would be short and, in fact, might even be drawing to a close. While admitting that unemployment was too high, the paper argued that part of the problem was that the area was so attractive to outsiders. It is "fair to assume that in a section with as easy transportation as Southern California, the majority of the unemployed have been drawn into Los Angeles." The editors of the paper also worried that hasty but well-meaning attempts to deal with the crisis might bring ill-advised reforms. A predictable consequence of the Depression, the paper warned, "is that it will bring forth a flock of schemes for unemployment insurance." The *Times* reminded its readers that "most human beings are naturally lazy and that working for a living is an acquired habit" and that unemployment insurance might encourage idleness among otherwise productive workers. "Work, not doles, is the true unemployment remedy."[11]

The paper pointed to the U.S. census taken in April as support for the view that Southern California was weathering the storm much better than other parts of the country. In June it reported that preliminary returns indicated that "Southern California as a whole may show up as one of the employment 'white spots' of the entire country." The count showed that fewer than 45,000 persons were unemployed in Los Angeles, only 3.6 percent of the total population. In contrast, Cleveland, the only other city reporting at this early date, had an unemployment rate of 4.5 percent. Furthermore, the paper felt confident that since the census takers had completed their work conditions had "improved considerably."[12]

The census returns do indeed show that in Los Angeles on April 1 those out of work and looking for work amounted to 3.6 percent of the total population. The *Los Angeles Times* deftly avoided reporting that, if one looked at what the census bureau called the "gainful population," meaning the working population, rather than the total population, unemployment was much higher, 7.7 percent. In all of its reporting on the unemployment figures of the census—in every article published over a period of months—the *Times* always reported the percentage of the unemployed out of the entire population. Furthermore, the paper did not report all of the unemployed. Census takers placed respondents to their survey in Class A "persons out of a job, able to work, and looking for a job" or Class B "persons having jobs but on lay-off without pay." The *Times* reported only the returns for Class A, but a more accurate employment figure is the sum of Class A and Class B—an unemployment rate of 8.8 percent. Even this figure may have been too low. Many of those who had lost their jobs in early 1930 may have told the census enumerators that they still had jobs because they believed that they would be called back in the spring.[13]

Whether or not the census figures are accurate, it is clear that the employment situation did not improve over the course of the year. The Metropolitan Life Insurance Company conducted an employment survey in the first week of December 1930. The company's agents visited 5,036 families in Los Angeles and found that of the wage earners sampled 21 percent were "wholly unemployed." In a second unemployment count conducted in January 1931, the census bureau sampled twenty-one urban areas nationally, including Los Angeles. The bureau asked the same questions as before and employed, as far as it was possible, the same enumerators. The results revealed that unemployment was much worse than reported previously. The percentage of the population in Class A, unemployed and looking for work, was 12.4 percent of the total population and 18.1 percent of the gainful population. Combining the figures for Class A and Class B increased the percentages even more—of the total population without work to 13.5 and of the gainful workers 19.7.[14]

As the spring of 1930 turned to summer and then to fall, economic conditions did not improve. Along with unemployment, according to the investigations of the Community Chest, "in one out of every four of the homes of these unemployed persons sickness is an additional burden, due to worry and mal-nutrition." Many unemployed workers and their families still had enough resources to get by—gardens to grow food, savings, relatives willing to help out—but these could not last. Despite the severity of conditions, the streets of greater Los Angeles remained mostly calm. Angelenos, like other Americans, were resilient. They still had confidence that they would be able to take care of themselves and that conditions would improve. But a kernel of worry began to grow. What if? What if things did not improve? What if the country entered another winter without a recovery in sight?[15]

Those who lost their jobs had few places to turn for help. Older unemployed workers, who made up about 40 percent of the unemployed, were in an especially difficult position. It was accepted as a truism that anyone forty years or older who lost their job would likely never work again. W. H. Holland, the superintendent of the county department of charities, told the *Los Angeles Record* that it was "next to impossible for men over 45 to obtain work." More than half of the unemployed had not reached the age of forty, and they would be the first to be rehired when the economy finally improved. For the older unemployed, the outlook was bleak.[16]

When the unemployed, elderly or not, used up all of their personal resources, there were few choices left: public relief, private charity, or hit the road and look for work elsewhere. The life of the bindlestiff (hobo) was not a practical alternative for women or older men. The stigma of turning to relief or charity was very real for those who worked all their lives and never expected to be standing in a bread line. The *Los Angeles Times* recognized the humiliation that many unemployed felt when forced to turn to others for assistance. The "present ranks of the destitute include thousands who until a year ago had never been faced with actual need. Self-respecting and independent, they hesitate to place themselves in the class of charity seekers and are going hungry and are in danger of being ousted from their homes."[17]

The California State Pauper Act of 1901 had made the counties responsible for the care of destitute residents. Municipalities had no legal responsibility for relief, although in hard times cities and towns sometimes appropriated funds for work in parks or other projects. Los Angeles had a social service commission but it only regulated the solicitation of funds for charities within the city limits and endorsed private social agencies. The State of California played a secondary role in caring for the poor. In 1928 the voters approved Proposition 19, a constitutional amendment that permitted the state to appropriate funds to assist the "needy blind." The following year, the legislature passed the nation's first mandatory old-age assistance law, but its benefits were meager. It required that a recipient be at least seventy years of age and a resident of the state for fifteen years. It limited the total aid that an applicant could receive to no more than one dollar a day, including income from all sources. Sometimes called a pension, technically it was not because recipients were expected to pay back any money they received if they found themselves able to do so. Also, the board of supervisors could take liens against any property the recipients owned, and if authorities found relatives financially able to support them they could be compelled to reimburse the county for any aid given. The law put an additional burden on county governments because the state expected them to pay for half the cost of the program. Over the course of the decade the legislature liberalized the provisions of this law, lowering the residency and age requirements and increasing the amount of the pension. By the end of 1938, the average monthly payment was about $32.[18]

The Los Angeles County bureau of welfare, part of the department of charities, administered outdoor relief, defined as assistance to indigents who were not residents of the county poorhouse. Relief was based on principles that went back to sixteenth-century English poor laws. It was intended for the "worthy poor"—the blind, the feebleminded, the elderly who had no relatives, and others unable to care for themselves. Unemployed individuals who were able to work, the "unworthy poor," were expected to find jobs, and it was assumed that they would be able to do so if they wanted. Funds for county relief came from property taxes. This meant that increases in relief expenditures went hand in hand with increases in property taxes. There was fierce resistance to such increases, not only from homeowners but from powerful real estate interests. This is one reason why relief payments never would be overly generous. Keeping relief expenditures low meant that county governments took great pains to limit eligibility. No one got relief unless they were self-supporting residents of the state for one year. If an applicant possessed $250 or more in personal property, he or she could not get relief unless the county placed a lien on the property. Anyone who owned $2,500 or more of real property could not receive aid at all. This meant that if the unemployed managed to hang on to their homes, they were in the position of paying taxes, if they could, to support a system that did not benefit them. In 1931 the legislature increased the residency requirement to three years in the state and one year in the county where the relief was provided. The county quickly took advantage of this and removed more than seven thousand cases from the relief rolls. To be rid of nonresidents, the county was perfectly willing to pay transportation costs back to their home state. Private charities generally provided transients with support for only about three days before cutting them loose.[19]

The alternative to public relief was private charity. Los Angeles and its surrounding communities did not lack for charitable organizations, including the Salvation Army, the Volunteers of America, Goodwill, the YMCA, the YWCA, the Jewish Social Service Bureau, the Catholic Welfare Bureau, the Midnight Mission, the Union Rescue Mission, and the Church of All Nations. Charity workers in the private sphere considered themselves more professional and better trained than their counterparts in the county. They believed that public relief was often politically motivated and too much under the influence of the business community. Commenting on the problem of lodging transient men, Dr. George Mangold, a member of the executive committee of the Council of Social Agencies, expressed some of this resentment when he said that the "private agencies are required to haul the coals out of the fire for the

Aimee Semple McPherson's dining hall was one of several private charities where the unemployed could receive a free meal in 1932. Los Angeles Daily News Negatives (Collection 1387), courtesy of the Library Special Collections, Charles E. Young Research Library, UCLA.

city." Despite the existence of this committed group of organizations and the men and women, paid and volunteer, who staffed them, Los Angeles had a reputation, when it came to charity, of not being particularly generous. "We live in a very cold-hearted and a very ego-centric community," C. A. Lyman, chairman of the 1930 Community Chest publicity campaign, remarked. He believed that people moved to Southern California for one reason—personal comfort—and put "their pleasures ahead of everything else."[20]

Most of the charities in Los Angeles were affiliated with the Community Chest. Founded in 1924, only five years before the Great Crash, the Chest was an effort to centralize and coordinate the city's charitable giving. The business community, especially the Chamber of Commerce, was behind the drive to create the new organization.

Business leaders complained that they were asked to give too much too often. The motivation of the organizers of the Chest, according to Lyman, was not to "do more good" but to be "bothered less." The Alliance of Social Agencies, representing the city's private social workers, feared that the Chest would be a business organization that would not appreciate the need for community planning or modern standards of social work. In spite of these feelings among professionals, the annual campaigns of the Community Chest soon became the single most important source of funding for affiliated charities. Even the cynical Lyman admitted that, though it began as a "business campaign without a great deal of heart in it . . . the desire to do good and to help" later grew into it.[21]

• • • •

These few attempts at public relief or private charity were the choices for the down and out in Southern California at the beginning of the Great Depression. Except to the *Los Angeles Times* and other advocates for free-market capitalism, it soon became clear that they were woefully inadequate. The *Times* continued with its line that the Depression had not affected Southern California severely and, in fact, that recovery had already begun. With the second Depression winter on the horizon, the paper managed to squeeze something positive out of news that most people would have found depressing. In October 1930, the paper published an editorial announcing that the end of the year brought "the best buyers' market that this generation has seen, or is likely to see." Prices had fallen so low on food, clothing, shelter, and most commodities that it amounted to "a 25 per cent increase in pay." This may have been good news to those who still had a job; it was less than exciting to the growing ranks of the unemployed.[22]

The spring of 1930 came and went, as did the summer. By fall it was clear to everyone that the city and county of Los Angeles faced a second Depression winter. Contrary to the optimistic bubblings of the *Los Angeles Times*, the economy was not improving. In fact, it was getting worse. The county, the city of Los Angeles, and the dozens of municipalities in the metropolitan region used every dollar available to create temporary work for the unemployed. These were pick-and-shovel jobs, available to local men only. It was not an uncommon sight to see workers in the field who seemed unaccustomed to manual labor. The writer John S. McGroarty reported seeing one such man along the road. He was working much harder but accomplishing less than an experienced laborer. "There have been a lot of men these late years working in ditches who don't know how," he wrote. They "have been glad to get any kind of a job at which they could eat."[23]

3

THE DOWNWARD SPIRAL

> Hoover gave the signal,
> Mellon rang the bell,
> Wall Street blew the whistle,
> And the country went to hell.
>
> Poem recited by children living in a
Los Angeles homeless encampment

Supervisor Frank Leslie Shaw, chairman of the county board of supervisor's charities committee, led the county's efforts to fight unemployment. He was hardworking and intelligent and infused new energy into the county's response to the job crisis. In 1930, Shaw was forty-seven years old. Born in a small town in Ontario, Canada, he moved with his parents to the United States when he was only six. His family settled in Joplin, Missouri. Shaw's extroverted personality made him a natural salesman. In 1908 he was working as a sales representative for a wholesale grocery firm when his employer transferred him to Southern California. When he retired from business, Shaw made a transition into politics. In 1925, with the support of both the reformist Municipal League and Kent Parrot, the political boss behind Mayor George Cryer's administration, he won a city council seat on a moderately progressive platform. Reelected to the council in 1927, he moved on the following year to a much more powerful seat on the board of supervisors. He was determined to do his best for his constituents but also saw politics as a potentially lucrative profession. John R. Quinn, who served with Shaw on the board of supervisors, recalled, "Very clever fellow, Frank Shaw was; good public servant; but as he said, 'Where the money goes, I go.'"[1]

Shaw declared that no deserving family would be permitted to starve in the county of Los Angeles. His program was to increase "work and to keep the bread line out of Southern California." Although he brought energy to the job, his ideas differed little from the voluntaristic schemes that others advocated. He repeated the business community's call to spread available work by adopting a five-day work week rather than the standard six days. He advocated fantasies such as the Man-a-Block program. The idea, not original with Shaw, was that each city block should hire an unemployed man to take care of lawns or do odd jobs. He also proposed a Woman-a-Block program to help with housework. At the beginning of December, Shaw announced the appointment of Harvey Fremming, deputy state labor commissioner and president of the Long Beach Central Labor Council, as "director of employment stabilization for municipalities within the boundaries of the county." Fremming was charged with creating a county job registration bureau and finding funds to create work. In the parlance of the twenty-first century, Fremming might have been called the county "unemployment czar."[2]

The unemployed who sought assistance through this new county program would not have to go through the indignity of becoming totally impoverished before accepting aid. In addition to the usual manual labor jobs, Shaw hoped to find work for "white collar" men and office women who were poorly served by most of the relief work the county and municipalities provided. Registration began at the beginning of 1931 at sheriff substations and fire stations. Registrants provided detailed information that helped create hierarchies to serve as guidelines to determine how funds, if found, were distributed. White male heads of families had the highest priority, single men next, minorities lower still. Nonresidents and noncitizens were at the bottom and not likely to get anything. The program also tried to find work for unemployed single women, although married men, who presumably supported families, had priority.[3]

Predictably, finding work for the registrants was the toughest part of Fremming's job. Shaw called a conference of the mayors and city managers of all incorporated municipalities in the county to discuss the distribution of jobs. Of the forty-one municipalities represented, only Beverly Hills did not request county money. (The representative of that city said that the only unemployed citizen living there was Will Rogers.) Most of the jobs were manual labor in county parks, roads, schools, and post offices and were temporary or part time. The county forestry department agreed to put men on relief to work at three dollars per day clearing firebreaks and similar work in the local mountains. Using its portion of the state gasoline tax and automobile license fees, the county appropriated $500,000 for road improvements in the municipalities and another $150,000 for work in the unincorporated areas. Businesses that converted to a five-day work week claimed to have created 954 new positions, and 6,963 other workers who might otherwise have been laid off were kept on the job. Despite the rule giving priority to male heads of families, Fremming managed to find work for several hundred unemployed women—a mere handful compared to the thousands of unemployed women desperately in need. In June, Fremming reported that since the beginning of the year he had found 25,402 jobs in the incorporated cities of the county and 5,117 in the unincorporated areas. Early in October, he claimed that since September 1 he had found work for another 63,456 individuals, but he also reported that there were still 145,000 unemployed in the county, 93,000 of these in the city of Los Angeles.[4]

Relief may have been a county responsibility, but the crisis was so severe that Mayor Porter thought the city needed its own plans to assist the unemployed. Political rivalries and clashing personalities kept Supervisor Shaw and Mayor Porter from cooperating closely. Porter's program did not include asking the city council to appropriate funds for relief. Instead, the mayor named Charles P. Visel, a private citizen, head of the Citizens' Committee on Unemployment Relief and charged him with creating a city registry with the names of 14,000 men who were ready to work should jobs ever materialize. Porter also expected city employees to contribute 1 percent of their pay to an unemployment relief fund. When the city attorney ruled that a mandatory salary deduction was illegal, the mayor made it voluntary. City workers proved exceptionally generous in helping those who lost their jobs. Over the twenty-five-month life of the program, they contributed over $200,000 to the fund.[5]

Acting independently of the mayor, the Associated City Employees Unemployment Relief Association donated apples to disabled women and men, who sold them on the streets. The sight of the destitute selling apples was common in American cities, so much so that the historian Irving Bernstein called the fruit an "absurd symbol of the depression." One might assume that such a seemingly harmless program would be above criticism, but N. P. Alexander, managing director of the Downtown Business Men's Association, considered the apple vendors to be unfair competition to downtown business. A letter to the editor in the *Times*, signed by "Navelencia," asked if the California orange, "the most glorious fruit grown anywhere on earth," might have been a better choice than the apple. As limited as it was, the program helped those who were living on the edge of starvation. In the two months that it lasted, participants sold two million apples, earning an average of about $90 for each person involved.[6]

At the suggestion of C. K. Steele, president of the Associated City Employees, the city council unanimously approved a $5 million bond issue for work relief to be placed on the ballot in a special election in early March 1931. The measure had broad support, ranging from the American Legion to the Socialist Party. Opposition came from realtors and from people who thought they had nothing to gain if it passed. In an angry letter to the *Los Angeles Times*, a reader named James Carlile Thompson wrote that, although unemployed, as a homeowner he would not be eligible to receive anything from the measure. "Am I benefited by this $5,000,000 bond? Not one cent!" Even so, it passed, as required for all bond issues, with two-thirds of those voting.[7]

Five million dollars was a lot of money in 1931 (almost $85,000,000 in 2019 dollars). Its supporters believed that amount was more than enough to keep the unemployed busy until the economy improved, but in less than seven months nearly all of it was gone. By year's end only about 15 percent of the city's unemployed had found work under the program, earning on the average about $300 each. The bond issue did have plenty of positive benefits. It enabled the city of Los Angeles to improve bridle paths, picnic areas, and parking lots, plant some 15,000 trees, and construct community houses, gymnasiums, swimming pools, bath houses, baseball diamonds, and life guard stations. When the money was gone, these improvements remained, but so did the unemployed.[8]

The city's private charities struggled under the weight of the unemployed. The Midnight Mission reported to Supervisor Shaw that during the month of January it served 71,075 meals to homeless and unemployed men—almost double the previous year. In its two downtown facilities, the Mission provided over 23,000 beds to homeless men. It was a sign of the times that the Mission, originally founded to serve the needs of transient men, saw an increase in the number of local residents who asked for help. Other service organizations such as the Salvation Army, the Red Cross, the American Legion, the Jewish Social Service Bureau, and the Catholic Welfare Bureau also experienced increased demands for their services. The county assisted private agencies as much as its resources allowed. The charities department provided fifty cents a day to the Midnight Mission for each man it served. "This gives each homeless man three meals, a bath, towels, soap and writing paper," according to social worker Mary Covell.

Early in 1931, financial support for the Community Chest began to dry up. The Chest's annual campaign in 1931 fell $500,000 short of its goal. As the economy worsened and the needs of charitable institutions grew, it became harder to raise money. A few months later, attorney Joseph Scott, éminence grise of charitable fundraising in Los Angeles, agreed to be chairman of a Chest emergency campaign to raise $265,000 specifically for those who lost jobs because of the Depression. The campaign flopped, achieving only about a third of its goal. The passage of the $5 million bond issue and the feeling that contributions were no longer necessary may have had something to do with the failure of these campaigns, but it was also true that more than a year after the stock market collapse Southern Californians were weary of the constant requests for money to assist the unemployed.[9]

In April 1931, Superintendent William H. Holland, head of county charities, asked the board of supervisors for an additional $1 million to carry his department to the end of the fiscal year. The board balked at this request. "I am not against feeding the people who are needy, but where is the money coming from to do it?" Supervisor Quinn asked. The supervisors granted Holland only $506,750. They complained loudly about the additional responsibilities the state had placed on counties without supplying the additional revenues to support them. These included programs for the blind, old-age pensions, child welfare, twelve new superior court judges for Los Angeles County, and pay raises for all of the county's superior court judges. But these additional responsibilities were not really the reasons for the county's financial problems. "It is unemployment," said Holland. "Fully 60 per cent of the people now on our charity list are there because of unemployment." Thirty-seven percent of county revenues went to relief—an increase of 11 percent over the previous five years.[10]

Even faced with demands for more assistance, the supervisors were under intense pressure from the Los Angeles realty board and other groups to cut costs and lower property taxes. The realtors pointed out that over the past five years the county tax rate had increased from sixty-six cents per $100 of assessed evaluation to eighty-eight cents and that municipal and school taxes also had increased over the same time period. They suggested that the board make cuts by eliminating county positions and reducing subsidies to the Chamber of Commerce and contributions to charitable institutions. The supervisors bridled at the realtors' suggestions. Shaw said that he did not understand, given the state of the economy and the demands on the county, how reductions could be accomplished. "There is nothing else we can do but take care of the people. . . . We cannot let them starve. If we let up for even six hours I hate to think of what might happen."[11]

At the end of May, Superintendent Holland approached the board and asked for another $350,000. The supervisors granted Holland only $100,000 and asked the county's bureau of efficiency to make a survey of the charities department to "determine whether all persons receiving aid are worthy, or if some of them have means of support and are hoodwinking county officials." The supervisors wrestled with the problem of what to do. Supervisor Wright wondered whether the county had a legal obligation to do anything other than provide for traditional charity cases. "There is no question what we should do with the people who are ill," he said, "but there is some question, under the law, as to our procedure in the case of those who are merely out of work." The board debated whether it should sponsor a $5 million bond issue similar to the one the city had just passed, or whether it should do the unthinkable and raise the county tax rate from eighty-eight cents to ninety-eight cents. The board did neither.[12]

Superintendent Holland continued to irritate the board with more requests for money. Early in June, he told them that the $100,000 the board gave him only a few days before did not include $25,000 for staff salaries and that he still needed the balance of the $350,000 he requested. Supervisors Mahaffey and Quinn seemed taken aback, maintaining that they thought the $100,000 covered staff salaries. The board reluctantly granted him the $25,000 but decided to deny the remaining $225,000. At 2 p.m. the next day Holland abruptly announced that he had run out of funds and closed his offices. He said that his department could not continue to operate unless the board of supervisors gave him another $250,000 to continue its work for the rest of the month. All work at the welfare department stopped. To say the least, the supervisors did not appreciate being blindsided by one of their department heads. "People are calling me up and telling me their aid has been stopped and that they are facing starvation," Supervisor Quinn announced to his colleagues. After a stormy session, the board appropriated the $250,000, taking the money from the county reserve. After granting the additional funds, the board ordered the auditor's office to install a new system of accounting in the charities department and to report at the end of each day how much was spent. In addition, the board hired a committee of special investigators—none of them involved professionally in the charitable community—and paid them $225 a month each, to survey cases in the charities department to determine if there were any persons receiving aid who were not entitled to it.[13]

On Shaw's recommendation, the county established a work test for able-bodied men on the county charity rolls. He argued that a work test benefited relief recipients because a work requirement preserved the self-respect of those who reluctantly accepted aid and weeded out the shameless deadbeats. "The test will not only satisfy the man who wants to work for the aid he is receiving, but it will eliminate the fellow who does not want to work, who has been using the depression as an excuse . . . to get a living without working," Shaw insisted. Eager to get out of what was a thankless job, Holland announced his resignation. The board drafted W. R. Harriman, head of the county poor farm, as his successor. He accepted reluctantly, pointing out that he had refused the position at least twenty times in the past.[14]

The committee investigating the department of charities issued its report on August 17. It did not deal with the larger question of how to cope with the unprecedented demands unemployment placed on the department. Instead, it focused narrowly on how to eliminate waste caused by administrative laziness and incompetence. The special committee seemed to feel all that was needed was to get rid of the deadbeats who were taking advantage of the county's good nature. They recommended that the casework that social workers usually performed be eliminated. The report noted that since 1925–26 "the county Welfare Department has conducted the 'Social Welfare' program. Under this policy each application for relief was developed into a social welfare case and 'the rendering of every possible service within the law and the solving of each problem or problems that caused the poverty.'" The committee objected to this practice for only one reason—it was expensive.[15]

It is hard to avoid the cynical conclusion that the supervisors selected a committee only to provide them with what they wanted to hear. The report, based on an examination of 5 percent of the recipients of county relief, concluded that largely because of administrative inefficiencies the department wasted thousands of dollars giving aid to people who did not need or deserve it. "There are families that have been receiving aid from the Welfare Department for many years," it stated. Children who were born into it "know nothing else than public relief." The report claimed that "indigents are pampered" and that county workers did not want to deny aid to individuals for fear of getting into trouble with their superiors. The committee pointed to individual cases of recipients they felt did not deserve aid: a family that owned an expensive radio and who had a son with "the most expensive type velocipede." At a home in Pasadena, two members of the committee walked up the driveway of a family on relief at the very moment that the family's two school-age sons "drove up in a Ford." Another woman, "besides owning an automobile," had two "very large and ravenous St. Bernard dogs that are being fed at public expense."[16]

The committee reported that the superintendent of charities rarely, "if ever," visited the offices under his supervision. There was little consistency from district to district office in the administration of relief, and there were no consistent criteria for granting aid. Districts operated independently with no "coherent, homogenous organization, nor standardized methods and practices." If transients were denied aid in one district, they could move to another one. "It is not an uncommon thing for a family, when confronted with the alternative of going to work or going without food, to pack up their meager belongings, move into another district, make application for aid and soon be on the county Welfare Department for care." The committee recommended standardizing practices across the county and interpreting the Pauper Act narrowly, to provide "simple relief for those who are in need and entitled to aid." The investigators made the hardly credible claim that such reforms would save $643,561 annually.[17]

Many Southern Californians believed that transients overwhelmed local resources. A 1936 State Relief Administration report, *Transients in California,* claimed that California was "at the top of the list . . . for unattached transients and families." The report noted that if transients have any sense "they start toward a state where climate at least will be favorable toward survival." Residency requirements for public relief made it illegal for counties to assist them—a restriction that the counties were perfectly happy to accept. These transients were passed on to the already overburdened private charitable institutions. A frequently suggested solution to the problem was the so-called work test—otherwise known as the "rock pile." As one charity worker put it, "Any man who is self-respecting, when he is given a bed and his meals in return for four hours work . . . ought to be willing in a time when thousands are unemployed to return that much to the city that shelters him."[18]

Transients, sometimes called "tramps," "hobos," or "bindlestiffs," were usually single men who hitchhiked or caught a free ride on boxcars, sometimes called "bum Pullmans." But as the Depression deepened, entire families began arriving in rickety automobiles. Rescue missions and charitable agencies such as the Midnight

Mission or the Salvation Army traditionally attended to the needs of these refugees. Los Angeles police chief Roy E. Steckel probably spoke for a majority of Southern Californians when he said that transients should not expect free room and board even in the city jails. "We do not intend to provide free lodging for flocks of vagrants in this city," he announced. "If they don't take the tip to stay away from Los Angeles . . . we will have to make some arrangements with the Police Commission and the City Council to provide a rock pile where they can be placed at good hard labor."[19]

Charles P. Visel, head of Mayor Porter's Citizens' Committee on Unemployment Relief, believed that as many as ten thousand of the unemployed in Los Angeles were "floaters" who drained resources that might otherwise go to residents. George H. Cecil of the Los Angeles Chamber of Commerce estimated that 20 percent of the charity cases in the county were chronic transients who came for "the sole purpose of becoming a charge upon us for charity." James S. Carter, in an article in the *Los Angeles Times* titled "The Incoming Hobo Army," wrote that these men, "the ones with the families hanging on somewhere, waiting for them to get a job, are the ones who will bear watching." They are "on the verge of desperation." Riding with them on the rails were the professional agitators, the "I.W.W.'s" who "never get particularly hungry or cold for they have ways of obtaining the makings of a mulligan and they know all the tricks of the road; their motto is, 'never work while you have your health'; and they get away with it." The policy of excluding transients reached absurd levels in 1936 with the "Bum Blockade," when Chief James E. Davis dispatched LAPD officers to the state's borders to intercept unwanted migrants entering the state.[20]

Even less welcome than native-born transients were the foreign born. As the Depression deepened, local and national political leaders persuaded themselves that foreigners residing in the United States took jobs and charitable resources that rightfully belonged to American citizens. Soon after his appointment in December 1930, William N. Doak, Hoover's secretary of labor, declared that he would deport all noncitizens residing illegally in the United States. He ordered the Bureau of Immigration, at that time part of the Labor Department, to hunt down and arrest aliens eligible for deportation. The secretary estimated that there were 400,000 living in the United

States. He argued that, if the country were rid of them, the nation's unemployment problem would be solved.[21]

Reenter Visel, who enthusiastically endorsed Secretary Doak's pronouncement. He believed that there were thousands of foreigners living illegally in Los Angeles and, if they were forced to leave, they would free up many jobs and relief money for "natives of this country and aliens who have made legal entry." He also felt that their expulsion would rid the city of troublesome people participating in unemployment demonstrations and "making heavy demands on the relief set-ups now operating." Visel invited Secretary Doak to send agents to Los Angeles and promised the full cooperation of local authorities in rounding up noncitizens who were in the country illegally. He announced this campaign in a publicity release that appeared in the newspapers on January 26. In this release, Visel said that trained members of the Bureau of Immigration's "Deportation Squad" would come to Los Angeles and assist W. E. Carr, head of the local Immigration office. In an attempt to appear fair and evenhanded, he added that not all aliens were deportable and reassured the Mexican community that they were not the targets of the campaign. Visel helpfully explained that deportable aliens included "Chinese, Japanese, Europeans, Canadians, Mexicans," and other nationalities. Despite these words, there was no doubt in anyone's mind that Mexicans were Visel's real targets.[22]

The deportation campaign found broad support among community leaders. Some thought that it might solve all of their problems. Supervisor Quinn believed that deportations could make the unemployment program "shrink to the proportions of a relatively flat spot in business." As a bonus, he thought that it would also rid the city of most of its communists. Chief Steckel and Sheriff William I. Traeger were less enthusiastic because they worried about the legality of rounding up individuals for no other reason than the suspicion that they were in the country illegally. In practice, they cooperated fully with Bureau of Immigration agents.[23]

At the end of January, William F. Watkins of the Bureau of Investigation and several federal agents arrived in Los Angeles. Watkins immediately sought a meeting with Visel and local law enforcement authorities. He soon discovered that Visel's estimate of the number of deportable aliens who lived in Los Angeles was grossly exaggerated. He disapproved of Visel's use of newspaper publicity because he felt, rightly, that it would drive their targets underground and make them more difficult to find. He soon learned that this coverage was an integral part of the city campaign. Visel wanted to do more than simply round up all of the deportable noncitizens he could find. He also wanted to create an atmosphere of fear and intimidation that compelled them to pack up and leave on their own. Watkins began his work early in February. A few days later, on Friday the 13th, Watkins's agents working with Captain William J. Bright of the sheriff's department launched a raid in the town of El Monte, east of Los Angeles. The authorities questioned three hundred people and took thirteen into custody; all but one of those arrested were Mexican citizens. Soon, the streets in East Los Angeles, a center of the Mexican population, were empty. On February 17, Miguel Venegas, a legal resident of the city, wrote his father in Mexico, "It's getting worse day by day, and the people are scared because there is an army of detectives searching to deport Mexicans who may have entered illegally which causes many to stay at home rather than go out in search of work; they do not understand that it is only those who do not have a passport that will be deported."[24]

In the afternoon of February 26, Watkins's agents and a contingent of LAPD officers surrounded the Los Angeles Plaza. The Plaza is a small park to the north of downtown Los Angeles that was the center of the original Spanish pueblo. After the American conquest, the city center moved south, but the Plaza remained a meeting place for speakers advocating various causes and where members of the Mexican community congregated and relaxed. The police refused to allow anyone to leave and began systematically questioning everyone present, asking for passports or other identification. A few curious spectators who wandered over to see what was going on were also detained. Mexican vice consul Ricardo Hill avoided arrest only because he had consular identification. The authorities hauled eleven Mexicans, five Chinese, and one Japanese person to the city jail. The surprise raid proved a spectacular failure at catching "deportable" aliens. Nine of the eleven Mexicans arrested were released. In retrospect, the whole episode seems pointless because noncitizens in the country illegally were unlikely to congregate in such an obvious place, or anywhere else, for that matter.[25]

When the federal campaign came to an end in February, the government had caught 389 noncitizens who were in the country illegally. Seven out of ten were from Mexico. To catch fewer than four hundred deportable aliens the authorities had rounded up, detained, and questioned three to four thousand people; the effort hardly seemed worth the bad publicity the Immigration Bureau generated in the process. Visel's ill conceived and poorly executed plan sputtered to a close, but, even so, he boldly declared victory. In a letter to labor secretary Doak, he bragged that the "exodus of aliens deportable and otherwise who have been scared out of the community has undoubtedly left many jobs which have been taken up by other persons (not deportable) and citizens of the United States and our municipality."[26]

In the midst of this atmosphere of fear and anxiety, Los Angeles County launched its own campaign to encourage Mexican nationals to leave. Supervisor Shaw was the first to come up with the idea of using county funds for a voluntary repatriation program. Mexican-born charity cases accounted for 9–11 percent of the relief load, and Shaw reasoned that if enough Mexican citizens could be persuaded to leave the savings would justify the expense. The county chartered special trains for those who volunteered to leave the country and enlisted the cooperation of the Mexican government, which allowed those who returned to bring, duty free, possessions such as automobiles and farm equipment. By early June the county program had repatriated some 1,350 individuals. An even larger number left on their own or with the assistance of private charity groups. The *Los Angeles Record* reported 29,000; the *Times* 40,000.[27]

Many of the children on these trains were born in the United States but lacked birth certificates or other documentation to prove their citizenship. They probably never returned—at least legally. George P. Clements, manager of the Chamber of Commerce's agricultural department, wrote that no "child could return, even though born in America, unless he had documentary evidence and his birth certificate and was able to substantiate this, the burden of proof being placed entirely on the individual." The county brushed aside the charge that some of the repatriated were American citizens. In the eyes of many white Americans, the issue of place of birth was irrelevant in any case. A Mexican was a Mexican, regardless of where he or she was born.[28]

Mexican citizens who took the county's repatriation offer did so with the understanding that someday they might be able to return, but officials were not entirely honest in making this promise. When the third train in the repatriation campaign left in August, the county issued departure cards to those on board. On the back, each card bore the stamp of the Los Angeles County department of charities. When presented for reentry, this stamp was accepted as proof that its bearer had been on welfare and would most likely be on welfare again. The possibility that an individual might become a "public charge" was sufficient grounds to deny entry into the United States.

Critics accused the charities department of simply dumping repatriates on the other side of the Mexican border, but it was not until after the ninth train departed that anyone looked into the issue. The county sent Rex Thomson, a deputy superintendent and a future head of charities, to investigate an agricultural colony for repatriates that the Mexican government proposed in Baja California. Thomson discovered not only that the land in question was unsuitable for cultivation but also that Governor Augustín Olachea adamantly opposed resettlement because he could not find work for residents already living there. The Mexican government also made abortive attempts to create repatriation colonies in the states of Guerrero and Oaxaca, but these efforts failed for various reasons.[29]

Although the number of Mexicans willing to be repatriated declined after 1934, the county never really gave up on the idea. As late as 1941, Supervisor John Anson Ford discussed continuing the program with Rodolfo Salazar, the Mexican consul in Los Angeles who, Ford admitted, "was rather touchy on the matter of repatriation." Even after the Japanese attack on Pearl Harbor, Ford went to Mexico to negotiate an agreement. On the last day of December, Mexican president Manual Avila Camacho announced his approval of Ford's repatriation plan, but the outbreak of war doomed any repatriation program. In March, Ford was dismayed to learn that California's U.S. senator, Sheridan Downey, suggested the possibility of importing 30,000–50,000 Mexican workers to meet labor shortages. The war changed everything. Unemployment disappeared, available labor became scarce, and repatriation became a thing of the past.[30]

A Los Angeles "Hooverville" squatter settlement located on a vacant lot on Alameda Street at Firestone in the early 1930s. Los Angeles Times Photographic Archive (Collection 1429), courtesy of the Library Special Collections, Charles E. Young Research Library, UCLA.

• • • •

Despite the optimistic statements of business and civic leaders, it became clear that as the end of 1932 approached better times were not on the horizon. The sad spectacle of people evicted from their homes became a common sight in Southern California. Those with nowhere else to go found shelter in makeshift huts made of tarpaper, scrap lumber, and burlap bags. Clusters of these houses assumed the character of semipermanent settlements. Some of the larger ones had names: "Hoover City," "New Haven Village," "Ragtown." These "Hoovervilles," as they were called nationally, differed from the hobo camps that existed even in good times along the Los Angeles River and elsewhere in the county. The inhabitants of these new places were not displaced single men—the tramps of pre-Depression America—but local families who had lost their homes.[31]

These victims of the economic collapse felt the pain of dislocation even more painfully because a world of plenty surrounded them. Dwellings that once provided shelter for evicted families remained unoccupied because no one could afford to rent or buy them. Dairy operators poured milk down the gutter rather than give it away. Citrus farmers disposed of unsold oranges in the Los Angeles River bed. Bakeries sold day-old bread to farmers who fed it to hogs. The county supervisors who wrestled with the choice of raising taxes or cutting relief opted for the latter. Charities department superintendent Harriman cut the 1931–32 average monthly relief payment to $19.12, and by the end of the fiscal year to only $13.00, an amount no one pretended was adequate. At the same time, the welfare load grew by 124 percent. Harriman found himself doing the very thing that cost Holland his job—asking the board of supervisors for more money. In the spring of 1932, two months before the end of the fiscal year, the county spent over $4 million on relief—a million dollars more than the amount budgeted.[32]

In the presidential election on November 8, 1932, Franklin Roosevelt carried Los Angeles County with 57.2 percent of the vote. President Herbert Hoover trailed far behind with only 38.6 percent. Only four years before, in what seemed another era, Hoover had swept the county with over 70 percent of the vote. Southern California, along with the rest of the country, waited to see what the new president would do. In 1932, Inauguration Day fell not at the beginning of the calendar year as it does today but on March 4. The four-month period between election day and the inauguration, sometimes called the Interregnum, was the darkest in the history of the Great Depression. Voters had tossed out the old and discredited president, but the plans of the new one, called the New Deal, remained a mystery. The future was uncertain. Southern Californians, a self-sufficient and resilient people, looked for ways to help themselves.

4

SELF-HELP

> We didn't know where we were going, but we were on our way.
>
> Member of a self-help cooperative

Local tradition has it that in the town of Compton in the spring of 1932, a man named "Shorty" Burchfield, a veteran of the Spanish-American War, planted the seeds of a movement that in a matter of months swept across the entire county. Self-help cooperatives, as they came to be called, put food on the tables of thousands of desperate families. Compton, a small town about halfway between Los Angeles and Long Beach, for most of its history was an isolated farming community. In the 1920s, the introduction of the automobile made it practical for workers to live in the town and commute to jobs in nearby oil fields and factories. During the decade, the town's population ballooned from 1,478 to 12,516. Land was affordable, and despite its explosive growth it retained a pleasant semirural character. The town possessed two important qualities that encouraged the growth of the self-help cooperatives—a tightly knit group of neighbors who looked out for one another and a location surrounded by richly productive farmlands.[1]

Burchfield was part of a group of aging veterans, members of the Disabled American War Veterans Association, who met regularly to discuss and complain about the state of world affairs. They were concerned most of all about how people could be going hungry when food lay rotting in the fields that surrounded their town. These "malcontents," as the future economist Clark Kerr fondly called them, did more than complain. They decided to do something to help themselves and others who were in a similar situation. During the winter of 1931-32, they placed baskets in local stores to collect donations for needy families. In February, one of the malcontents, possibly Burchfield, picked up an empty gunny sack and made the rounds of local truck farms. (No one remembered for certain who actually did this, but as one member of the group explained, "It all had to have a beginning so we selected Burchfield.") He traded his labor for any surplus produce the farmers were willing to give him and returned home that night with his bag bulging with vegetables. The following morning his friends joined him. At the end of the day they brought their families more food than they could eat. Much of the produce they collected was below market grade, but it was still edible and very welcome in homes where there was little or nothing on the table. For the most part, the Japanese Americans who operated the farms in the area were cooperative because they were also loath to accept charity and sympathized with those who were willing to work. They were also getting a good deal—cheap labor paid for with produce they would have thrown out. These farmers were central to the success of the early self-help movement, a fact not lost on those who depended on them. One Compton resident said that the "Japanese treat us better than the white people do."[2]

Burchfield and his fellow veterans expanded their group to include anyone who wanted to join. In the beginning there were no rules or formal organization. Members worked as much as they could or wanted, and food was divided on the basis of need rather than hours worked. A veteran named Bill Downing, owner of the Compton Moving Company, donated a building and a truck and informally assumed the responsibilities of manager. The movement spread quickly to neighboring communities—Bellflower, South Gate, Huntington Park, and then across the entire county. Growth was slower within the Los Angeles city limits because urban neighborhoods lacked the advantage of close proximity to farmlands. The Unemployed Aid Society, a group under the influence or control of the Communist Party, organized some of the city units. The membership of the majority of cooperative units was white. Of 110 units that Kerr surveyed, eighty-eight were made up of whites, but some units had racially mixed memberships. Only one specifically excluded minorities as a matter of policy; in theory, at least, all of the others followed a policy of "no race or color lines." Even so, in a city and county where residential segregation was universally enforced, the membership of the cooperatives reflected the racial makeup of the surrounding neighborhoods. Kerr reported that at year's end there were ninety barter units in Los Angeles County serving 25,000 families.[3]

The Compton self-help cooperative was an entirely local and spontaneous phenomenon, but it was not the first such group in the United States. Credit for that probably goes to the students and staff of the Seattle Labor College, who early in 1931 organized a barter cooperative called the Seattle Unemployed Citizens' League. Unemployed workers also formed barter exchanges in Idaho and Utah. Burchfield and his friends in Compton had no connection or even knowledge of these other efforts, and Southern California proved to be an exceptionally fertile ground for the cooperative movement. In December 1934, when UCLA sociologist Constantine Panunzio completed his fieldwork for a study of the movement in the area, there were 139 self-help units in Los Angeles County, constituting over 44 percent of all cooperatives in the United States.[4]

Panunzio gave several reasons why the self-help cooperative movement was so popular in Southern California. In the 1930s, Los Angeles County was still an important agricultural region and farms were close to suburban communities. The movement appealed especially to older residents who were not likely to find work even if the economy improved. (Panunzio calculated that the average age of the membership in the units he studied was 52.4 years.) Many of the participants were property owners not eligible for relief even if they were inclined to accept it. The failure of the business community and local government to deal effectively with the crisis left people with few alternatives. The aging and conservative population of Southern California rose to the occasion and produced leaders who were willing and able to step forward to help themselves and their neighbors.[5]

Of the more than a thousand people Panunzio interviewed, over 80 percent were American born and most were from the Midwest.

Panunzio called them "a plain, average, matter-of-fact folk, trying to make the best of a bad economic situation without resorting to private or public charity." The movement had no place for radicals. Downing, manager of the Compton cooperative, made it clear that this "is no place for radical expression against duly authorized American law and order." One of the participants in the early movement told Kerr that charity "is for abnormal people in normal times. We are normal people in abnormal times. We want work." The movement was an expression of a long American tradition of self-reliance and the Christian obligation to help others in time of need. A member of Wilmington Cooperative No. 12 declared himself 100 percent in favor of the cooperative movement, but he was not in favor of charity. "I believe that they (the Government) should cut out charity and say 'Work if you want to eat.'"[6]

In 1933, about a year after it began with one man and a gunnysack, the Compton cooperative had five hundred active members representing a broad range of skills and professions. "We started with nothing," Downing said. "We had to sell the idea to everyone we came in contact with, and until the last three or four months it has been a tough fight to keep things going." Their aging building housed an office, a kitchen where workers got lunch every day, and a warehouse divided into large wire-partitioned bins and refrigerator boxes for food storage. The cooperative distributed milk at three in the afternoon every day. There was a 10,000-gallon tank for gasoline in the back of the property. Anyone who showed up in the morning to work got in a truck and rode around until they found a farmer willing to hire them.[7]

Kerr reported a typical take for one day's work in the fields: "One crate of beets, two tons of cabbage, sixty-six boxes of celery, four lugs of corn, twelve boxes of carrots, three sacks of cucumbers, seventy boxes of pears, fifteen sacks of potatoes, two crates of lettuce, six sacks of onions, thirty-nine boxes of peaches, five crates of radishes, one sack of salt, fourteen lugs of tomatoes, one and a quarter tons of rhubarb, eleven boxes of turnips, and other miscellaneous fruit and vegetables."[8]

In the beginning, there were no elected leaders, no accounting system, no registration, and no monetary value assigned to the various kinds of produce. Such an informal system could not last. When the cooperative became large enough to require full-time leadership, the members formally elected officers. Downing became its first elected manager. The growing organization required the registration of members and their dependents and the formulation of rules about how much work members were to perform. Two days of work a week became the accepted contribution of labor expected of all members, but food continued to be distributed according to need rather than hours worked. The cooperative added services in response to the needs of members, the abilities of its leaders, and available resources. Special contact men, many of whom were former salesmen, went out in advance and lined up farmers willing to cooperate. "Carrot pullers" did the actual harvesting. Older men stayed in the warehouse to sort produce. Early in 1933, the members decided that those who found work outside of the unit could remain in good standing provided they contributed 10 percent of their pay to the cooperative. The general philosophy was that "he who works not, eats not." The cooperative became a social center as well. Members organized dances, card parties, and other recreational activities to boost morale and raise funds.[9]

The Compton self-help cooperative was one of the most successful and well-run of such groups in Southern California. Others followed a similar pattern of development with variations depending on available resources and the dedication of its members. Generally, they had no formal recruiting program. Many new recruits joined after seeing "a notice that anyone could get food for work." Like the Compton group, most were organized democratically, but there were exceptions. Kerr described the manager of one Los Angeles cooperative as an "embryo storm trooper." "We need army discipline," this manager explained. "As long as I am here, what I say goes." Some special-interest groups organized cooperatives. Unemployed artists and actors formed the Arts and Professions Cooperative, and motion picture extras organized the Hollywood Assistance League. At least three of the squatter settlements in the Los Angeles area, the Hoovervilles, formed cooperatives. Members usually worked diligently, but there were always a few who put in their time hanging out at headquarters and socializing rather than working. Individual units ranged from clean and inviting to dark and dirty. Sometimes the buildings were filthy and in poor repair. Kerr vividly described the dining hall in one such place: "Men reeking with sweat help serve the food.

Women with disheveled hair and with red sores on their arms pass you the salt pork gravy . . . and serve coffee in cups without handles by sticking their thumbs and dirty finger nails into the cups. . . . Cull foods, poorly prepared, cockroaches underfoot and flies over head—these are the conditions found in the unit mess hall."[10]

In the early days of the cooperative movement, most people in Southern California supported what they were doing. Even the *Los Angeles Times*, usually suspicious of any movement independent of the business community, approved. In September 1932, the paper ran a long appreciative article that compared the cooperatives to pioneer communities. "What appears to be one of the most workable plans yet devised for combating the effects of unemployment is now in operation in Southern California. Its success is all the more remarkable from the fact that no one in the beginning seems to have thought it out—it 'just grew.'" After all, what was there not to like? The cooperatives did not cost the taxpayers anything, and so far as anyone could tell they were clean of the taint of radicalism.[11]

Over time the self-help cooperative movement drifted inexorably away from its roots. The cooperatives found it necessary to supplement the simple barter of labor in exchange for food and other necessities of life with requests for donations. To acquire things that were difficult or impossible to obtain through trade, they approached businesses and local governments for donations of commodities such as milk, meat, and gasoline. This was called "chiseling," a word that originally meant nothing more than asking for something for free, but, as businesspeople and others grew weary of individuals and organizations asking for handouts, the word came to take on negative connotations. Some cooperatives also experimented with production. In November 1932 a cooperative bakery began operations in south Los Angeles. Families brought flour that the Red Cross gave them and turned it in to the bakeries in exchange for orders for bread. One bag of flour was good for thirty-four loaves. Planting gardens was also an easy form of production. Generally speaking, the business community disapproved of the cooperatives going into production. Picking crops in exchange for submarket produce was fine, but competing with businesses on the free market was something else altogether. Some cooperative members also balked at the idea of going into production because they feared that businesses might retaliate by discontinuing donations; some worried that competition with the private sector could eliminate jobs and reduce their chances of getting work.¹²

Rank-and-file members may have rejected radicalism, but this did not mean that they lacked a sense of class solidarity with other workers. In 1933, self-help cooperative workers refused to scab against Mexican strikers in the El Monte berry fields—even though the pickers struck against Japanese growers who often employed them. As one might expect, the cooperative movement naturally attracted the interest of communists who were eager to get a foothold in this people's movement. Following the idea that it was easier to organize "around a turnip" than slogans, the party followed the policy of "boring from within." Although it never controlled a single cooperative, the party claimed to have "at least three of our members in every unit" in the city of Los Angeles. In some cases, communists may have been able to push individual cooperatives in the direction of more militant action. In south Los Angeles some of the cooperatives formed "home guards" to prevent evictions. In one case, sheriff's deputies removed a pregnant woman and her child from her home and left her and her possessions on the sidewalk. A committee of members arrived on the scene and in defiance of the authorities moved the family back inside. Their leader, a man named Haddon, said that "I am not a Red or a Bolshevik. I believe in law and order, but only as long as it places the value of a human life ahead of that of an old shack or shanty."¹³

As the number of self-help groups proliferated across Southern California, individual units attempted to cooperate with each other. This began with the simple "swapping" of goods and services. The county board of supervisors lent a hand with an appropriation of $10,000 for the purchase of gasoline and oil. In July 1932, representatives of units in the communities of Bell, South Gate, Lynwood, Maywood, Huntington Park, and Compton organized the Unemployed Cooperative Relief Association (UCRA). In honor of its pioneer status, Compton became Local Unit No. 1. The association grew rapidly, and it soon became what Kerr called "the strongest federation of unemployed persons in the state of California."¹⁴

The UCRA issued a statement of fourteen principles that read like a Sunday school lesson plan or a Boy Scout pledge. They promised to "guard the Laws of God, Nation, and Nature," to follow

Women working in a self-help cooperative office in the early 1930s. Los Angeles Daily News Negatives (Collection 1387), Library Special Collections, courtesy of Charles E. Young Research Library, UCLA.

the Golden Rule, to be fair in dealings with people, to care for "widows, orphans, cripples," to "sacrifice all personal feelings for the good of the whole," to abolish idleness, and so on. The founders pledged to keep all operations simple and to use "man-power hours" as far as possible. They reassured labor that they would support a living wage and promised business that they would "protect and assist all existing business establishments in securing a reasonable return on their investment." These principles were not so much a plan of action as an attempt to enlist the sympathy and support of government officials, businesspeople, and the citizenry in general.[15]

The UCRA did not attempt to control the activities of individual units. Its purpose was to carry out functions that were difficult or impossible for local groups to manage. The association served as the official representative for cooperatives when approaching businesses and private charities. In a move that had important long-term consequences, it established a warehouse to coordinate the distribution of surplus goods. A considerable amount of goods, mostly vegetables, fruit, and milk, passed through the warehouse. During a three-week period in the fall of 1932, workers in the warehouse handled about twenty tons of food. The warehouse also distributed donations of tires, batteries, and other hard-to-obtain items.[16]

The UCRA was supposed to be a statewide organization, but most of its affiliated cooperatives were in Los Angeles County. As it grew, most of its membership shifted away from the rural and suburban communities to the city of Los Angeles. Pat May, a natural politician and head of the central warehouse, outmaneuvered his rivals until he controlled the UCRA. A midwesterner by birth and about fifty years of age, May claimed to have been an Industrial Workers of the World (IWW) organizer before the war and a participant in the 1919 Seattle general strike. Rumors circulated that he was a strike leader in the beginning, but when the tide turned in favor of the employers he switched sides. True or not, the story illustrated his reputation as an opportunist who did not hesitate to abandon those who no longer served his purpose. One who knew him said that "Pat never stays with a sinking ship. He will play the winning side."[17]

During the 1920s, May moved to Huntington Park, not far from Compton, where he worked as a contractor and painter. With the help of the Salvation Army, he organized one of the pioneer self-help cooperatives. A forceful and belligerent orator who beat down his opponents with a loud voice and personal abuse, May used his position as head of the warehouse to create a nucleus of loyal followers and to expand his power. He controlled disbursements of donations passing through the warehouse, a power that he did not hesitate to use to his own advantage. As one manager recalled, "Pat used to say, 'You voted against me and God help you when you come to the warehouse.'"[18]

Politicians soon woke up to the fact that the cooperatives represented a sizeable number of potential voters. May, who tended to favor conservative Republicans, liked to brag that he controlled 100,000 votes. Stanley Fenton, a member of Mayor Porter's Citizens' Committee, told a convention of the UCRA that we are "behind you as long as you support law and order and are not Bolsheviks." A few months before the municipal elections in May 1933, the city council, with the support of the mayor, authorized the purchase of groceries to be distributed to cooperatives within the city limits. Porter's supporters distributed the goods, carefully including campaign literature with the packages of food. May helped things along, explaining that he did not tell people how to vote, but "we do tell 'em who their enemies is." The assistance abruptly ended after the elections.[19]

The cooperative movement also attracted the attention of the Los Angeles County board of supervisors, who saw cooperatives as a way to reduce or at least slow the relentless growth of relief expenditures. The board created the county Food Administration, which worked directly with individual units, thus avoiding the May-controlled warehouse. The cooperatives that chose to align with the Food Administration, most of which were located in the suburbs, formed a new federation called the Area Conference. The Area Conference required that the units be democratically organized and avoid producing goods or services in competition with private business. The most valuable assistance the Food Administration offered the cooperatives was the distribution of gasoline and oil as well as grants to pay gas and water bills. It assisted in the distribution of surplus products such as milk that producers had been pouring into the gutters at a rate of 20,000 gallons a day. It also created a division to organize community gardens and helped more than thirty units begin vegetable production on donated land. May, who supported Mayor Porter, considered the Food Administration nothing more than a political instrument of Supervisor Shaw, a rival of the mayor.[20]

In 1933 the Food Administration fell by the wayside after Congress created the Federal Emergency Relief Administration (FERA). The new agency, one of the most important measures passed during Roosevelt's first one hundred days in office, disbursed federal relief money to the states. The State of California created the State Emergency Relief Administration (SERA), later simply the State Relief Administration (SRA), to handle the infusion of federal money. Although distributed through the county charities department, the federal money was not subject to the restrictions placed on county relief, and it carried less of a stigma because it was tied to work projects. Cooperatives generally allowed these workers to keep their memberships active while receiving this relief.

The SERA administrator appointed Harry L. Jones, a former stockbroker and salesman, the director of cooperatives for Southern

California. Jones created yet another federation, the Unemployed Cooperative Distribution Association (UCDA), which absorbed the UCRA, the Area Conference, and some independent units. Between September 1933 and April 1934, the UCDA received grants of federal money totaling $120,000. Jones ignored FERA guidelines that stipulated that these funds be used for production projects. Instead, he used the funds to purchase staples that he distributed to the cooperatives as direct relief. He admitted that his new policy was not in the original self-help spirit of the cooperatives, but he felt that an emergency existed and that aid needed to be delivered as quickly as possible. "When it came time to allot the money, we might have given it for production or for relief," he explained to Kerr. "We decided in favor of the latter. These people were hungry and needed food at the time."[21]

Units outside of the city of Los Angeles joined the UCDA only reluctantly. One manager explained that "Jones forced us to join. . . . if we didn't join, God only knows when we'd get anything." Cooperative members received more assistance with less effort, but accepting handouts was not part of the original cooperative spirit. One member complained that we "started out to be self-sustaining but we are becoming just another charity racket." Jones's policy also introduced distinctions that divided workers. The new arrangement created two categories of membership: "white slip" members who were not on county relief and "pink slip" members who received county relief but continued to work in the cooperatives. Those on relief were not eligible to receive staple groceries purchased with the FERA grant money.[22]

The changes affected rank-and-file morale. Workers often showed up just to log in their hours to get food rations, then did little or no work. The new system increased the power of the managers because they had the authority to distribute government-issued food. One member complained that none "of these units are democratic any more. Just let one of these boys on the bottom try to get things changed at the office and see what happens to him." The *Los Angeles Daily News* saw similarities between the Jones regime and Italy under fascism. It "compares most favorably in diplomacy, statesmanship, and good old-fashioned bludgeoning with the successful methods by which Mussolini transformed a semi-liberal, laissez-fair nation into a socialist-fascist state."[23]

The Jones regime came to an end in May 1934, when FERA sent Winslow Carlton, an idealistic young Harvard graduate, to investigate cooperatives in Southern California. He soon became director of a newly created SERA division, the Self Help Cooperative Service. Carlton's appointment began yet another phase of the cooperative movement. He let it be known that SERA would make grants only to individual units, basically putting an end to the UCDA. May, who dominated the board that oversaw the UCDA, considered the new program an attack on his power and threatened to throw Carlton's representatives out of the cooperatives, branding them "skunks and stool pigeons."[24]

Carlton made it clear that the federal program was not intended to distribute relief payments but to create production programs leading to eventual self-sufficiency. The first step was for the government to supply funds for the purchase of equipment. This "might appear as a step backward from a complete cooperative system," Carlton explained, "but was absolutely necessary to meet the urgent needs of the cooperators." Once the equipment is in place and production began he expected that a completely "self-sufficient system will result. This is the final stage, the goal of cooperatives."[25]

Carlton's tenure as head of the SERA's self-help division coincided with an increase in popular interest in cooperatives, one brought on by Upton Sinclair's 1934 campaign for governor of California (see chapter 9). The heart of Sinclair's platform, called End Poverty in California (EPIC), was a statewide system of agricultural and industrial cooperatives that would replace all other forms of relief. Sinclair considered the self-help cooperatives to be a version of his program in miniature. Although he lost the general election, other progressive candidates championed the cooperative idea. Los Angeles County voters elected John Anson Ford and Herbert C. Legg, supporters of the self-help movement, to the board of supervisors. They joined board member Gordon McDonough, also a supporter. Ford, in particular, saw great promise in the cooperatives. He summarized his position succinctly: "Let the unemployed help themselves."[26]

The new liberal majority on the board created a department of rehabilitation to coordinate all county efforts related to cooperatives. With great fanfare, the department announced the opening of a pilot program in Glendale to employ a hundred workers. The plans included a bakery, cannery, possibly a dairy, as well as facilities for making and repairing clothing. Despite high expectations for the new department, the board of supervisors did not provide adequate funding and it never accomplished much. The Glendale pilot program lasted only a few months. After only about a year in operation, the county board of efficiency declared the rehabilitation department a failure and recommended its abolition. Instead, as part of a general reorganization, the supervisors folded it into the department of charities, where it languished for a number of years without a clear mission. Rex Thomson, who became head of the department of charities, kept it alive hoping that one day it would "repay the cost of its continuance."[27]

Suburban units, located near agricultural areas and possessing strong leadership, were more successful in receiving grants for production projects than those in Los Angeles with fewer resources. In a report published in December 1934, Carlton drew a contrasting picture of the two types of cooperatives. One of the city units presented a dismal picture: "A broken-down store building; old, battered wood, forming an irregular partition around a marred desk and patched chair; reverse side of old hand bills substituting for stationery; a few scattered piles of withered carts, cabbage and oranges; a half dozen old ladies sitting in the dark, intent on the rag rug in their laps; five men leaning over a hand-styled Ford truck which was once a roadster." A suburban unit that had received a production grant left an entirely different impression: "A renovated warehouse; an office partitioned off housing a clean, shiny desk; stationery printed with a seal; a room containing piles of labeled canned goods; another room full of fruits and vegetables; another steaming with the fragrance of tomato relish boiling in a huge vat; thirty women cutting tomatoes; men actively working with machinery in the process of canning 'number 10's'; men loading a shiny new five-ton truck with boxes of scanned goods. Those are two cooperatives."[28]

The city units survived by collecting cast-off produce from wholesale warehouses and collecting old newspapers and junk. "Chiseling" continued but became increasingly difficult as merchants tired of being asked for handouts. Bakeries that in the past donated bread to cooperatives out of fear that they might start their own bakeries stopped donating when they no longer feared the possibility of competition. By 1938 the number of city units had dropped from approximately seventy-five to about thirty. Those that remained experienced an increased turnover in managers. A few lucky members found work, those who could accepted relief, and others simply drifted away. "We have been living on celery and carrots too long," one of them said.[29]

Only democratically organized cooperatives were eligible for FERA production grants, but "democracy" under the new system differed from what it was originally. Kerr described it as changing from a town-meeting style to a city-manager style government. Formerly, the cooperatives elected managers and directors at irregular intervals ranging from a few weeks to a few months. Under the new system, cooperatives that received grants adopted a standardized constitution providing for the election of a board of directors that in turn selected the manager. Grants were for capital equipment and similar expenses and not for salaries or staple goods. FERA required the producers to maintain reasonable wage levels, set at about thirty cents an hour. Cash sales were supposed to provide funds for the purchase of new materials and eventual self-sufficiency. The Self-Help Cooperative Service's *Bulletin* stated the goal clearly: "The present Federal program anticipates the time when the self-help cooperatives may produce all the necessities of life, and provide self-employment which will result in an adequate standard of living as well as maintain self-respect." Achieving this goal was nearly impossible given FERA's requirement that no products be sold on the open market. This was a galling restriction in view of the fact that cooperative members were unemployed because private businesses could not provide them with work. The permitted markets for the sale of cooperative-produced goods were very limited. Sales could be made to cooperative workers, dependents of workers, other cooperatives, and government agencies. The lack of adequate markets, despite the general high quality of the products, meant that income generated was not sufficient for the cooperatives to operate at full capacity.[30]

Operating cooperatives according to business principles was contrary to their original purpose, which was to help people in need. Cooperatives expected their members to produce according to their abilities and were rewarded according to their needs. They put people to work who were not employable in the private market. If they were run like a business, managers would be obliged to turn away those who did not have the desired skills and even to reduce the workforce if necessary. Production required specializing in one activity, whereas the original cooperatives gathered together as many skills as possible in order to cover a variety of activities. Under the new system, too many members and too many skills were problems rather than assets. The division of the workforce into "white slip" and "pink slip" workers meant that, even if the cooperatives were run on a business-like basis, not everyone received the same compensation. In Los Angeles County, about 40 percent of the workers in the grant cooperatives were on relief.[31]

During the last three months of 1933 and the entire year of 1934, FERA gave out a total of over $400,000 in grants in California. Los Angeles County received, by far, the largest amount, almost $165,000. The fifty-one grant cooperatives in Los Angeles County employed more than 15,000 people. The most popular types of production projects were sewing, farming, gardening, canning, and baking because they required the least amount of capital investment and raw materials. When units received grants they often began with a burst of enthusiasm, but with rocky starts because of poor planning and the lack of experienced workers. One Los Angeles unit that intended to produce clothing found that it had no workers who knew anything about tailoring. Another that planned on catching seafood had only one person with deep-sea fishing experience; on their first trip, they managed to return with a small catch only to find that they had neglected to make provisions for cleaning and preserving the fish. The quality of the workforce varied widely among the cooperatives. All units had people who thought of the cooperatives as social centers and hung around playing cards and generally not working. Everyone was required to put in two days a week but, because they could show up when they wanted, on some days there were too many workers and on others not enough. The cooperatives were undercapitalized and operated with outdated equipment. Bakeries produced only a fraction of bread that a commercial bakery produced, canneries had old equipment, dairies did not have enough cows. Dealing with government bureaucracy was difficult. Grant funds were often delayed because they had to pass through many levels of approval. The government accounting system was extremely complicated and hard to understand.[32]

The production cooperatives formed a loose federation, the California Cooperative Units, Los Angeles County, to facilitate trade, but it proved inadequate to the job. Distribution between units never worked the way it was supposed to. Units did not know what was available to trade or what other units needed and wanted. In some cases, especially with agricultural units, products were seasonal, leaving some cooperatives with nothing to sell or trade year around. Relief agencies proved to be a poor market because most agencies provided relief in the form of cash rather than in goods. The agencies that did use goods, such as the Federal Surplus Relief Corporation and the Federal Transient Service, purchased in larger lots than the cooperatives could supply. It was difficult to deliver to work camps such as those of the Civilian Conservation Corps because they were widely scattered.

Carlton thought he knew how to solve these problems. To overcome the lack of sufficient capitalization, he proposed loaning the cooperatives over $4 million to be repaid over a three-year period. He also wanted a more effective central warehouse to facilitate interunit exchange and coordinate production. He suggested solving the lack of an adequate market by creating cooperative stores where members could purchase goods with credits earned from work. In addition, he wanted people on relief to receive two-thirds of their payments with credits redeemable only at the cooperative stores.[33]

Carlton was not able to sell this plan to state and federal officials. It was expensive, and critics doubted that cooperatives could meet the standards of private business. SRA administrator Frank McLaughlin thought that the cooperatives attracted people who failed in private business. Most "of the Cooperators," he wrote, "represent men who have either been unsuccessful in private industry or whose skills, physical condition, or other factors have made it impossible for them to compete successfully with those better equipped." Businesses objected to using tax money to underwrite potential competitors. They even opposed the sale of cooperative goods to relief agencies because they felt that this was an invasion of their market.[34]

In March 1936, Carlton resigned as state director of the Self Help Cooperative Service. Under the conservative administration of Republican governor Frank Merriam, the very idea of cooperative activity came under fire. Harold Pomeroy, the new state relief administrator, had little love for the movement. In 1932, as mayor of South Gate, Pomeroy was one of the organizers of an early cooperative unit, but he fell out with its manager, who became his personal and political foe. This experience seems to have turned him into an enemy of the entire cooperative movement. He even objected to the use of the word "cooperative" and had the name of the Self Help Cooperative Service changed to the Department of Self Help. In the eyes of FERA officials, the phrase "production for use, not profit" only meant socialism.[35]

W. B. Hughes, the new director of the Department of Self Help, shared Pomeroy's feelings. He believed that cooperatives were a "social accident" that resulted from the inability of county government to meet the relief need. He gradually weeded out troublesome managers and forced those who remained to keep a low profile. One of them said, "I've been keeping my mouth shut." Social workers investigated members and kept case records. Cooperative members had never been subjected to this kind of scrutiny before. Hughes expanded the kinds of workers assigned to the cooperatives. They included Works Progress Administration workers, those receiving money through FERA, and others temporarily assigned because they happened to have needed skills. All were paid differently. At the same time, he purged the cooperatives of anyone who did not meet membership qualifications. These included useful workers such as doctors and barbers who provided services but did not put in the required number of hours, anyone temporarily inactive, and old and incapacitated members who received products while not working. The state claimed ownership of all equipment and sometimes confiscated it when it felt a cooperative was not performing properly. The state strictly controlled all sales, most of which went to single men's relief camps that SRA operated. The camps frequently did not pay for the products they received, making the relief camps cheaper to operate, which was the true goal of the administration. At the end of 1937, the relief administration began closing cooperatives. It shut down fifteen in Southern California in November and asked for the return of equipment purchased with state funds.[36]

At the beginning of 1938, Pomeroy proposed shutting down all state aid to all units, effectively ending their ability to continue operating. Alarmed at this prospect, the Los Angeles County board of supervisors asked for a federal investigation of the SRA's administration of the cooperatives. The state department of finance called the state agency's handling of the self-help program a "managerial fiasco." C. C. Smith, a new director of Self Help, instituted reforms and pulled the cooperatives back from the brink of extinction.[37]

In the November 1938 gubernatorial election, state senator Culbert Olson defeated Republican Frank Merriam. Olson, the first Democratic governor of California since 1894, had won his senate seat in 1934 on Sinclair's EPIC program. He was a believer in the idea of "production for use." The centerpiece of Olson's administration was to replace traditional relief by requiring recipients to work on cooperatives. In exchange for work, they would be paid with credits to be used to purchase staples at a network of cooperative stores. The governor's ambitious plan fell victim to an intense partisan battle over the future of the SRA. Accusations of corruption and charges of communist infiltration hobbled the Olson administration's efforts to carry out its program. In addition, falling unemployment levels convinced the so-called economy bloc in the legislature that the SRA was no longer necessary and pressed for its abolition. In an editorial, the *Los Angeles Times* proclaimed that "there will soon be no need for the S.R.A." On June 30, the legislature shut down the SRA, and sole responsibility for relief went back to the counties. Other than a single cooperative store located on San Pedro Street south of downtown Los Angeles, Olson's plan for state-sponsored self-help cooperatives never materialized.[38]

The end of the SRA was the final blow to the cooperative movement. The state finance director ordered the return of state-owned equipment and the distribution of food stored in cooperative warehouses. Some cooperatives, such as a print shop in Los Angeles, attempted to continue operating as privately run businesses, but the state soon shut them down. A Glendale city councilman asked the board of supervisors what to do with a herd of cows left after the closing of a cooperative dairy. He thought that if the county took over "human clients of the SRA it might also take over its livestock."[39]

• • • •

The self-help cooperatives began as a grassroots movement. Without assistance from government authorities or any other external authority, groups of neighbors came together to find ways to feed their families and to avoid taking charity. This democratic movement spread with surprising speed across Southern California, leading the nation in the creation of self-help cooperatives. As it grew, and as ambitious individuals, politicians, and social theorists became involved, it moved away from its spontaneous and democratic origins. The production cooperatives of the late 1930s bore little resemblance to what the movement's founders in Compton had envisioned. Partisan battles in the state legislature and an improving economy put an end to the cooperative movement. The fact that the cooperatives existed at all calls into question the widespread view among many writers that Southern California was a region with no cohesive community. Many of these writers—Mencken, Wilson, West, Fogelson, and others—were themselves outsiders who, for whatever reason, could not see the community beneath the suburban sprawl and the endless avenues of the region. The self-help cooperative movement could only emerge in a place where neighbors helped one another in a time of need.

5

THE GOD THAT FAILED

(in this case, capitalism)

> Capitalism is a purely cultic religion, perhaps the most extreme that ever existed.
>
> Walter Benjamin, "Capitalism as Religion"

Of all the systems of belief that claimed to have the answers to fix the economy and bring the country out of the Depression, the devotees of the free market were the most numerous. For the defenders of unregulated capitalism, true freedom came from understanding, accepting, and submitting to the impersonal workings of the market. Ignoring or interfering with its operations was the road to certain disaster. One might ignore the rules in the short term, but the market always prevailed. The system was harsh, but it was absolutely fair because the rules applied to everyone with no exceptions. The role of government was limited to providing an orderly and peaceful environment so that business could operate in an atmosphere of safety and stability. Organized labor, because it sought to fix wages and hours in defiance of the workings of the law of supply and demand, had no place in the free-market system.

Believers in the free-market system held that the failure to follow the true path was evidence of a flawed moral character. Speculators and irresponsible businesspeople who ignored the discipline of the market eventually failed. Punishment usually came in the form of loss of wealth and personal disgrace. Workers who refused to do an honest day's work for an honest day's pay but instead lived on the labors of others also felt the wrath of the market. Accepting charity even in the hardest times was a sure sign of failure. Government welfare programs undermined the character of workers and destroyed personal initiative. The unemployed were victims not of an unfair economic system but of moral failures. Those who really wanted to work, even in the hardest of times, could surely find a job. Unemployment was evidence of a flawed moral character.

Before the arrival of the New Deal, most national, state, and local governments were friendly to if not firmly under the control of business. This was certainly true of the city of Los Angeles, the Los Angeles County board of supervisors, and the city councils of most of the surrounding municipalities. The enemy of the free market was organized labor, especially the American Federation of Labor (AFL) and its affiliated unions. Los Angeles had a national reputation as the city of the open shop, or the American Plan, as its supporters liked to call it. The *Los Angeles Times*, the leading mouthpiece of free-market capitalism in Southern California, defined the open shop for its readers. "The open shop denies the right of a labor union to force any worker to become a member of it by any form of coercion," the paper explained. "It insists that every worker shall be free to join or not join, as he sees fit, and without being penalized for either choice."[1]

Business leaders reacted angrily to the charge that the open shop was anti-union. John Austin, a director of the Chamber of Commerce, insisted that the term did not mean that at all. "Open shop means you reserve the right to yourself to hire men or women whether they belong to a union or whether they don't and to set your own wage scale, but this open shop situation has been twisted to mean non union when it doesn't mean that at all." This description of the open shop did not, however, match the reality of the workplace in Southern California. Despite how fair-minded the business definition sounded, in practice it meant that unions were strictly forbidden. Regardless of what a *Times* editorial might say or what a director of the Chamber of Commerce might claim, workers at an open shop who tried to join a union or even spoke favorably of organized labor were very likely to find themselves suddenly unemployed.[2]

The defenders of the free-market faith thought of the open shop as an ideal that made it possible for the entire community—worker, employer, and everyone else—to live in harmony and prosperity. Appearing before the United States Commission on Industrial Relations in 1916, the secretary of the Merchants and Manufacturers Association (M&M), Felix J. Zeehandelaar, said, "The open shop in Los Angeles is neither an experiment nor a theory. Our faith in the open shop in this community is so strong that we absolutely are sure that our prosperity . . . is based upon that one factor." And to make sure the commissioners understood his point that the open shop benefited everyone, he added "that whatever is of benefit to the employer classes must be a direct benefit to the employees or the working classes."[3]

The patron saint of the open shop in Los Angeles was Harrison Gray Otis, publisher of the *Los Angeles Times*. He began his career in small-town print shops in Ohio and then in Kentucky at the antislavery Whig paper the *Louisville Journal*. After the Civil War, Otis worked in the U.S. Patent and Government Printing Office (where, for a brief time, he was a member of the International Typographical Union), edited the *Santa Barbara Press*, and chased seal poachers in Alaska. In 1882 he found his way to Los Angeles, where he became editor and eventually the sole owner of the *Times*. As the city grew, so did Otis's paper, becoming one of the most powerful institutions in Southern California.

Although Otis made his fortune in the newspaper business, his military service was the defining experience of his life. He enlisted as a private in the Union Army and served until 1864, when he was mustered out with the rank of brevet lieutenant colonel. He fought in fifteen battles and was wounded twice. "In time of peace, prepare for war" was one of his favorite maxims.[4] He insisted on being called Colonel Otis and referred to his office staff as the phalanx, his home as the bivouac, and his country house as the outpost. He allegedly kept an arsenal of fifty rifles in the *Times* offices and drove around town in a car with a working cannon mounted on the hood. When the United States went to war with Spain in 1898, he volunteered for service and wrangled a commission as brigadier general. Although the war ended before he saw action, he participated in the bloody suppression of the Philippine insurrection. When he returned home, he insisted that he be addressed as General Otis.[5]

Otis's greatest war was with organized labor. In 1890 he locked the union printers of the International Typographical Union out of his plant and hired a strikebreaking outfit to supply replacement workers. This was the beginning of what the historian Grace Heilman Stimson called "an almost endless controversy" that was to "dominate the local labor scene for years to come." Otis assumed the leadership of the open-shop forces and recruited powerful allies such as the M&M and the Los Angeles Chamber of Commerce. The business elite of the booming city eagerly followed Otis and his *Times* into a long and ultimately successful battle against organized labor.[6]

Otis advocated a view of labor-management relations that had little connection to the real world. "In employing men we come face to face," Otis explained. "We find out what he is and what he can do, and he finds out whether he wants to work for us, and we get together a good deal like two men trading horses. And we say to him, 'What wages do you want?' Well, he wants so and so. Well, we dicker with him, and finally get together. We may yield to him and he may yield to us, but finally we get together, the rate is fixed, and we pay the rate." Otis denied that in this situation the employer had the upper hand. He believed, or claimed to believe, that it was a mutual, noncoercive arrangement. "Well, the decision is left to each side, isn't it?" he explained. "In other words, if the workman feels that he cannot accept the wages, the treatment, the hours, he does not continue in our employ. Of his own volition he leaves our employ."[7]

In the early hours of October 1, 1910, a bomb exploded in the *Los Angeles Times* building. The blast ignited barrels of highly flammable ink housed in a passageway called ink alley. The explosion and the resulting inferno completely destroyed the building and killed twenty employees. Several burned alive while trying to escape the flames. The police also discovered two other bombs, one at Otis's home, which exploded doing little damage and harming no one, and a second at Zeehandelaar's residence that proved defective and did not detonate. On Christmas Day, another bomb destroyed the Llewellyn Iron Works. The plant's owner, John Llewellyn, was one of the city's most outspoken nonunion employers. Authorities arrested two union men, John J. McNamara, secretary of the International Association of Bridge and Structural Iron Workers, and his younger brother James for planting the bombs. Neither of the men were from Southern California and had no connection with the Los Angeles labor movement. They probably targeted the *Times* because it was a national symbol of the open-shop movement. Otis blamed the entire union movement, not just the McNamara brothers, for the crime. The "real character of the sinister forces aligned against the peace and welfare of Los Angeles ultimately was dragged to light. It was the turning point in a war of forty years for a city's freedom."[8]

On October 1, 1929, the nineteenth anniversary of the bombing, the *Times* published a thirty-three part series titled "Story of the Forty-Year War for a Free City." It described in meticulous detail the history of "a war for a city's freedom." As the *Times* saw it, under the enlightened leadership of the businessmen of the Chamber of Commerce and the M&M, Los Angeles became a mecca for freedom-loving American workers. Eastern cities that suffered under the iron rule of the AFL, the story went, produced a steady stream of workers to Los Angeles. All were "tired of having union tribute arbitrarily deducted from their wages without their consent to pay large salaries to union officials and to maintain other workers in strike-idleness, tired of being 'regulated' in every act by a walking delegate and especially tired of being told, as free Americans, where, when, how, for whom and for how much they could or could not work. They came to Los Angeles because this city was heralded as a place these things did not exist."[9]

The paper argued that outside forces inspired labor's campaign to unionize the city's workers and to turn the open shop into its dark opposite, the closed shop. As long as Los Angeles remained a bastion of nonunion employers, it would be a threat to organized labor everywhere. The eastern unions would never stop sending their minions to the sunny city in the West, but with the exception of the motion picture industry, which seemed to follow its own rules, the city was victorious in keeping them at bay. The *Times* series concluded with an editorial cartoon showing the hands of Capital and Labor (Goodwill and Cooperation) clenched in a firm handshake. Under the open shop, the article confidently concluded, "mutual suspicion is replaced by mutual confidence, opposition and oppression by cooperation and recognition of the other's rights, hostility and misunderstanding by friendliness and understanding."[10]

Otis died in 1917 at age eighty. At his interment in Hollywood Cemetery, a squad of riflemen fired a three-volley salute and Spanish-American War veteran Sgt. James Sykes played "Taps." Otis's successor, his son-in-law Harry Chandler, was already in place. Chandler, whom Otis considered "a jewel in the family and just the man for me," had an entirely different style from his father-in-law. Whereas Otis was argumentative and enjoyed a fight, Chandler was much less confrontational, operating quietly behind the scenes. One of his political enemies, William Bonelli, found him charming and urbane, but ruthless. "There was nothing crass about Harry Chandler in action or words," Bonelli wrote. "When, in his level voice, he let you know that he would have his way or destroy you, there was always an over-larding of regret. It was as though you were forcing him to do something he didn't really want to do and whatever happened to you was your fault." Bonelli claimed that throughout Chandler's long career it would be hard to find a single altruistic act. What Chandler cared about more than anything else in the world was making money.[11]

In 1882, Chandler, the son of New Hampshire farmers, enrolled as a freshman at Dartmouth College. His education ended abruptly when on a dare he jumped into a cold vat of liquid starch. This foolish act seems totally out of character—unless a monetary wager was involved. Whatever his motive, the stunt changed Chandler's life. He developed a case of chronic bronchitis and on his doctor's advice headed for Southern California. He was nineteen years old, sickly, and had very little money—just the kind of penniless transient that in the 1930s he urged the police to turn back at the California border. He eventually took up residence in a tent at the southern end of the San Fernando Valley and earned his keep by picking fruit and tending horses. He received his pay in the form of surplus fruit that he sold to threshing crews. As his health improved, he managed to save $3,000. This was the beginning of the fortune that one day would make him the richest man in Southern California.[12]

Chandler acquired a *Los Angeles Times* delivery route and eventually bought several routes, including one for the *Herald*, disguising his ownership by purchasing it through a partner. He used this route to strangle the *Tribune*, the main rival of the *Times*, by steering subscribers away from the *Tribune* to either the *Times* or the *Herald*. The *Tribune* lost so many readers that it soon folded, and Chandler, like a circling vulture, moved in and bought the paper's equipment and distribution routes. The young man rose rapidly in the Colonel's estimation and began courting the old man's daughter, Marian, whom he married in 1894. Chandler gradually took over management of the *Los Angeles Times* and served as publisher and general manager until he died of a heart attack in 1944. As his wealth grew, Chandler arguably became the most influential man in Southern California. He was active in many businesses, but his largest investments were in real estate in Southern California and in Mexico. In 1938 he estimated that his land holdings exceeded a million acres.[13]

Otis and Chandler worked closely with the M&M, a powerful advocate for the region's business interests. For many years it was under the direction of Otis's close ally, Felix Zeehandelaar, known in labor circles as Crazy Zee. In its early years, this association defined its mission broadly as a promoter of local business interests, but, over time, the M&M narrowed its focus to the all-important role of fighting unions. The organization pledged itself to fight for "freedom and independence," in other words "the principles of the 'open shop.'" It promised "no discrimination against honest American workmen" and pledged to never tolerate the "interference of agitators and strife breeders" and to "protect employers in their right to conduct and manage their business as they see fit." The M&M used its power to pressure municipal governments to pass anti-labor measures such as Los Angeles's strict 1910 anti-picketing ordinance. It was one of the chief lobbyists behind the passage of the notorious 1919 California Criminal Syndicalism Act, a draconian law that made membership alone in the IWW a crime punishable by up to fourteen years in prison. The M&M used its influence to provide moral and financial assistance to firms during strikes. It also used its power to bring businesses into line that deviated too far from open-shop policies. Its leaders pressured the mayor and the chief of police to deploy extra police during strikes. It helped recruit strikebreakers and raised funds to bring in security guards to beef up police protection and to hire detectives to spy on strikers.[14]

The Los Angeles Chamber of Commerce worked in tandem with the M&M. It was as uncompromisingly open shop as the M&M,

but its mission was broader. Founded in 1888 in the aftermath of the boom of the eighties, the organization promoted Los Angeles as an ideal place to live and do business. It spread the word about Southern California through newspapers, magazines, books, pamphlets, exhibitions, and word of mouth. The Chamber sent a trainload of citrus trees to the 1893 Chicago World's Fair and planted a temporary lemon grove in the stadium. For years, a "California on Wheels" exhibit toured the East, showing off the products of what Angelenos liked to call America's Italy. The lobby of the Chamber's headquarters in Los Angeles housed an exhibit of local products that included, among other things, a life-size elephant made of walnuts and a thirty-foot wine bottle. The county board of supervisors approved an annual appropriation for these activities—support that continued even when it came under fire during the financially tight years of the Great Depression.[15]

The Chamber's magazine, *Southern California Business*, published articles on the region as well as statistics on employment, housing construction, and manufacturing. The board of directors appointed various committees to study and report on specific problems of the day. Several departments focused on publicity, agriculture, foreign trade, and other areas. Most important were an industrial department, founded in 1919, which concentrated on attracting manufacturing to the region, and a research department that conducted surveys, compiled information about the Southern California economy, and maintained a library. A special education committee kept its eye on teaching and the administration of the schools with the purpose of keeping them free of "undemocratic" (i.e., radical) influences. One of the Chamber's directors said that he had been told that "at UCLA 60% of the teachers and professors were foreign born," some of whom preached an "insidious propaganda against our form of Government."[16]

The Chamber maintained a very close relationship with the Los Angeles Police Department. The offices of Capt. William "Red" Hynes, head of the LAPD intelligence squad, better known as the Red Squad, were in the Chamber of Commerce building. Chief James E. Davis told the Chamber's board of directors that his desire was to provide Los Angeles with the kind of stable conditions that made secure investments possible. He assured them that he was not afraid to take firm action against radical elements. "I will tell you quite frankly," he said on one occasion, "that I would use machine guns if I had to take 100 or 500 lives if in my judgment I thought it was necessary to do that to save the lives of a great number of law abiding people and protect property generally in the city. Now sentimentalists may not agree."[17]

Another group, the Better America Federation (BAF), focused on educating the public in the principles of unregulated capitalism. Its founders were the traction millionaire Eli P. Clark and Reese Llewellyn, owner of the Llewellyn Iron Works. Harry M. Haldeman, president of the Pacific Pipe and Supply Company, was president of the organization for many years. Lieut. Col. Leroy F. Smith, director of the speaker's bureau, described the BAF as "nonprofit, nonpolitical, and nonsectarian." Its mission was to remind Americans of the responsibilities of citizenship, to oppose any attempt to change the government as outlined in the Constitution, to oppose expressions of class consciousness, to show that the interests of employers and employees were the same, and "to defend the right of private property the only practical incentive to the full exercise of individual energy, skill, and thrift." The BAF opposed communists, socialists, and all labor organizers. The organization saw the difference between communists and socialists only in their methods, not their goals. Col. Smith wrote that the socialist "would cut the tail off of the cow an inch at a time; the communist would cut the tail off the capitalistic cow at one fell swoop." The organization regarded almost any kind of reformer—even those who championed relatively moderate ideas such as the initiative, referendum, and the direct election of U.S. senators—as subversive. It reserved special venom for the American Civil Liberties Union (ACLU), regarding it as nothing less than a front for "the organized forces for revolution, lawlessness, sabotage, and murder." It considered strikes and labor disturbances illegitimate and in almost all cases the work of criminals or Bolsheviks. The BAF opposed the abolition of child labor. It was against compulsory education beyond the age of fourteen because this was all that most people needed and too much education was more of a "handicap" than a help. It considered the eight-hour work day and forty-hour work week unwise because they resulted in too much leisure and were detrimental to morals. "Satan finds some mischief still for idle hands to do," a BAF pamphlet warned. Laws that prohibited night work for women and minors were unfair because they interfered with the fundamental rights of the intended beneficiaries. Minimum-wage laws were useless because only the workings of the free market could determine the cost of labor. The BAF conceded that labor had the right to collective bargain, but only if employers decided who they bargained with and had the right to refuse to bargain. The BAF displayed a distrust of democracy in general, arguing that the founding fathers created a republic, not a democracy.[18]

The Chamber of Commerce coordinated the response of the business community to the collapse of the economy. It followed the lead of President Herbert Hoover, a believer in a voluntaristic approach in dealing with the crisis. Hoover asked business leaders to invest in construction and other projects to maintain wage levels and keep people in their jobs. His most radical idea, which shocked leading industrialists, was the suggestion that preserving wages came before maintaining profit levels. The president also asked the country's businesses to try to spread available work. The Chamber enthusiastically adopted this idea because it was voluntaristic and did not require government intervention or tax increases. In theory, reducing the normal six-day work week to five enabled employers to avoid layoffs even in the face of declining business revenues. The idea was the centerpiece proposal at a meeting of civic leaders that county supervisor Frank Shaw called in November 1930.[19]

The *Los Angeles Times* endorsed the plan as long as the shorter hours came with a wage reduction. The idea of workers receiving the same pay for five days work that they had received for six days violated the natural workings of the economy. In any case, the *Times* reassured its readers that the reduction of working hours would not involve a pay cut because prices had fallen so much over the past year that, even though workers earned "one-sixth less," they "will buy more goods now." Chandler cited Ricardo's venerable iron law of wages, which dated from 1817, as support for the idea that with a reduction of working hours there always would be a corresponding reduction of wages. Ricardo, who earned his living as a stockbroker, maintained that wages always rose or fell to match the cost of living. When prices went up, wages rose. When prices went down, wages fell. His "law" dictated that workers always received in pay what they needed to live and no more or less. To try to keep wages high artificially, for example, through the efforts of organized labor or just by being a soft-hearted employer, was contrary to the natural workings of the free market and always led to disaster. As far as Chandler was concerned, this settled the question.[20]

The Chamber's secretary-manager, Arthur Arnoll, told the board of directors that spreading the work was the organization's priority. "We are getting here every day men who have been with these private corporations for five, six and ten years who are apparently thrown into the street with hardly a week's notice." Some businesses adopted the program. The Firestone tire company went to a four-shift, six-hour-day plan that the company claimed saved several hundred jobs. Other employers resisted what seemed, on the surface, to be a simple idea. For one reason or another, some found it difficult to implement changes in shifts or the work week. One employer argued that it was easier to encourage his Mexican employees, "aside from those of particular value to us, to go back to Mexico." Arnoll complained about the lack of support for the idea: Our "Unemployment Committee was set up with twenty prominent men and they tried three times to meet and the third time the committee got disgusted as they couldn't get over three people there. That is the attitude of mind so what are you going to do?" The subcommittee of the Chamber's construction industries committee warned that the five-day week bore too close a resemblance to organized labor's long-standing demand for a five-day week. It "would be unwise for the Chamber of Commerce to push any further on that."[21]

Franklin Roosevelt's bold actions during his first one hundred days in office left the Los Angeles business elite badly shaken. It soon became apparent that the new president's program taking shape over the spring and summer of 1933 represented a drastic departure from the past. The New Deal was pragmatic, experimental, and unburdened with concerns about ideological consistency. Roosevelt's immediate object was to provide relief to the thousands of Americans out of work as quickly as possible. He cared little that, for the most part, his program ignored the sacred laws that governed the free market. Roosevelt's actions lifted the mood of the country, but they had the opposite effect on the business elite.

In Los Angeles these leaders fell into despondency, depression, and fear for the future. Apocalyptic visions of doom and destruction emanated from the front offices of Southern California businesses.

As FDR's programs began to dominate the national conversation, the Southern California business community fell back on moralistic solutions. In August 1933 a *Los Angeles Times* editorial argued that the real recovery involved returning to the path of "justice, truth and righteousness." Unemployment was a problem, but, the paper somewhat irrationally suggested, "We can't coax recovery back by jobs. Charity is necessary and helpful; yet we can't return prosperity with handouts." The problem lay in the moral character of the nation. "There is one immutable law—honesty, then prosperity. We talk of goods—but do we have goodness?" In the eyes of the business community, the national trend was away from honesty toward dictatorship. In September 1933, Byron Calvin Hanna, a lawyer and director of the Chamber of Commerce, complained bitterly that the president was "the most powerful and autocratic ruler in the world today." He believed that the past battles to preserve the open shop were "inconsequential" compared to the new challenges. "We are facing the possible breakdown not only of our National Government but of our civilization."[22]

William Clinton Mullendore emerged as the leading Southern California apostle of the free-market religion. Tall and lean, with blue eyes and a scholarly manner, Mullendore was born on his father's farm in Kansas in 1892. He earned undergraduate and law degrees from the University of Michigan and practiced for a time in Winfield, Kansas. When war broke out in 1917, he joined the United States Food Administration and became friends with Herbert Hoover, the agency's director. After the war, Hoover appointed Mullendore special representative with the American Relief Administration in London and Berlin, and when Hoover became secretary of commerce under President Warren G. Harding he made the young lawyer his personal assistant.[23]

Mullendore served with Hoover until the end of 1923, when he resigned and moved to Los Angeles to practice law. He eventually became special counsel for Southern California Edison and in 1930 became a vice president and, then, executive vice president. He was a firm believer in individualism, personal responsibility, and unregulated capitalism. He preached the faith regularly at various forums in Los Angeles and other cities. By all accounts, Mullendore was a persuasive and charismatic man. Leonard Read, assistant manager of the Western Division of the Chamber of Commerce, visited Mullendore, hoping to persuade him to soften his criticisms of the National Recovery Administration. He failed miserably. After an hour's meeting, Read emerged a changed man, having experienced something like a conversion experience. He joined Mullendore in rallying the business community to battle the growing forces of government paternalism and socialism.[24]

Mullendore considered criticism of the free-enterprise system on the same level as treason. In 1931 he told a meeting of the League of Women Voters that the "man who breaks down public confidence in private business is as guilty of a crime as the man who tries to blow them up with explosives at night and he should be dealt with in the same manner." He vehemently attacked the critics of the so-called power trust—the giant holding companies that controlled most of the nation's power and light production. These highly leveraged corporate structures allowed financiers such as Samuel Insull of Chicago to control vast empires with minimal investment of their own money. These complex organizations were beyond government control because state regulations applied only to the operating companies that actually produced electricity. The devious "political agitators" that Mullendore thought should be treated as criminals were such men as Nebraska senator George W. Norris and Pennsylvania governor Gifford Pinchot, who wanted to bring the country's power companies under public control.[25]

Mullendore told a meeting of the Western States Chamber of Commerce that the New Deal inflicted permanent damage on the character of the American people through the policy of "officials leading and encouraging its citizens into a position of dependency upon government." He considered FDR's first hundred days in office as the "greatest revolution" in American history and "a denial of the lessons which our whole history had taught." For Mullendore, the New Deal philosophy was nothing more than "an easy way to pay for an entire nation's economic sins . . . to drink yourself sober, to borrow and spend our way out, under the leadership and direction of government."[26]

Mullendore believed that the Great Depression was not an economic crisis but a spiritual one. The problem was not the cost of living but the "cost of high living." People forgot the value of thrift, of living on what one earned, and not going into debt. Our "disrespect for the older guides and laws was not limited to material and economic affairs. There was at the same time a growing indifference and skepticism in our religious and moral or spiritual life." Like a preacher of the old-time religion, Mullendore laid the blame squarely at the feet of the sinner:

> Who was it that lived beyond their means and overextended their credit? Who bought and sold in the stock market? Who speculated? Who bought and who sold automobiles that we could not afford? Who built and who patronized the surplus number of motion-picture palaces? Who started the miniature-golf craze and similar stunts? Who built the extravagant country clubs, and golf courses, and the beach clubs and mountain clubs, and hunting clubs, and women's clubs, the resplendent big hotels and palatial office buildings, etc., and so on? Who urged the enormous expenditures on roads and schools, and public buildings, and parks and playgrounds, and who benefited from these things? Who raised our taxes and created our public debts? Who patronized the bootlegger, and allowed the rackets to grow which sprung up in that dizzy era?

Mullendore refused to acknowledge that the system had failed. It was the individuals who ignored the fundamental laws of the free-market system who were failing. The solution to our problems, Mullendore warned, was not to expect government to solve them for us. "If we choose Government control we are admitting individual failure. . . . We are saying we no longer want freedom because the responsibilities of freedom are too much for us. We are asking for a boss because we are tired of self-reliance."[27]

Mullendore seemed to enjoy his role as the Cato of American capitalism—warning his listeners of the impending collapse of society. "I have been accused of being a pessimist," he admitted. "But pessimism usually is the mere relating of unpleasant facts." Mullendore believed that nothing less than a spiritual awakening could revive the old virtues of self-reliance and individualism and save civilization. He relished his role as the harbinger of doom, but he was not the man to lead a crusade. This was the job of the clergy.[28]

Southern California had a large Catholic population, a substantial Jewish community, and a few liberal social gospel crusaders, but most of the region's church-going population was conservative, even reactionary, and Protestant. The seven-foot-tall neon-red Jesus Saves sign that for decades graced the top of the Church of the Open Door in downtown Los Angeles was a visual reminder of this fact. Churches were on the front lines when it came to dealing with the human consequences of the Depression. Helping the needy was the traditional role of the church in a society that had few other relief programs. The Protestant denominations, as well as the Catholic Welfare Bureau and the Jewish Social Service Bureau, offered aid to thousands, often helping many who did not share their religious beliefs. Unlike county relief and Community Chest charities that limited support to residents of the city and county, many religious organizations did not distinguish between locals and outsiders when offering help. Aimee Semple McPherson's Angelus Temple provided assistance to everyone, even nonresidents. To cope with the large numbers of those in need, the evangelist converted a warehouse once used by the Yellow Cab Company into a center with a soup kitchen, employment office, and medical clinic. The Union Rescue Mission, an independent Protestant mission, operated without the support of the Community Chest and served thousands of indigents each year without questioning where they came from. Such generosity irritated the directors of the Chamber of Commerce and county welfare officials, who felt that such assistance attracted destitute migrants to Los Angeles. Many congregations acted independently, doing what they could in small ways. Typical of this were the "poundings" that took place when a congregation loaded the pantries of needy parishioners with foodstuffs and other necessities. Some churches raised funds through programs such as the Church of the Blessed Sacrament's "hard-times party," a musical program that accepted donated food as the price of admission.[29]

Conservative religious beliefs and conservative economic beliefs reinforced one another. Other than a few dissenters on the left, most clergy saw no conflict between the god of the free market and the religion of Jesus Christ. Rev. Horace B. Sellers, pastor of the Euclid Heights Methodist Church, told his flock that the "business or professional man who thinks only of himself and not of service to his customers or clientele will soon have no customers or clientele to think of." Henry Ford sold so many cars, he believed, because he "placed the thought of service to the public ahead of private gain. More and more the truth of Jesus' words is becoming apparent in our business and economic world and business success is being adjudged today by service to the people rather than by private wealth attained through business ventures."[30]

James W. Fifield Jr. was pastor of the First Congregational Church, the city's oldest Protestant congregation and well known as the church of the wealthy. Fifield's views on economic issues so perfectly matched those of the business elite that he became known as the "Thirteenth Apostle of Big Business" and "St. Paul to the Prosperous"—titles he proudly embraced. Tall and lean, he reminded people of Jimmy Stewart. From boyhood, Fifield understood the value of establishing relationships with the rich and the powerful. He sprinkled his autobiography with the names of famous men whom he claimed to know well. J. C. Penney, George Pepperdine (founder of Pepperdine University), Douglas MacArthur, Benito Mussolini, Will Durant, and Senator Arthur H. Vandenburg were a few.[31]

The First Congregational Church occupied a massive Gothic revival structure on the edge of Lafayette Park in Los Angeles. Its 157-foot concrete tower, topped with four 19-foot pinnacles, gave the structure the look of an English cathedral. Completed in 1932, the church was intended to impress observers with the wealth and power of its parishioners; the costs of building and maintaining this magnificent structure drove the congregation into near bankruptcy. At night, Fifield's predecessor, Dr. Carl Safford Patton, tried to cut expenses by roaming the building turning off lights. Fifield intended to rescue the church from its burdensome debt and halt the decline in membership. He approached the job as if he were the head of a corporation, asking for a generous salary and a $100,000 line of credit from the Security First National Bank. Fifield decreed that all lights in the church were to stay on all night. "When so many felt discouraged, defeated, burdened or frustrated, they might look and see me turning on another light." He invited representatives from the Jewish, Catholic, and other Protestant churches to his installation ceremony because he wanted to establish relationships with the city's leading religious figures. All represented important Los Angeles religious constituencies: Rabbi Maxwell Dubin, rabbi at Temple Immanuel; Rev. W. Bernard Stevens, bishop of the

Protestant Episcopal Diocese of Los Angeles; and the venerable Joseph Scott, the Catholic attorney who was a fixture of Los Angeles public life for decades.[32]

Fifield believed that no one, other than communists, could deny that capitalism was "the best system ever devised for the acquisition and distribution of wealth." In *The Single Path*, his guide to Christian living, Fifield wrote that a "system that provides so much for the common good and happiness must flourish under the favor of the Almighty." If capitalism had the divine blessing, then it was obvious that God must approve of its methods as well. "One can argue from this, then," Fifield wrote, "that the practices of capitalism are also moral, aimed at the highest good for owner and worker alike."[33]

Fifield believed that wealthy people were most comfortable around people like themselves. To that end, so he claimed, he rode around town in a chauffeured car and joined the California Club—the "best" club in town. (He claimed that his membership over the years enabled him to raise more than $10 million.) When he moved to Los Angeles, Fifield and his wife purchased a home in exclusive Fremont Place that Gatsby would have admired. Built for a million dollars in the 1920s, it came with imported tiles, wood paneling, Tiffany stained-glass windows, a swimming pool, colonnade archways, and extensive lawns.[34]

Fifield conducted a growing radio ministry, spoke to audiences around the country, wrote for publications, and served on boards and committees. He left the "task of mingling with the people" to his assistant ministers. By 1941 he had paid off the mortgage on his church and quadrupled its membership. Weekly worship attendance averaged about three thousand. Unlike the Angelus Temple, the First Congregational Church had no soup kitchens or clinics for the poor. "We had a full time cafeteria at the church," he recalled, "which served lunches to businessmen." The church helped the unfortunate indirectly, he said. In "line with my conviction that real help is to help one help himself, most of our assistance work was channeled through the excellent operations of Goodwill Industries, which received great support from our people."[35]

Fifield's views on Roosevelt and the New Deal mirrored those of his wealthy parishioners. During the president's second term, Fifield abandoned any pretense of nonpartisanship and his public utterances took on an increasingly strident political tone. He worried about the New Deal's threat to personal freedom and the dependency on government programs. In *The Tall Preacher* he recalled that it "seemed that people could not do anything without asking the government. Instead of recognizing the creative and dignifying power of Freedom under God, the people were crying for those who would give them freedom from fear, freedom from exploitation, freedom from competition—and even freedom from an eternal God."[36]

In 1938, Fifield decided to go national with his message. He incorporated a nonprofit group called Spiritual Mobilization, with its headquarters at the First Congregational Church. He issued a pamphlet, "Christian Ministers and America's Future," that called on the nation's clergy to take a leading role in combating the rising dangers of totalitarianism. By this he did not mean just the fascist dictatorships in Italy and Germany and Communist rule in the Soviet Union but also developments closer to home. He warned that Americans, because they sought security over freedom, were blind to the "perils" of the New Deal. "Every concentration of power in our national government," he wrote, "especially in its executive branch, represents a reduction of freedom for the individual citizen and for the constituent States."[37]

Early in December 1940, with the help of his old friend J. C. Penney, Fifield received an invitation to address the Annual Congress of the National Association of Manufacturers at the Waldorf Astoria Hotel in New York City. The title of his talk was "The Religious Foundation of True Americanism." His message was that the regulatory state threatened the free-enterprise system and individual liberty. Businesspeople were not to blame for the Great Depression; on the contrary, they were its saviors. The god of the free market and the god of Christianity were one and the same. The message that they were on the side of the Lord pleased the industrialists, and at the end of his speech the audience burst into applause. Fifield's Waldorf Astoria speech made him a national figure.[38]

During the war, Fifield became increasingly active in politics locally and nationally. In 1943 he took a leadership role in forming the Los Angeles Better Government League. The peak of the influence of Spiritual Mobilization came after the war. The number of affiliated ministers nationally increased from more than four hundred in 1944 to more than 1,800 a year later. It attracted the financial support of wealthy business leaders such as J. Howard Pew Jr., president of Sun Oil. Fifield wrote a weekly newspaper column that appeared in over two hundred newspapers, and his voice could be heard on over five hundred radio stations. His views became increasingly conservative, taking on a social Darwinist slant. He argued that government programs interfered with God's plan by supporting the weak. He also opposed government programs that sought to end racial discrimination. He opposed the creation of the California Fair Employment Commission, dismissing claims of racial discrimination in employment. Spiritual Mobilization continued its work through the 1950s, spreading its message through its magazine, *Faith and Freedom*.[39]

• • • •

Other than a weak effort to save jobs by spreading the work, the Los Angeles business community had no plan to deal with the Depression. A real program would mean government involvement in the economy and the possibility of taxes—both of which were out of the question. Instead, the apostles of the free market blamed the victims. They believed that the problem of the Great Depression was not an economic one at all but a moral one. The unemployed were unemployed because they deserved it. In good times they squandered their wealth on consumer goods such as radios, cars, and other luxuries. The punishment may have been severe, but it was not undeserved. There was nothing to do but let the natural working of the free-market economy bring a return of prosperity. In the meantime, the unemployed would have to survive as best they could.

6

SALVATION FROM THE LEFT

> We were confident that we alone were tapped by history to fulfill its mission for humanity's liberation from exploitation and oppression.
>
> Peggy Dennis, *The Autobiography of an American Communist*

Southern California communists did not believe that the Wall Street crash was a temporary market correction. They believed that it was more in the nature of a death rattle. They did not puzzle over the question of when the economy would recover because they had no doubt that the world was experiencing the final crisis of capitalism. While the capitalist press preached optimism in the face of disaster, communists celebrated the imminent collapse of the old order. The business elite accused them of orchestrating a whispering campaign with the intention of undermining faith in the economic system. Los Angeles County district attorney Buron Fitts warned that spreading malicious rumors about the health of financial institutions was a criminal offense punishable by a $1,000 fine or one year in jail. Communists saw such threats as proof of the desperation of the capitalist class.[1]

The Communist Party in the United States dates from a split in the Socialist Party of America in 1919. The issue in question was whether or not the Socialist Party should affiliate with the

Third International (otherwise known as the Communist International, or Comintern). The Comintern, headquartered in Moscow, was an international association of Communist parties. Its ostensible purpose was to promote world revolution, but its real function was to assure Moscow's control over international communism. The debate in the party in the United States divided along national and linguistic lines. Most of the Socialists that supported affiliation with the Comintern were foreign born and members of the party's foreign-language federations; most opponents were native-born English speakers.

In California the disagreement was so rancorous that it led to the temporary demise of the state Socialist Party. In Southern California a Russian immigrant named M. J. Golos and others of Russian or Eastern European birth formed a new Communist Party. Many of the recruits to this new party were Jews who came to Los Angeles by way of New York to work in the garment industry. Many of them lived in Boyle Heights. Located on the east side of the Los Angeles River, not far from the garment district, Boyle Heights was a polyglot neighborhood of Jews, Japanese Americans, Mexican Americans, African Americans, and Russian Molokan Christians.

Communist Party headquarters was located in a brick building on Brooklyn Avenue (now Cesar Chavez Avenue) in Boyle Heights. Party membership was very small. As late as 1937, the Los Angeles County Communist Party convention set a modest goal of increasing its size to 1,500 members. The party also had difficulty hanging on to members after they joined. The number of new recruits barely kept up with those who left. The real strength of the party was not its size but the dedication of its core members, otherwise known as the party cadres. Communist Party cadres lived in a world separate from, but interacting at various points with, the larger society. Bound together through family and marriage, these cradle-to-grave radicals placed loyalty to the party above all else.[2]

Regina "Reggie" Karasick, otherwise known as Reggie Carson, Reggie Ryan, and later Peggy Dennis, belonged to the Los Angeles cadre. Born in New York City, she and her family moved to Boyle Heights in 1912, when she was three years old. Her parents, Meyer and Berta Karasick, were revolutionaries who fled Russia in 1904 and never abandoned their radicalism. Meyer worked as a cloak maker and sometimes ran his own cleaning business. When her health allowed, Berta worked in the garment trade as well. The couple enrolled their two daughters in the Socialist Sunday school at the Labor Temple and, like other parents, in the local public school. Of the two, Reggie later recalled, the "former was more important." Although of Jewish heritage, her family was defiantly nonreligious. Meyer and Berta sent their daughters to school on all Jewish holidays. "Each year I was mocked for being the only Jew at school on Hebrew holidays, just as I was scolded during the war years for refusing to buy war savings stamps." The girls always skipped school on May 1, the international day of revolutionary solidarity, and refused to use the easy excuse of sickness to cover their absences. Reggie attended Roosevelt High School in Boyle Heights, where the children of communist parents made up a sizeable bloc. Even for students, being a member of the party was dangerous and inevitably led to collisions with school authorities. On at least one occasion, Arthur Gould, the assistant superintendent of schools, refused to allow a young communist to graduate solely on the grounds that "his citizenship was not satisfactory."[3]

In the small world of the radical left, party activities made up a large part of daily activities. Bill Schneiderman, who as an adult became the California party secretary, and his siblings—Emma, Harry, and Louis—spent their free time selling papers and handing out leaflets on city streets. Not infrequently, the police arrested them and threw them in jail for infractions such as violating the city handbill ordinance, blocking the sidewalk, or disturbing the peace. Reggie and her older sister walked picket lines with their mother. Their social life "revolved around fund-raising concerts for Soviet Russian famine relief, beach picnics for the *Daily Worker*, and dances in support of mine and textile strikes in faraway states."[4]

When they reached the age of eight, boys and girls joined the Young Pioneers League, where they participated in extracurricular activities. At an older age they moved up to the Young Communist League (originally called the Young Workers League)—the usual step before adult membership in the Communist Party. At age thirteen, Reggie perfected her speaking skills as a YCL spokesperson. As a bright, young student she lived a double life as a party member and student in public school. She recalled giving orations denouncing capitalism at Communist-sponsored meetings and reciting the poems of James Whitcomb Riley at PTA meetings. For those not raised in the party, the YCL often provided young people their first exposure to Marxism and to like-minded people of their own age. This was the case for Meyer Baylin, who recalled singing revolutionary songs at meetings, going to jazz clubs, attending dances, and—perhaps the main goal—meeting young communists of the opposite sex—including Vera, his future wife.[5]

Los Angeles communists operated a summer camp in the San Bernardino Mountains east of Los Angeles. Except for the economics classes that Yetta Stromberg, the nineteen-year-old manager, conducted, activities differed little from any other camp. It did not last very long, but it is remembered today for a landmark case in the history of American civil liberties law. Local authorities viewed the very existence of the camp as an outrage. In 1929, at the alleged instigation of the LAPD Red Squad and the Better America Federation, George H. Johnson, the San Bernardino County district attorney, and a group of American Legionnaires raided the camp. They found a small number of adult supervisors and about forty children ranging in age from six years to the teens. Johnson arrested six women, including Stromberg. They also arrested Isadore Berkowitz, the camp handyman.

Johnson had no idea what kind of charges he would bring against the seven people he arrested. A search of the camp uncovered little incriminating evidence other than a box of Communist literature belonging to Stromberg. This box, which contained material advocating the overthrow of capitalism and the U.S. government, suggested the possibility of prosecution under the criminal syndicalism law. Further investigation suggested another possibility. The district attorney discovered that each morning Stromberg assembled the children and conducted a ceremony involving the raising of a small red flag and the reciting of a pledge of allegiance to the "cause for which it stands." This was a clear violation of California's anti–red flag law prohibiting the public display of any "red flag, banner or badge." Since its passage in 1919, no one had been charged under this law, but Johnson decided that the time had come.

Except for one of the women who happened to be visiting her daughter at the camp on that day, a jury found all of those arrested guilty. Everyone except Stromberg received sentences ranging from six months to five years in San Quentin for conspiracy to display the flag. The young camp manager got ten years because the jury found her guilty of conspiracy to display the flag plus the act of displaying it. After the verdicts, Berkowitz the handyman, who suffered from disabilities resulting from service in World War I, committed suicide. The ACLU appealed the convictions in the California courts on the ground that the anti–red flag law was an unwarranted limitation on free speech. The appeals court dismissed all convictions for conspiracy, upholding only Stromberg's conviction for the charge of displaying the flag. The ACLU then appealed the case to the U.S. Supreme Court. On May 18, 1931, in *Stromberg v. California*, Chief Justice Charles Evans Hughes, writing for the majority of the Court, ruled that the state anti–red flag law violated the First and Fourteenth Amendments to the Constitution. This historic decision was the first time the Court struck down a state law because it violated the free-speech clause of the Constitution.[6]

The communist cause was often a family affair, but when the choice was between family and the party, the party usually prevailed. As a young woman, Reggie married Frank Waldron, a rising star in the Communist Party. In 1930, on party orders, the couple left Los Angeles with their infant son for New York and then Moscow. Over the next four years they traveled, separately or together, on assignments in Europe and Asia. They left their child in an orphanage, where he spoke only Russian. When it came time to return to the United States, the party ordered Reggie and Frank to leave their son behind. The party leadership thought that an English-speaking couple with a child who spoke only Russian might attract attention from American authorities. Without protest, the two abandoned their son and left him in the care of the Soviet state.[7]

Despite the party's efforts to recruit new followers, almost everyone in Southern California despised communists—not only their natural enemies, businesspeople, and the police but also socialists, trade unionists, and the general population. This antipathy can be traced back to the so-called Red Scare that began in June 1919, when bombs exploded in eight cities across the United States—allegedly the work of foreign-born anarchists. Whoever planted the bombs targeted several prominent public officials, including U.S. attorney general A. Mitchell Palmer, who was not injured. Over two days in January 1920, Palmer retaliated by dispatching federal agents to thirty-three American cities to arrest foreign radicals. The raids rounded up several thousand men and women, although fewer than six hundred were ever deported as undesirable aliens. In Los Angeles, agents arrested Benjamin Ling, a Lithuanian, and E. Louis Lieberman, a Russian. Both were members of the Communist Party. Ling, according to the *Los Angeles Times*, was "one of the most dangerous enemies to the American government." The paper argued that more would have been arrested if the American Legion had not already run so many radicals out of town.[8]

One result of this outburst of anti-radical and anti-foreign hysteria was the passage of the California Criminal Syndicalism law in 1919. The main target of this legislation was a revolutionary syndicalist union, the IWW. The law tossed out the distinction between word and deed, making it a felony to advocate through speech or the printed word the violent overthrow of the government or to belong to an organization that advocated such a goal. With the decline of the IWW, the criminal syndicalism law fell into disuse, but it remained on the books. In the 1930s, prosecutors revived the law as a useful weapon in their battles against communism. Also dating to the Red Scare period was the LAPD Anarchist Bomb Squad, later renamed the Intelligence Bureau and popularly known as the Red Squad. The unit became the LAPD's primary instrument for monitoring and suppressing radical activity. The Red Squad worked so closely with the business community that it was considered an arm of the Chamber of Commerce. It acted as an almost independent agency of the police department and did not limit its activities to the boundaries of the city of Los Angeles.[9]

George E. Cryer, who served as Los Angeles mayor for nearly all of the 1920s (1921–29), was an avowed enemy of any form of radicalism. John Clinton Porter, who followed him as mayor in 1929, was even less tolerant of radicals. He had no understanding of why communists or anyone sympathetic to them (for example, the ACLU) had any rights at all. No "organization which is against the government of the United States has any rights in this city," he told the *Los Angeles Times*. Chief of police James "Two-Gun" Davis, who served from 1926 to 1929 and again from 1933 to 1938, was a no-nonsense law-and-order man. He considered constitutional rights to be of use only to criminals. He wanted the authority to fingerprint everyone living in the city and did not understand why anyone other than lawbreakers would object. Davis was also an anti-Semite who believed that the Jewish communists of Boyle

Heights were a greater danger than Nazis. Roy "Strongarm Dick" Steckel, who served as chief between Davis's two terms, believed that his officers could hold suspects without charge for at least forty-eight hours—despite the fact that this was a violation of the state constitution.[10]

In 1927, acting detective lieutenant (later acting captain) William "Red" Hynes became the commander of the Intelligence Bureau. A veteran and a member of the American Legion, Hynes was twenty-six years old when he joined the LAPD as a patrolman in 1922. His first big assignment was as an undercover officer during the 1923 IWW-led strike at Los Angeles Harbor. He infiltrated the union, won the trust of his fellow workers, and became secretary of the strike committee and editor of its bulletin. All the while he spied on union activities and acted as an agent provocateur. While head of the Red Squad, he regularly attended local Nazi meetings and, like his chief, considered Jewish communists a far greater risk to the country than Nazis. Hynes's undercover activities earned him the nickname "Red" and a reputation as an expert on radicals. His knowledge of radical activities was no doubt extensive, but the young officer's popularity with his superiors in the LAPD and the Chamber of Commerce probably had more to do with his willingness to bust heads when he felt the need to do so, which was often.[11]

Hynes's policy in dealing with communists was simple. He broke up any Communist-sponsored meeting or gathering on the grounds that any organization that advocated the overthrow of the U.S. government had no constitutional rights. He also applied this rule to any organization that he considered a front for the party—and his definition of a front was very broad. It did not matter if these meetings were held in a public hall, in a private home, or on a street corner. In situations where the authorities felt constrained by law, Hynes counted on the assistance of the American Legion as auxiliary police. Excessive violence against anyone who opposed them was standard operating procedure for the Red Squad. Clinton J. Taft, director of the Southern California Branch of the ACLU, summarized the Red Squad's treatment of the Communist Party in testimony before a congressional committee:

> Their meeting places have been raided; their headquarters have been raided without search warrants; they have been

arrested in platoons now and then, dragged into jail, beaten up as they were arrested, unnecessarily beaten; they have been beaten up after they were taken to jail, held incommunicado so that not even a lawyer could see them for hours and hours at a time, and for several days they have been held incommunicado sometimes and then released without any formal charge being placed against them. Every constitutional right guaranteed in the Bill of Rights has been denied those communists.[12]

Southern California Communist Party members followed the Comintern's policy of infiltrating existing capitalist institutions—in the terminology of the time, "boring from within." Communists in the United States formed the Trade Union Educational League (TUEL) to coordinate activities in American trade unions and an aboveground and legal political party, the Workers Party of America (eventually renamed the Communist Party USA). Organized labor did not look with favor on the idea of communists "boring from within" their unions and sometimes entered into unholy alliances with the police to root out party members within their ranks. Early in 1924, the TUEL sponsored a lecture by Ella Reeve Bloor, a prominent member of the Workers Party. About thirty union men and women attended. The LAPD and U.S. Justice Department agents burst into the meeting and arrested everyone present. The LAPD took names and union affiliations of all those arrested and turned this information over to an AFL representative. Shortly thereafter, everyone who attended the meeting was expelled from his or her union. The raid was a cooperative effort between police and the AFL to identify and purge communists from union ranks.[13]

William Schneiderman learned how willing conservatives in the labor movement were to work with the police when it came to dealing with communists. At the AFL's 1927 annual meeting in Los Angeles, young Schneiderman had the honor of representing the upholsterers union local at the convention. When he arrived at the Alexandria Hotel, he was directed to a conference room where he expected to meet with the credentials committee. Instead, he was surprised to find two top AFL officials, secretary-treasurer Frank Morrison and vice president Matthew Woll. He was even more surprised by the presence of "Red" Hynes, who identified

Schneiderman as a communist. Morrison perfunctorily banned the upholsterers union representative from the convention. Their business finished, three men abruptly left the room.[14]

The policy of boring from within ended abruptly in 1928. At its Sixth World Congress the Comintern announced that capitalism had entered its Third Period. In communist theory, the Third Period marked the breakdown of capitalist stability and the approaching collapse of the free-market system. This was the communist equivalent of the evangelical Christian end of days and the second coming of Christ. The Comintern directed party members to abandon the policy of boring from within and to become much more confrontational with the authorities. Following this new policy, American Communists formed the Trade Union Unity League (TUUL), a federation of Communist-controlled unions paralleling the unions affiliated with the AFL. In many trades, workers found two unions competing for their attention. In the Los Angeles garment industry, the Communist Needle Trades Workers Industrial Union and the Socialist-dominated International Ladies Garment Workers Union competed for the allegiance of workers. In the political sphere, the party rejected any cooperation or alliances with other parties. Communists coined a special term, "social fascists," for all non-Communist reform groups.[15]

Even before the Great Depression began, unemployed councils were the primary means through which the Third Period Communist Party reached out to those it considered the victims of capitalism. These councils appeared in all major American cities, including Los Angeles. The unemployed councils attempted to mobilize the unemployed around specific issues, such as evictions, the administration of welfare, or racial discrimination. Sometimes the issues—such as the recognition of the Soviet Union, freeing political prisoners, or protests against militarism—seemed far removed from the needs or interests of the city's unemployed. The councils also served as a way to involve those who were sympathetic to the party but were not members. Through these councils, the party reached out to the most neglected and oppressed groups in society. In Los Angeles the party was one of the few organizations with a predominately white membership that made the needs of the African American community a priority.

Meyer Baylin began his long career in the party as an unemployed council organizer. He began by leafleting and "soapboxing" on skid row, preaching to homeless unemployed who lived on the streets or in flophouses. To avoid being arrested for violating city ordinances against street speaking and leafleting without a permit, Baylin rented a vacant lot from a sympathetic landlord for $20 a month. He paid the rent with dues collected from new members. Nearby, the Salvation Army served donuts and coffee, providing refreshments for the unemployed while they listened to his speeches.[16]

In the African American neighborhoods bordering Central Avenue in the southern part of the city, the unemployed councils defied authorities when they restored water or power to homes cut off for nonpayment of bills. The unemployed councils also blocked county authorities when they evicted families from their homes. In March 1933, a group calling themselves the League of Homeless Youth seized an empty house on the south side and moved in. In another dramatic episode, when deputy sheriffs tried to evict Ezra F. Chase and his wife and child from their home on 59th Street, the Junior League of the Unemployed Council of America intervened. According to the *Los Angeles Times* account of the incident, although they were "loudly abused" by the occupiers, deputies managed to remove Chase and his family. Chase, a veteran, spoke to a large crowd after being put out in the street.[17]

The county welfare department was a repeated target of communist protests. A young unemployed council organizer, Dorothy Healey, wrote that "every week we would take a new delegation of unemployed down to the metropolitan welfare office to demand higher relief payments or jobs. Every week 'Red' Hynes and the red squad would be there, and people would be beaten up. But every week we'd go back again. We were determined we would outlast them." On one notable occasion in January 1933, about one hundred unemployed entered the county welfare offices on North Broadway in downtown Los Angeles. Ezra Chase, the very same man evicted from his home the previous August, led the group. Chase confronted the unfortunate assistant in charge, one Horace D. Roberts, and demanded immediate food relief. When the police intervened, the invaders fought back with fountain pen tear gas guns. The *Los Angeles Times* considered the fight "one of the most desperate between radicals and police in recent years." Furniture was smashed and "blood was strewn over the rugs and desks, chairs and windows." The police arrested five protestors. Eight men, four of them police officers, went to the hospital.[18]

Third Period doctrine required Communist parties to focus on demonstrations—otherwise known as mass proletarian revolutionary action. In February 1930, the executive committee of the Comintern declared February 26 to be International Unemployment Day and ordered Communist parties around the world to hold massive demonstrations. The Comintern later changed the date to March 6, leaving local groups confused and uncertain as to what to do. Los Angeles communists decided to hold demonstrations on both dates.[19]

On the afternoon of February 26, party members and sympathizers assembled at the Plaza. The plan was to march the short distance to city hall and demand an audience with the mayor. The demonstrators expected police resistance and following Comintern instructions formed self-defense committees to protect themselves. Frank Waldron, one of the leaders of the demonstration, stuffed his cap and lined his peacoat with newspapers to protect against police clubs. The crowd was large, but it is difficult to know how many were participants and how many simply showed up to watch. The press reported wildly differing estimates of the numbers. The *Los Angeles Daily News* reported two hundred, the *Herald* five thousand, and the *Times*, which as a matter of editorial policy always exaggerated the communist threat, put the number in the "thousands."[20]

Mayor Porter and Chief Steckel, who considered any demonstration the same as insurrection, had no intention of allowing it to proceed. As soon as a young communist named Carl Sklar climbed on a wagon to address the crowd, the police moved in. The *Los Angeles Daily News* reported that night sticks "were drawn and tear gas bombs were thrown by the officers. The screaming mob battled to the southeast corner of the Plaza." The *Los Angeles Times* description of the event makes lurid reading: "Thousands of Communists and Red sympathizers defied reserve police squads in one of the most stubborn riots in the city's history last night at the Plaza in which billy-clubs, tear-bombs and rough-and-tumble fighting of the severest character were necessary to the hard-pressed officers to subdue the milling, screaming throngs that ran wild in the streets."[21]

The *Los Angeles Times* considered the police the victims of the riot, reporting that though few of the "Reds" had been injured the LAPD suffered considerable casualties. Many "of the 300 hundred officers in the battle nursed numerous bruises and lacerations," the paper reported. It appears that the authorities were not prepared for the marchers' fierce resistance, yet it seems unlikely that the police, armed to fight with billy-clubs and tear gas, came off worse. In an editorial comment, the paper blamed the entire demonstration on foreigners. "Virtually all of those arrested here, it was noticeable, bore Russia names and the majority are presumably aliens. In Russia such demonstrators would be court-martialed and shot with a minimum of ceremony or delay. This being a capitalist nation with no mercy on the proletariat, a few will presumably serve short jail sentences with food and clothing supplied at the taxpayers' expense."[22]

Hynes was determined not to be caught off guard again. He prepared for the upcoming March 6 demonstration by raiding the offices of left-wing organizations and arresting suspected communists. Among those hauled off to jail was Vratian Galalian, a suspected Soviet agent, held for possible deportation proceedings. In the garment district officers raided the headquarters of the Trade Union Unity League and the Needle Trades Workers Industrial Union. At the International Labor Defense headquarters they arrested about a dozen people. The police also broke up "secret meetings" in San Pedro where communist agitators were allegedly organizing longshoremen.[23]

The worldwide mass demonstrations on March 6 took place as scheduled. On "Red Thursday" in England, the unemployed turned out in London, Manchester, and other major cities. Communists also marched in Berlin, Hamburg, Munich, Vienna, and Seville. In the United States, the size of the turnout surprised everyone. The unemployed marched in New York, Detroit, Chicago, Boston, Milwaukee, Baltimore, Cleveland, Washington, D.C., and Seattle. The demonstrations in New York and Detroit ended badly with pitched battles between the police and the marchers.[24]

Los Angeles communists planned a repeat demonstration. On the morning of March 6, Mayor Porter arrived at his office accompanied by an armed police officer, a chauffeur, and his son Lee, who also carried a gun. Porter refused to address the unemployment demonstration or to meet with Leo Gallagher, an attorney for the ACLU. The police department deployed one thousand men to confront the marchers. About five thousand spectators ignored warnings to stay away and showed up to watch. The *Illustrated Daily News* reported that so far "as a radical demonstration was concerned, the day was a complete flop." The police arrested about twenty-three people, mostly for blocking sidewalks and shouting slogans.[25]

For the next few years, Communist-sponsored demonstrations became a regular feature of Los Angeles life. The combination of the confrontational approach of the Communist Party during the Third Period and Hynes's policy of breaking up all Communist-sponsored meetings and demonstrations inevitably led to an increase in the number of violent clashes with the police. There seemed to be few limitations on Hynes's authority to decide what qualified as a communist meeting and the amount of force he could use in breaking it up. Hynes interpreted his mandate broadly and monitored all left-leaning organizations to be sure that communists were not behind them. On three separate occasions the Red Squad broke up seemingly harmless public meetings where attorney Leo Gallagher spoke about his trip to the Soviet Union.[26]

The African American journalist Loren Miller described an abortive meeting of the Friends of the Soviet Union at Los Angeles Polytechnic High School. The school board allowed a group opposing recognition to use the high school's auditorium and out of fairness agreed to give the same courtesy to the other side. (In November 1933, President Roosevelt officially recognized the Soviet Union.) Captain Hynes protested, but the board permitted the meeting to go ahead. About 1,700 people showed up. Outside the hall a number of American Legionnaires gathered with blackjacks in their hands while others took seats around the auditorium. Before the meeting could begin, the lights went out and the Legionnaires inside the hall began shouting and booing and stamping their feet. The audience gamely responded by singing "There's a Long Trail a-Winding" and "America." Hynes showed up and ordered everyone to go home, claiming that his men could not protect them.[27]

The 1932 Olympics, held in Los Angeles, was an irresistible opportunity for local communists to make a public statement. The Games were simply too big and too important to ignore. When the final parade of nations began, five men and two women wearing

One of many Communist Party demonstrations during the Depression, this one a hunger march for the unemployed and poor in 1933. Harry Quillen, photographer. Los Angeles Photographers Photo Collection, courtesy of the Los Angeles Public Library.

track suits jumped from the stands and began running around the track shouting "Free Tom Mooney!" Two men followed, carrying a large banner bearing the same words. A booing crowd in the bleachers clearly showed their disapproval. (Earlier, when Luigi Beccali of Italy raised his arm in a fascist salute after winning the 1,500-meter race, there was little protest.)[28]

The Mooney case was the cause célebre of the American left during the 1920s and 1930s. At the time of the 1932 Olympics, the former San Francisco unionist was serving a life sentence in San Quentin for the bombing of the 1916 San Francisco Preparedness Parade. His trial was blatantly unfair and it was obvious to any reasonable observer that he was falsely convicted, but a succession of Republican governors refused to grant Mooney a pardon.

The police quickly arrested the Olympic protestors and hustled them off to jail. Of the nine participants, the police booked six, four of whom were members of the Communist Party. The protestors, all in their twenties or younger, received sentences of nine months in prison—the maximum permitted by law.[29]

In February 1933, the Red Squad crashed a meeting of the John Reed Club in Hollywood. The John Reed Club was named for the radical journalist and author of *Ten Days That Shook the World*, a book favorable to the Bolshevik revolution. Hynes claimed that his men intervened to prevent an attack by American Legionnaires who were about to invade the meeting. He insisted that all members of the John Reed Club either belonged to the Communist Party or were sympathizers. On this particular day, the club in Hollywood was holding a "Japan Night" that included martial arts exhibitions. The master of ceremonies was Karl Hama (later known as Karl Yoneda), a local Japanese American communist. The Red Squad invaded the building, smashing doors and vandalizing works of art and confiscating Springfield rifles and bayonets later revealed to be stage props. Hynes arrested Hama on the charge of violating the criminal syndicalism law.[30]

A few days later, representatives of the ACLU, including Clinton J. Taft, president of the Southern California branch, and attorney Leo Gallagher appeared before the Los Angeles City Council to protest the raid. Accompanying these representatives were about fifty members of the John Reed Club and the Workers Ex-Service Men's League. The audience became unruly and the council president ordered the room cleared. The Red Squad jumped into action and in the process of removing the spectators shoved Gallagher into an adjacent room and beat him up, leaving him with broken glasses and two black eyes.[31]

Hynes and his superiors in the LAPD and in city hall believed that the Communist Party posed a real threat to society. Mark Pierce, a member of the police commission, said that "Communists have no Constitutional rights and I won't listen to anyone who defends them." In its columns the *Los Angeles Times* did not connect the protests to the depressed economy but blamed the agitation on foreigners, especially Russian immigrants. The *Times* praised Hynes's work. He "has broken up more Communist demonstrations and prevented more Communist mischief than any other dozen policemen here and perhaps anywhere." A reader of the *Times*, lacking any other source of information, could not be blamed if he or she concluded that class warfare was being fought on the city streets. The *Los Angeles Herald* took a more level-headed view of the communists. The paper editorialized that the Red Menace was a "mere bugaboo, such as used by parents sometimes to frighten children."³²

Dorothy Healey, a prominent figure among Los Angeles communists, recalled that, if "you were a Communist, you simply did not have a right to free speech." It was not only communists and their supporters who believed that the police were out of control. The ACLU, the Los Angeles Bar Association, the Los Angeles Ministerial Association, the Methodist Ministers Association, and the Municipal League lodged protests with the mayor's office against the activities of the Red Squad. They claimed that the police raided and broke up meetings without warrants, were brutal in their handling of the arrested, and denied citizens the right of peaceful assembly and petition. None of this mattered to Mayor Porter, who gave the police his unconditional support. He believed that those who complained were "defending an organization which preaches the overthrow of our government. Therefore I see no reason why I should recognize their demands."³³

The illegality of some of the LAPD's methods disturbed the Los Angeles Bar Association, a more conservative group than the ACLU. Rather than focus on the defense of radicals, as the ACLU did, the organization examined the department's methods—especially the use of the "third degree." A junior bar association composed of younger attorneys investigated police wrongdoing. They went into the lockups and interviewed prisoners and police officers. They discovered that the police routinely held arrestees without charges for forty-eight and sometimes seventy-two hours. They also found that the "third degree" was commonly used in special "incommunicado" cells from which sounds of screams could be heard. These investigations received a great deal of publicity and generated a large number of complaints. The attitude of the police was that criminals did not have rights and so if their law enforcement methods were illegal then they should be made legal. One police captain wanted a "whipping post and the cat-o'-nine-tails—'cut them deep and then rub handfuls of salt into the cuts.'" The bar association's investigations made it into President Hoover's Wickersham Commission report on illegal police activities, and they may have been responsible for the department's requirement that all newly hired officers have at least a high school diploma.³⁴

The courts also lost patience with Hynes. On March 11, 1933, the Red Squad shut down a meeting where candidates for various public offices were scheduled to speak. Hynes had decided that this was a Communist-sponsored event. Organizers were still setting up tables and putting out refreshments when his officers arrived to shut down the meeting. The police ordered everyone to leave, turned out the lights, and locked the door. The organizers of the meeting sued the City of Los Angeles for damages resulting from the cancellation of the meeting. The fact that Hynes's men shut down the meeting before any speaker, communist or otherwise, uttered a word disturbed municipal court judge B. J. Sheinman. Sheinman ordered that the damages be paid. He showed his outrage in his summary of the case:

> This is an unwarranted invasion of the right to assemble and an unjustifiable assumption of authority. The authority of the police officer goes only this far in a case of this kind—to arrest upon a violation of the law by words spoken or acts done.... But to allow him to speculate, and base his action on mere suspicions or beliefs, is the indulgence in an unconstitutional and unlawful procedure calculated to deprive citizens of a fundamental and basic right, and to place the officer above that constitutional structure upon which our freedom as a democratic nation is predicated.[35]

A few days later, superior court judge Emmet H. Watson issued an injunction prohibiting the police from interfering with a similar meeting. Federal judge Harry Holizer also issued an injunction ordering the police not to interfere with a meeting of the Friends of the Soviet Union. These decisions did not prevent the Red Squad from disrupting Communist-sponsored meetings, but they did make the city government more reluctant to close down meetings without clear proof that speakers advocated the overthrow of the government—an act that remained a violation of California law.[36]

Mayor Frank L. Shaw, elected in June 1933, established a free-speech zone in the Plaza where speakers could say what they wanted without fear of police interference, but he also appointed the fiercely anti-radical James E. Davis as LAPD chief and kept Hynes as head of the Red Squad. Mayor Shaw had friendly relations with the conservative AFL; he had no tolerance at all for its more aggressive rival, the Congress of Industrial Organizations (CIO). During Shaw's time in office the Red Squad continued to serve as an arm of the Chamber of Commerce to help to break strikes and interfere with the CIO's organizing drives. In 1938, Fletcher Bowron, who defeated Shaw in a special recall election, fired Chief Davis and abolished the Red Squad.[37]

In 1935, the Seventh World Congress of the Communist Party declared an end to the Third Period. The Comintern reversed its former policy and announced the creation of a People's Front, better known as the Popular Front, and instructed party members around the world to work with and join non-communist groups. Reform groups were no longer to be considered "social fascists" but instead allies in the fight against the real fascists. The Trade Union Unity League and its constituent unions were dissolved and their members ordered to join non-communist unions.

In the mid-1930s, the CIO began organizing unskilled workers in the mass production industries. The rise of the new labor federation led to a deep rift between the CIO and the AFL. The latter organization traditionally focused mostly on skilled workers, whereas the CIO organized unskilled workers in the mass production industries. A new wave of labor militancy spread across the United States. The CIO, often using unorthodox tactics, won a number of important victories in previously union-free corporations. Notable was the General Motors sitdown strike in 1936–37, when workers seized the plant and refused to leave until the corporation recognized the new union. Southern Californians soon found themselves swept up in this new organizing drive. The CIO targeted the region's large industries such as Douglas Aircraft, Goodyear, Goodrich, Firestone, and the Long Beach Ford assembly plant.

Many of the new labor federation's most talented organizers were communists out of work after the Comintern's dissolution of their unions. John L. Lewis, the head of the CIO, cared little about the political affiliations of his organizers. When criticized that he brought in too many communists, he responded with a folksy remark: "Who gets the bird, the hunter or the dog?" Party members became influential in the Southern California CIO. Philip M. "Slim" Connelly, a communist and one-time leader of the Los Angeles Chapter of the American Newspaper Guild, became head of the CIO's Los Angeles Industrial Union Council. Party influence was so strong that some union leaders called the Los Angeles CIO an "outpost" of the Communist Party.[38]

• • • •

The influence of the Communist Party on the lives of ordinary residents of Southern California is difficult to measure. The confrontational tactics of the Comintern's Third Period may have been cathartic for the participants and entertaining for the general public, but they did little to advance the cause of communism. The regular invasions of the county welfare offices did nothing to persuade the Los Angeles County board of supervisors to increase welfare payments or find jobs. Moving people back into their homes and restoring utility services may have helped some unfortunate families in the short run, but in the long run they provided no permanent benefit. During the Third Period, political theater seemed to be the only thing the communists did well.

It was not until the time of the Popular Front that the party became involved in activities that made a difference to some Southern Californians. Communist organizers doubtless had a part in many of labor's victories during this period. The party also became deeply involved in what it called "Negro work." Communist organizers hoped to open "wide the doors of the Trade Union movement to the Negro people" with educational campaigns to "eradicate any discrimination of the Negro people on the job and in the Trade Unions." The party did not end racial discrimination in the union movement, but it may have contributed to the advances that were made. The party was one of the few mostly white organizations in Southern California willing to declare itself unequivocally in favor of African American rights to better housing, increases in welfare benefits to the level of those that whites received, and demonstrations against employment discrimination in African American neighborhoods.[39]

The party was an abject failure in the only mission that mattered to its members—persuading Southern Californians that the capitalist system had failed and needed to be replaced with a communist one.

7

The Utopian Society

> Utopia. A plan for or vision of an ideal society, place, or state of existence, *esp.* one that is impossible to realize; a fantasy, a dream.
>
> Oxford English Dictionary

Sometime during the summer of 1933, Merritt T. Kennedy and Walter Reausaw began thinking about forming an organization that they would call the Utopian Society. Both saw this new organization as a way to make money. Kennedy was a stock promoter who, according to one acquaintance, sold oil securities of questionable value—sometimes called "banana oil" stocks. Reausaw also worked as a securities salesman. His personal history was somewhat questionable. At the time the two men began discussions to form the Utopian Society, Reausaw had at least seven outstanding bench warrants ordering him to appear in Los Angeles municipal court. In one case, a judge ordered him to explain why he could not repay a widow who loaned him her life savings to invest in various promotional schemes. Reausaw, whom the *Los Angeles Times* described as "handsome and well-dressed," did not give the appearance of being destitute yet explained that he was broke and forced to live off of his mother-in-law's inheritance. A third man, Eugene J. Reed, a bond salesman recently relocated from Denver, also was involved in the creation of the new organization. He later claimed to be the sole mastermind behind its origins—an assertion that others angrily denied.¹

In planning the Utopian Society, Kennedy, Reausaw, and Reed borrowed heavily from a movement called Technocracy. Technocracy was wildly popular in Southern California for a few months during the darkest days of the Depression—between Franklin Roosevelt's election in November 1932 and his inauguration the following March. Technocracy was not so much a philosophy as an engineer's fantasy as to how society should be managed. It promised the elimination of every bad thing that plagued humanity. If the world were run according to Technocratic principles, there would no longer be poverty or hunger. Individual greed would disappear and universal leisure rather than the struggle for survival would become the new human condition. Technocracy promised this revolutionary change without the inconvenience of a revolution. It was a technical problem best left to technicians who understood the laws of physical science. The engineer and the slide rule replaced the revolutionary and the gun.

It was largely through the efforts of Manchester Boddy, publisher of the *Illustrated Daily News* in Los Angeles, that Technocracy became known to Southern Californians. Boddy launched a campaign in the pages of his newspaper promoting Technocracy as the way to end the Depression. He falsely implied that the new president would make Technocracy the centerpiece of his recovery plan. The first two issues of the *Illustrated Daily News* that carried stories about Technocracy sold out completely. In *Glory Roads*, Luther Whiteman and Samuel L. Lewis describe crowds that gathered around the doors of the newspaper's offices, eagerly waiting for copies hot off the press. "Men fought and scrambled. Dollar bills in the rear were often waved over the heads of those in front. Edition after edition would be sold out. Technocracy had taken hold." This confirms, if nothing else, Boddy's well-known prowess as a judge of how to boost his paper's circulation.²

The leader of the Technocrats was a somewhat mysterious man named Howard Scott. He led a group called the Energy Survey that worked from borrowed offices at Columbia University. The Energy Survey produced charts that showed the amount of employment, production, and energy consumed in American industry over the previous one hundred years. Supporters of Technocracy claimed that the construction of the charts was not a simple matter. It involved the "integration of physics, chemistry, geology, geophysics, thermo-dynamics, zoology, biophysics, biology and physiology." The mathematics involved was supposedly "more complex than that of Einstein's unified field theory" and its implications for mankind greater than Darwin's theory of evolution.[3]

What, exactly, was the nature of this Technocratic society that was supposed to end the Depression? The sole purpose of the state in a Technocracy was to "guarantee each member of the community a proportionate share of the energy production of the community." The exact energy value of all commodities or services would be calculated by exacting scientific standards. The energy dollar, the x-erg, would replace traditional money. Every year each adult citizen would receive a certificate for so many x-ergs. In exchange for these certificates, the citizenry would be required to perform a small number of hours of labor. These energy dollars would have to be spent by the end of the year. Saving or hoarding energy dollars would not be allowed, thus making it impossible to accumulate wealth. In a Technocracy this would, in any case, be unnecessary because all reasonable human needs or desires were satisfied. The state would track all expenditures, even the smallest, and deduct each one from the holders' certificates.[4]

The creation of the Utopian Society dated from a meeting held in a private home in August 1933. In addition to Kennedy and Reausaw, the attendees included James B. Hollis, Maxwell P. Smith, H. R. Hadfield, and a man known only as Mr. Ellis. Hollis ran an advertising agency. His slogan was "Advertising Modernized." In a letter to Upton Sinclair he claimed that he and Smith were the final authors of the "organization, plan, aims, and preliminary procedure" of the organization. Smith was an insurance salesman brought into the group when Kennedy asked for advice about a plan, later abandoned, to sell policies to members of the proposed society. Hadfield was a member of the executive committee of the Continental Committee on Technocracy, California Division. He asked the committee's permission to help form a society to promote technocratic principles. The committee withdrew its endorsement when it realized that Hadfield was only interested in the money he could earn from the sale of memberships. They expelled Hadfield from the Committee on Technocracy on the charge of racketeering. Nothing is known about Ellis, but one member of the group left when he could not persuade the others to exclude Jews as members of the new organization. Since nothing was heard from Ellis again, he may have been the one who left.[5]

This small group of men debated various ways to exploit the public interest in Technocracy. They considered opening a bookstore. Hollis wanted to raise money to produce a film version of *Looking Backward,* Edward Bellamy's utopian novel. The group rejected these ideas in favor of forming a secret society similar to the many fraternal orders popular at the time. Initially, they planned to organize a sales force to sell memberships for ten dollars each, but Smith argued that the fee was too high and, in any case, there was no incentive for people to join such an organization. They finally concluded that the best way to attract members was to create a society that gave the appearance of being exclusive. The names of its members were to be kept secret. There would be no advertising in the newspapers, radio, or anywhere else. All recruiting would be done on a person-to-person basis. Members would be identified only by a number—the lower the number the higher the prestige because it indicated greater seniority. For example, Smith received the number 2 x 1 because he was the second person to join the first committee.[6]

In February 1934, Kennedy, Reed, and Reausaw filed incorporation papers with the California secretary of state to form a nonprofit organization called the Utopian Society, Western Division. The articles of incorporation gave the three men complete control over the affairs of the organization, including the authority to create bylaws, fix fees, and distribute these fees. In May, Kennedy, Reed, and an attorney named Forrest Hartley set up another corporation called the National Foundation of the Utopian Society of the United States. This second corporation did not replace the earlier one but, instead, was a bald attempt to corral some of the money that might flow in from chapters in other parts of the country. Although the vast bulk of its membership was in Southern California, the Utopian Society spread to San Francisco, Oakland, Denver, Pittsburgh, Cleveland, Dallas, Chicago, and a few other cities. According to its charter, the National Foundation received 20 percent of the revenue of the Utopian Society. The articles gave the trustees of the

National Foundation the authority to pay themselves "reasonable salaries" and included provisions "for pensions and annuities" for incapacitated trustees or their widows and dependents.[7]

Secrecy allowed the infant organization to grow unnoticed by watchful groups such as the LAPD, the American Legion, the Better America Federation, and the *Los Angeles Times,* who feared any potentially subversive organization. The Utopian Society was not exclusive at all. It was open to all American citizens, regardless of race, sex, or religion. It was one of the rare organizations in 1930s Los Angeles that admitted African Americans on an equal basis with whites. (Hugh Macbeth, an African American attorney, became the Utopian Society's legal counsel.)[8]

The Society recruited members through small group meetings in private homes. Invitations came from friends, neighbors, or coworkers who already had gone through their first meeting. The potential members were ushered into a darkened room where an American flag was prominently displayed. The person who conducted the meeting, known as the reader, solemnly informed his listeners that much of the Society's business would be "conducted in secrecy" and that only "men and women who have vision, judgment, and courage" could join. Attendees were required to swear an oath of secrecy and of loyalty to the U.S. Constitution. The reader then revealed for the first time that the organization was a fraternal order called the Utopian Society of America (U.S.A.).[9]

The reader explained that the Society's aims were full employment, a decent standard of living, the elimination of poverty, care of the sick and aged, strengthening the American family, education for youth, eliminating the need for charity, ending crime, eliminating speculation, and preventing the accumulation of wealth in the hands of a few. The remainder of the meeting required each prospective member to be blindfolded and quizzed privately on his or her eligibility for membership. Depending on the size of the group, the organizers of the house meeting asked the successful graduates to form themselves into one or two committees. The members of these committees received written instructions and were then authorized to conduct their own house meetings. This "chain-letter approach" to recruiting new members was fabulously successful. Carey McWilliams, one of the first to report on the Society, estimated that at it was not unusual for at least 250 house meetings to be held in Los Angeles every night. By the end of 1933, he claimed, the Utopian Society had recruited about 500,000 members. Although this figure is surely an exaggeration, the real numbers were very large. Almost overnight a mass movement with thousands of followers appeared on the scene—all without the knowledge of the newspapers or local government officials.[10]

The house meeting was only the first step in the process of becoming a member of the Utopian Society. All who attended one of these meetings and served on a committee that organized another meeting were eligible to receive the "Revelations and subsequent Cycles of secret work." The Revelations consisted of weekly dramatic dialogues presented before meetings of the initiates. The dialogues reviewed important points of the Technocratic analysis of the economy. This gave house-meeting graduates something to do while they progressed to full membership by passing through the Second, Third, and Fourth Cycles. (The house meeting was the First Cycle.) Initiates who completed these three Cycles advanced to the full membership of the Fifth Cycle.[11]

The men who created the Utopian Society were caught off guard by their success in recruiting thousands of prospective members in such a short time and scrambled to write the scripts for the dialogues. Kennedy went to see Reed. While sitting in his car in front of Reed's apartment, he asked him if he thought that he could write the scripts quickly. Reed, a member of the Masons and familiar with the rituals of that fraternal order, pondered the request and then agreed to do it. In a few days he roughed out some ideas, but before he began writing he became seriously ill. Pressed for time, Kennedy and Rousseau visited Reed as he lay in his hospital bed. They took his notes and worked furiously to finish the scripts. As the performances of the Second Cycle began, they had not yet finished the Third and Fourth Cycles.[12]

The Cycles were a series of allegorical plays set in the fifth century. They portrayed the plight of people caught in the grip of a depression and their deliverance through the principles of Technocracy. Putting the performances together on short notice was as great a challenge as writing the scripts. Costumes were made from gunnysacks held together with safety pins. First Cycle graduates were the performers. A narrator read their lines while the pilgrims acted in pantomime. For the first performance, the organizers rented a hall in a Masonic lodge on Wilshire Boulevard.[13]

Only graduates of house meetings were admitted to the performances. Those who attended greeted one another by their numbers. Each Cycle began with the oath of secrecy and allegiance to the Constitution used in the house meetings. The Second Cycle performance exposed the misery and unfairness of the capitalist economy. Five pilgrims carrying lanterns—one of them a woman with a baby—wander across the stage in search of the Hermit Reason. Along the way they encounter a grain merchant and a cloth dealer, who refuse to help the pilgrims. (The merchants later go bankrupt and join the pilgrims.) A moneylender loans them money, requiring them to wear the shackles of debt. They are arrested and found guilty of not paying taxes. A magistrate confiscates the money they borrowed from the moneylender and sends them on their way. At last they meet the Hermit Reason, who tells them "of a wonderful land where the heavy work is done by machinery, and where there is an abundance for all."[14]

The Third and Fourth Cycles pick up the story as the Hermit, pilgrims, and bankrupt merchants arrive at the gates of Utopia. The Hermit gives the head pilgrim a new name—the Forgotten Man—a phrase borrowed from one of President Roosevelt's radio talks. The Coordinator of Government appears, removes Forgotten Man's shackles, and then begins to explain the various departments of government. Forgotten Man wants to know the nature of the revolution that brought the Utopian world into being. The Coordinator of Government explains that the new society did not come into being through violence. Instead, it was "an intelligent and peaceful revolution."[15]

"Production for Consumption!" was a slogan often associated with the Utopian Society. In the Technocratic economy, production for profit was a thing of the past. Once the people accepted the irrefutable logic of the new order, a flourishing economy would emerge that did not require profit. Newton Van Dalsem, author of a history of the Society, described this new world: "Wheels hummed.—Motors whirled.—Trains roared into the night.—Women sang.—Children danced to school on well-shod feet.—The cloud of debts was driven back.—The fires of Greed and Profit smothered.—The pure air of opportunity quickened the pulse of men.—They leaped forth to conquer."[16]

The Fourth Cycle production closed on this optimistic note. Candidates who passed through all four Cycles were eligible to enter the Fifth Cycle—full membership in the Utopian Society. Those who paid a three-dollar membership fee (about $56 in 2019 dollars) were directed to a room where they were given an armband, a secret grip, words, and sign." The new members paid dues of ten cents a month.[17]

The number of people attending the Cycles soon outstripped the capacity of the Masonic lodge and facilities available at other fraternal orders, such as the Elks and the Eagles. The Society, by charging a small admission fee, could afford to rent the Shrine Auditorium, but even with a seating capacity of over six thousand it was not large enough. Van Dalsem reported that on one day in June the Shrine hosted nine meetings. Even then thousands were turned away. Estimates of the Society's membership at its peak range from 250,000 to 500,000. Whatever the actual number, it was most certainly very large. Stanley Moffat, an attorney from the town of South Gate, claimed that the Society's membership in his community was about six thousand. The 1930 U.S. Census showed the population of the city to be 19,632, so about a third of the city's residents, amounting to almost all of its adult population, were members of the Utopian Society.[18]

By the middle of 1934, the Utopian Society had grown too large to remain a secret to the general public. With cash pouring in from the hundreds of thousands of members who paid the three-dollar initiation fee, the organizers set up headquarters in a house west of downtown and later in a two-story office building on La Brea Avenue. The Society's coming out party was a gathering of 25,000 people who filled the Hollywood Bowl. The event featured music including "Song of Utopia," composed by John T. Boudreau, band director at Loyola University. Charles N. Fielder and Roy G. Owens wrote the lyrics. Fielder was a composer with numerous works to his credit, including "Hymne Olympique," or "Now Sing of Virile Games," the official song of the 1932 Olympics. The speaker of the evening was Jonathan F. Glendon, a Society trustee and a former silent film and stage actor active in the Technocracy movement.[19]

According to Van Dalsem, Glendon's address was "delivered with great skill." He analyzed the causes of and cures for the national economic crisis from a Technocratic point of view. The development of modern machinery, he said, eliminated jobs and ensured that the country had "a vast body of citizens who cannot possibly ever again find employment." The government's response—presumably the relief programs of FDR's New Deal—was to create "synthetic jobs" paid for with "synthetic money." As a consequence of spending money that could never be repaid, the nation was on the verge of bankruptcy. "Is it possible for the human mind," Glendon thundered, "to conceive a situation more ridiculous, more tragically silly, in which the supposedly intelligent people of a great nation find themselves?" Government can "fumble, experiment, and juggle, in order to keep things going after a fashion," but these efforts do not address the real problems. It must have been reassuring to the American Legionnaires in the audience, who carefully monitored his remarks for any hint of communist sympathies, that Glendon made a point of rejecting violent revolution. "Violence, overthrow of government, tirades of crimson agitation, tinkering with effects in ignorance of causes; destruction of machinery—these things will get us nowhere."[20]

Glendon said that all that was required to fix the situation was the "setting up of a COMPLETELY NEW economic system" based on the principle of production for consumption, not for profit. And how was this revolutionary switch to be accomplished without revolution? Simply by adopting the Technocratic energy dollar. It would be easy to do this because "the constitution provides that congress shall have power to coin money, issue currency, and determine the commodity upon which the currency shall be based; therefore, it can be based upon the total goods produced for each twelve month's period, by perfectly regular and legal procedure." This simple reform would usher in a new society. Glendon assured his listeners that this Utopian paradise "is not a dream. It is not theory. It is not politics. It is a plain, simple, mathematical proposition, worked out by engineers, scientists and economic authorities.... Science is READY to answer the requirements of the times. Nothing can longer delay its action. The consciousness of the people is at last awakening."[21]

The little group of men who dreamed up the Utopian Society created a machine that was marvelously successful at recruiting members. The flaw in their plan was that there was nothing for members to do after they entered the Fifth Cycle. Other than the privilege of paying dues, learning secret grips, words, and signs, and wearing armbands, the Utopian Society offered no other benefits for its members. It may have been that the Society grew so rapidly that its founders did not have time to formulate a long-range program. More likely, the real goal was always nothing more than bringing in money.

The Society's founders may have seen the new organization solely as a way to make money, but many joined because they believed in its message. A large number of these "true believers" thought of the Utopian Society as a vehicle to bring about the vision of the future as described in Bellamy's *Looking Backward.* Van Dalsem asserted that "the philosophy of Edward Bellamy and that of the Utopian Society of America are identical."[22]

Bellamy championed a type of native-born socialism very different from European Marxism. In his novel, a young man named Julian West falls asleep in the year 1887 and awakens in 2000. He is surprised to find a society where private property has vanished—all vice, want, and war gone with it. This revolution did not come about through a violent upheaval but by a process of gradual evolution. All of the great business corporations combined until only one huge corporation remained. The government then stepped in, took over, and operated the giant corporation in trust for the people.

Bellamy's book was a best seller and was especially popular among the middle class. *Looking Backward* inspired many of its readers to form clubs that were part of the Nationalist movement, as it was called, that spread rapidly across the country. Local Bellamyites formed Los Angeles Nationalist Club No. 1 in 1889. This club was basically a reading and discussion group composed of middle- and upper-class men and women. There were separate branches for workers and the foreign born. The club had only limited involvement in politics. An exception was H. Gaylord Wilshire's 1890 congressional campaign. He was the first person in American history to run for Congress on a socialist platform.

Almost immediately after the Hollywood Bowl extravaganza, the Utopian Society began to fall apart. The *Los Angeles Times,* previously unaware of the Society's existence, became very interested in anything negative about its activities. Money, the paper reported, "proved to be the root of much evil for Utopians." Some members expressed outrage at incorporation of the National Foundation, which they saw as a blatant money grab. Owens took aim at the pensions and annuities that the Foundation provided for the trustees and their dependents. He said that the money to fund them came from the pockets of "the unemployed and those on charity rolls." After a tumultuous meeting, the National Foundation idea was scrapped and the incorporation articles modified. The amended charter provided for a president and fifteen-member board of directors that included Kennedy, Reed, and Reausaw. Owens became one of the directors, as did Glendon, who also became president.[23]

Other questions arose as to how the Society spent its money. Alonzo J. Riggs, a director, led a fight against the clause in the incorporation papers that permitted a salary of $5,200 for officers and against high fees paid to those who provided services for the organization. He complained, in particular, that Boudreau, composer of "Song of Utopia," received a two-thirds royalty on the sale price of the sheet music that sold for thirty cents per copy. Riggs protested that the Society should not be run for the "benefit of concessionaires."[24]

Glendon and Owens soon resigned their positions amid accusations of financial incompetence. Glendon's critics pointed out that he had declared personal bankruptcy in 1931—proof that he was a poor money manager. For a time both men continued to have influence as the leaders of one of the factions that jockeyed for control of the Society. In September, Owens was one of several individuals who applied to the California secretary of state's office for the incorporation of Utopian National Dated Money. Apparently not affiliated with the Utopian Society, this new organization was to campaign for the creation of a currency, like the Technocratic energy dollar, carrying an expiration date. The secretary of state rejected the application. Owens returned to the concept of a dated currency in 1938 when he emerged as the "engineer-economist" of Ham and Eggs, a pension movement to be discussed in chapter 10. Glendon's career ended abruptly with his premature death in 1937.[25]

Men whom Van Dalsem described as having "shifty eyes, hard faces and deceitful hearts" filled the Society's headquarters. In

August, Smith visited Kennedy there and found it an armed camp, full of nervous men divided into small groups, "all of them casting suspicious glances at the others." When Smith walked up behind Kennedy and tapped his friend on the back, he "jumped a foot off the floor." The *Los Angeles Times* described the atmosphere at headquarters as comic: "The business office corridors of the society headquarters on a busy day look like the Tonnerville Sheriff's office with Laurel and Hardy in charge. Ex-policemen, ex-Coast Guards, ex-private detectives, ex-marines and ex-army privates loiter about the halls, their pockets bulging with guns." Reed, fearing for his life, left town for a few days. He went to the train station in the company of "a squad of armed men."[26]

Stories that business interests were out to destroy the Utopian Society appeared regularly in the *Utopian News*. The paper claimed that someone hired Florian De Donato, a Chicago import of questionable background, and his firm, the California Intelligence Service Bureau, to spy on the Society. The *Utopian News* charged that De Donato's operatives infiltrated the Society's meetings to find evidence of communist or other subversive activities and to inform businesses if they found their employees at Utopian meetings. Many businesspeople, not knowing what the secretive organization was all about and fearing that it might be subversive, tried to keep their employees from joining. Bullocks, a large department store, put up a notice that any employee found to be a member of the Utopian Society would be discharged. When two hundred employees stepped forward and said that they had joined, the store backed away from its threat.[27]

The editors of the *Utopian News* admitted that they did not know who was paying De Donato, but they pointed to Harry Chandler or, perhaps, Chief Davis, who allegedly had a "secret fund" to finance such things—or possibly the Chamber of Commerce, the Pacific Mutual Life Insurance Company, Standard Oil, Union Oil, or the Safeway or Ralph's grocery chains were behind the campaign. All the accused denied that they had anything to do with any attempt to discredit the Society.

By the end of August 1934, the pool of potential new members had dried up because almost everyone who considered joining had done so already. Utopian membership declined. Keeping the seats filled at the Shrine Auditorium became the overriding goal of fundraising. When filled to capacity, a performance grossed about $2,000, but as the size of the audiences declined so did revenue. Income fell to less than $50 for each performance.[28]

The directors desperately looked for new ways to raise money. They experimented with a "block system" that involved flooding Los Angeles with field workers assigned to individual city blocks to recruit people to attend the Shrine meetings. This approach did not have much success. In any case, some members objected to the idea of sending recruits directly to the Shrine to watch the Cycles because it eliminated the house meetings, which they felt necessary for the proper training of new recruits. Others disagreed, feeling that house meetings were no longer necessary and that the public should be taught Utopian Society principles solely through the Cycle performances.[29]

Revenues continued to spiral downward. The directors were forced to lay off staff. They could no longer support the "veritable army of clerks, stenographers, bookkeepers, guards and executives" packed into the headquarters. By the end of August, John G. Wenk, the new president, assembled the employees and informed them that the Society could no longer afford to pay their salaries. (He added that those who could not find other jobs were welcome to come back and work for free.)[30]

The conmen and racketeers abandoned the organization and drifted away, looking for greener pastures. Reed took up residence in Greenwich Village in New York City, where he applied for a charter under New York law for the Utopian Society of America (East). He did this without the permission or knowledge of his associates in California. Kennedy and Reausaw disappeared from the pages of the Los Angeles newspapers. The 1936 *Los Angeles City Directory* listed Walter Reausaw as a Utopian Society speaker. He continued to live with his wife, Gertrude, in Los Angeles until 1938. The 1940 directory shows Merritt T. Kennedy still residing in the city with his occupation listed as "engineer."[31]

The Society moved into smaller headquarters. The directors gave up on holding meetings at the Shrine Auditorium, and the Cycle dramas moved to smaller venues. In January 1935 the Society collected $1,849.50 (about $36,000 in 2019 dollars) in dues. If the dues were still ten cents a head, this means that the membership had fallen to fewer than 20,000 individuals.[32]

As the grifters left, those who remained behind were the true believers. They outlined their program through the publication of weekly *Revelations*. The *Revelations* consisted of dialogues read by two readers. One was designated as Pilgrim, the other was Reason, otherwise known as the Coordinator. In these dialogues, Reason explained to the Pilgrim, who seemed to have forgotten or misunderstood what he learned in the Cycles, the basic principles behind the Utopian Society.[33]

The directors assured the members that the Utopian Society would remain a nonpolitical, educational organization, but how the directors defined "nonpolitical" was problematic. President Wenk assured the membership that the Society would not endorse candidates for public office or engage in political controversies, but, at the same time, it would be "interested in all matters having to do with the public weal." It was difficult to be interested in "all matters having to do with the public weal" without being political. In January the directors announced a program of action "to help protect those unfortunate people who are being inadequately nourished and clothed." They assured the members that this kind of action was "not entering politics, but it was simply using its moral force and its large membership to bring the proper pressure to bear through group action."[34]

The plan of action included several programs. A first-aid unit called the White Legion gave medical aid to members in need. In cooperation with a local funeral home chain, the Society arranged for free funeral services for members who had no money. The Utopians maintained a labor registry department to help place members in jobs. Some of the programs stretched "nonpolitical" to the limit. One of the aims of the Society was to "eliminate graft and corruption." To do this, the directors began monitoring the actions of the Los Angeles City Council. "HOW DID 'YOUR' COUNCILMAN VOTE ON THE GAS FRANCHISE EXTENTION? [sic]," asked the *Weekly Bulletin*. The Society also encouraged its members to monitor their members of Congress on important issues such as the Public Utility Holding Company Act that was before Congress in the summer of 1935.[35]

The directors created a legislative committee to watch over the activities of the state legislature. "Bills proposed in the State

Legislature must be studied before passage. In some cases it requires many weary hours of tedious effort to find the joker hidden in some innocent sounding proposal." The *Field Bulletin* warned that hundreds of "potential Fascist bills were introduced in the last session of the legislature" and claimed that through the influence of its large membership the Society defeated fifty-two of them. The *Bulletin* bragged, "We were in the fore-front of the fight to repeal the sales tax on food-stuffs; and the success of your Society against the attempt to take the vote away from those people on relief is well known."[36]

The Utopians opposed several measures before the legislature that put limitations on the right of free speech. The Society's *Bulletin* warned that there were bills pending in the state assembly that would "carry on where the Criminal Syndicalism Act leaves off." One made it a crime to interfere with the faculty or authorities of any educational institution. Another made it a felony to encourage anyone to refuse to bear arms or to train in their use. The intent of these bills, according to the *Bulletin*, was to place pacifists or opponents of ROTC "in cells at San Quentin." Other proposed bills made it a crime to simply be present at any meeting where speakers advocated the violent overthrow of the government or to have in one's possession books or pamphlets that did the same.

During the summer of 1935, Wenk and Macbeth, the Society's legal counsel, traveled to Washington, D.C., to seek a personal audience with Franklin Roosevelt. The purpose of the five-minute conference the two men hoped to have with the president was to ask him to consider the "Sparks Plan." Named for Fred Sparks, a Southern Californian, the objective of the plan was to resettle unemployed workers on unused farmland in Los Angeles County. The Utopian Society considered it a useful temporary measure "until final victory is won in the existing War for Economic Freedom, and the new order of social and economic conduct is finally approved and installed." After living in a hotel for a month, Wenk and Macbeth received a short note from the president indicating that he was sorry he did not have time to meet with them, but that he had read their documents. The Federal Resettlement Administration eventually built two communities in Southern California. One was located in San Fernando with forty homes and another in El Monte with one hundred. They were located in semirural areas where the residents could supplement their incomes with garden produce. It is unlikely that these projects were what Wenk and Macbeth had in mind. The man behind them was Ross Gast, who wrote a column in the *Los Angeles Times* Sunday supplement. The homes sold for $2,600–$3,000 ($51,000–$59,000 in 2019) and were open only to "white gainfully employed workers."[37]

Even among the true believers, there continued to be dissension in the Utopian Society. A vociferous faction demanded an elected board of directors. The dissidents also insisted that the Society adhere to its policy of being an educational society and avoid "all political tendencies." The *New York Times* took delight in the travails of the Utopian Society, noting wryly that "propagandists for new social orders seem to have a difficult time getting along together."[38]

Under pressure from the discontented elements in the Society, which Wenk referred to as "that 'crew,'" the directors formulated a plan of democratization to give the membership a larger voice. This plan involved setting up lodges with a membership of at least five hundred each. These lodges, much like a labor union, were to choose the board of directors. It is not known if this plan ever went into effect.[39]

Around May 1935, the *Revelations* began to appear in mimeograph form instead of letterpress, and they had abandoned the dialogue form of exposition. The essays focused more on topics such as income inequality and the connections between the rise of fascism and the capitalist system. They also warned that, just as capitalism inevitably leads to depression and unemployment, it also "drives just as inevitably to war."[40]

• • • •

By the end of 1935, the Utopian Society had quietly faded away. Its effective life span was only about two years—from mid-1933 to late 1935. It rose like a rocket, exploded in a gaudy display, and then vanished. The *Los Angeles City Directory* listed the Society's address at 1919 S. Western Avenue until 1940, when the listing disappeared. Those who joined the Utopian Society were a mixture of hustlers looking for easy money and a larger group who looked for a way out of the Depression. They were of that "white-collar lower middle-class element" which, Carey McWilliams reported, was the source of most of its members. They were people who the capitalist economy had cast aside—the ones Glendon referred to in his Hollywood Bowl speech as those who would never find jobs again. They were those self-respecting and independent people that the *Los Angeles Times* admitted were "going hungry and are in danger of being ousted from their homes." They attended house meetings, went through the Cycles, and paid their initiation fees and dues because they saw in the Utopian Society the possibility of a way out of a desperate situation that government and business leaders were powerless or unwilling to solve.[41]

The promises of the Utopian Society were left unfulfilled. Its organizers never explained how the Utopian or Technocratic revolution would become a reality. The idea that a new society could be summoned into being without conflict seems ludicrous in retrospect. The Utopian Society was an object of derision not only from contemporaries but also from later historians. What most of these commentators miss is that thousands of otherwise conservative Southern Californians were willing to cast aside capitalism and adopt a radical solution to their problems. They embraced a peculiarly American form of radicalism. They wanted drastic change but remained solidly middle class. They rejected the concept of class struggle and violent revolution.

8

The Townsend Plan

> We suspect that citizens are eager to adopt this plan, not because they have read it and analyzed it, but because they are victims of economic insecurity, and would grasp at any straw that would prevent them from sinking.
>
> *Covina Argus*, June 29, 1934

On September 30, 1933, Dr. Francis E. Townsend, a retired physician, published an article in the *Long Beach Press-Telegram* outlining a plan that he believed would end poverty among elderly Americans and at the same time benefit everyone by stimulating the economy. All American citizens age sixty or older, regardless of sex, who were retired or otherwise unemployed were to receive a lifetime pension of $150 a month "or more." Funding was to come from a new federal sales tax. He placed no restrictions on how the estimated fifteen to twenty million beneficiaries used the money. The only requirement was that all of it be spent before the end of each month. No saving (or hoarding) of cash was allowed. The genius of the doctor's plan—at least in his mind—was that the monthly injection of so much money into the economy would provide a stimulus so great that it would put an end to the Depression. As Townsend explained it, his plan provided not only pensions for the old but jobs for the young. "Age for leisure; youth for work," became the motto of the Townsend Plan. Between September 30, 1933, and February 20, 1934, Townsend wrote a total of eight letters to the *Press-Telegram*. He also busied himself selling pamphlets for twenty-five cents each, circulating petitions, speaking to small groups, and taking up collections to further the cause.[1]

Like the Technocrats, Townsend believed that modern technology had replaced workers with machines and developed a permanent class of the unemployed. In a second letter to the *Press-Telegram* he wrote, "Machines have supplanted muscle. Brains have supplanted brawn." The challenge was to find a way to restore consumer buying power. Townsend had little faith in free-market solutions such as rationing jobs or in New Deal programs that regulated business through NRA codes or minimum wage legislation. He also rejected the free-market idea that government stay out of the economy. "Our attitude toward government is wrong," he wrote. "We look upon government as something entirely foreign to ourselves. . . . But the fact is, we must learn to expect and demand that the central government assume the duty of regulating business activity." Although Townsend called for government regulation of the economy, he did not reject capitalism itself. His plan depended on a revival of the capitalist economy. In the final formulation of his plan, Townsend set the pension at $200 a month (about $4,000 in 2019). He said that he chose this amount because his calculations showed that a pensioner, spending that amount every month for a year, would add one job to the economy. Simply by spending his or her allotted $200 every month, each pensioner would create enough jobs to end the Depression. A few months later, in an unguarded moment, he told a *New York Times* reporter that the real reason that he decided on $200 was because no competitor "would come along and offer more."[2]

Townsend believed that his plan, if adopted, would change the human condition. In a November 4 *Press-Telegram* letter, he wrote that "happiness and honor" could become "the lot of mankind at the latter end of life instead of a drab, vegetative existence in pauperism that faces so many today." Criminality would disappear because no one "would jeopardize his chances of retiring in honor and affluence." The pension plan would "do away with the desire to accumulate great wealth." Freed from the need to provide for security in old age, men and women would be free to enjoy life in an egalitarian and worry-free world.[3]

Townsend claimed that he was the sole author of the plan, that it sprang fully developed from his brain. (Some of his followers considered the plan a revelation from God.) He often said that the inspiration hit him one morning when he was shaving. He happened to glance out of his bathroom window and saw three old women going through the garbage looking for something edible. The sight so outraged him that he burst into profanities and began yelling at the top of his voice. His wife warned him that the neighbors could hear, but he said, "I want God Almighty to hear me! I'm going to shout till the whole country hears!" Like so many things about Townsend's life, it is impossible to know if this incident ever took place. Most historians consider it fictional or at best an experience modified to fit his version of the origin story.[4]

The ideas embodied in the plan were not original to Townsend. He borrowed from the Technocrats the idea that modern machinery created unemployment. Money that had to be used in a specific time period is similar to Technocratic energy currency, which expired in one year. Irving Fisher, a noted Yale economist, wrote about the limited use of a dated currency in a widely circulated pamphlet that Townsend may have read. Townsend also may have borrowed the idea of giving money to the elderly from two other sources. One was Stewart McCord, a Seattle dentist, and the other, C. H. Douglas, a British engineer. McCord, in the widely read essay "A Lecture—Mercy Death for Surplus Labor," argued that the aged should be taken out of the labor market by giving them a monthly government payment. Douglas, the author of the so-called social credit plan, noted that workers' pay always lagged behind the cost of the goods they produced, thus undermining their purchasing power. He proposed to fix this by having the government distribute money to everyone to make up the difference. Townsend may have borrowed the idea of a government payment to the elderly from one of these men—or he may not have. He did not credit them if he did.[5]

A likely source for Townsend's ideas could have been the article "How to Fix Everything," from *Vanity Fair* magazine. The author was Bruce Barton, an advertising executive who is best known for his book *The Man Nobody Knows*, which portrays Jesus as a master salesman. In his article Barton tells the story of a reporter who on a slow news day suggests that a cure for the Depression might be found in switching bananas for the apples that street vendors sell. All of the banana peels tossed aside on the streets will result in many people slipping and falling down. These falls will cause torn clothes as well as injuries such as sprained ankles and broken legs. These unfortunate accidents will provide employment for tailors, textile workers, retail workers, doctors, nurses, medical supply manufacturers, and, possibly, lawyers. The chain of events that began with the sale of bananas stimulates the economy and brings prosperity "slipping in on a banana peel."

Barton agreed that what the country really needed was more spending power, but banana peels were not necessary. He argued that everyone should retire at age forty-five and be paid not to work at a rate based on half of their salary over the preceding five years. (Barton chose forty-five because he was nearing forty-five himself.) The influx of cash his plan provided would stimulate business and provide employment. In a variation of the Townsend Plan motto, he wrote, "Let young men work and old men loaf." There is no evidence that Townsend read Barton's satirical article, and the suggestion that it inspired his plan infuriated him.[6]

It does not really matter where Townsend got his idea. What matters is that it found a receptive audience. Southern California was fertile ground for any plan that favored the elderly. The 1930 U.S. Census shows that over 9 percent of the population of Long Beach was sixty-five or older. The figure for Los Angeles County was 7 percent, significantly higher than the national average of about 5 percent. The elderly faced extraordinary economic hardships. In October 1934, Los Angeles County had 29,295 people age sixty or older on welfare or living in county institutions. The cost to the county was over $400,000 a month. Unlike the United Kingdom, Germany, or France, the United States had no national pension system. Some federal civil service employees received a small pension, as did veterans who served in wartime and their widows. Private pensions were uncommon and not particularly generous. In 1929 the California legislature had the distinction of passing the country's first mandatory old-age pension law, but its benefits were meager (see chapter 2). Administered through the counties, the measure limited the total aid from all sources to no more than one dollar per day. Recipients had to be at least seventy years of age and a resident of the state for fifteen years. They were expected to pay the money back if they were able, and, if officials discovered that recipients had relatives financially capable of supporting them, they could be compelled to reimburse the county.[7]

Townsend found a receptive audience among the Long Beach elderly in part because he was one of them. When he began promoting his plan, he was sixty-six and unemployed, with no prospect of finding a job. Unable at times to even pay the family's electricity and gas bills, his wife took on work as a nurse to make ends meet. Tall and thin, Townsend spoke with a soft voice, projecting the image of a plain country doctor. Russell Owen, an experienced *New York Times* reporter, described him as a "kindly, simple man, who began this movement out of a desire to do good. There can be no doubt of that, unless he is the most consummate faker who ever lived." "Consummate faker" may have been a more apt description than Owen realized. Beneath the façade of the good doctor was a thin-skinned and egotistical man who bridled at criticism and seldom forgave those whom he thought did him wrong. It could be that he actually believed in his plan or, more likely, came to believe in it as time went on, but there can be no doubt that his main goal was to make a buck.[8]

Convincing his audiences of the economic feasibility of his plan was not necessary. The prospect of receiving $200 a month, with the only requirement that they spend it right away, was enough to persuade seniors to support the idea. That was a lot of money in 1933. The responses to his early efforts were so encouraging that Townsend turned to a young real estate agent, Robert Earl Clements, for help. Clements was kind enough to lend Townsend a desk in his office but was reluctant to become a partner in the pension business. Clements was not an economist and did not pretend to be one, but he knew how to organize a marketing campaign. After some thought he concluded that he could sell the idea. In any case, he needed some income; in the fall of 1933, the real estate business was dead.[9]

The two men were a contrast in age and appearance. Townsend was in his mid-sixties, "rather withered," and as likely to be interviewed in his "blue-striped pajamas" or bathrobe as in the plain suits that he usually wore. Clements was a smooth, soft-spoken man of thirty-nine who had the look of a successful businessman. A reporter described him as wearing "a modishly cut" brown checked suit with a red tie, handkerchief peeping from his breast pocket, and "sport shoes in two tones of brown." Townsend became the movement's public voice and Clements the behind-the-scenes manager. Despite Townsend's claim that the plan was his creation alone, it was in reality the work of both men. The newspapers widely recognized this partnership, referring to Clements as the plan's "co-author," "co-founder," or "chief organizing expert." In 1936, after disagreements over its direction, the former friends parted, never to speak again. In his 1941 autobiography, Townsend does not mention his ex-partner except once, when he quotes Clements, identified only as a young real estate man, as saying, "Doc, you're a better man than I am!"[10]

Nearly all of what we know of Townsend's life comes from his autobiography, which portrays him in a very positive light. He was born in 1867 on his father's farm in northern Illinois. His childhood appears to be typical of rural farm life in the Midwest in the late nineteenth century. The family was poor, self-reliant, the father a strict disciplinarian, and so on. Townsend left home as a young man, drifting around the country working as a farm hand, homesteading, teaching in a one-room school, mucking in a Colorado mine, selling cast-iron ranges to Kansas farm families. In 1890 he went back to school and graduated in 1893 at the age of twenty-six. Quite "mature for a high school senior," he admitted. In 1899 he enrolled in Omaha Medical College. He was thirty-one years old—the oldest student in his class. He worked his way through school by keeping books and delivering newspapers. One of his professors, an "ardent believer in the Socialist philosophy," loaned him money so that he could complete his studies. Townsend claimed that his exposure to socialist ideas planted in him a "hope that in a poverty-free world we might see an end to vice and disease." This may have been the case, but it is difficult to reconcile this professed sympathy for socialist ideas with his later hostility toward socialists such as Upton Sinclair and his courtship of reactionary politicians like William Lemke and Gerald L. K. Smith.[11]

After graduation, the only work he could find was as a replacement for a physician on leave in Belle Fourche, a town in the Black Hills of South Dakota. His temporary job became permanent and he remained in the Dakotas for sixteen years. His patients were scattered throughout the remote parts of what was still a raw frontier. In his autobiography he wrote that it was not unusual for him to travel fifty miles by horseback or buckboard to take care of some ranch family's medical needs. He built a house in the hamlet of Nisland and married his nurse, Minnie Bogue. He adopted her daughter and they had a son of their own. The rigors of this life eventually wore him down and, in 1919, he packed up and moved to Long Beach.

The weather was better in Southern California, but Townsend's poor health prevented him from keeping up a regular medical practice. He lived off of his small investments and dabbled in various money-making schemes. One was a plan to sell dry ice to fishermen to help them preserve their catches during the hot Southern California summers. Townsend raised some funds, but the project collapsed and the money disappeared. In 1930 he found a job with the City of Long Beach as one of a group of physicians who visited the indigent in their homes. Townsend wrote that the experience made a deep impression on him. "I saw children—children of fine Americans—doomed to be weak, physical runts due to malnutrition. I saw children denied milk. I saw them sent to school without breakfast, because their parents were too proud to beg." In the summer of 1933, a new city administration ended the program and Townsend lost his job. A few weeks later, as he recounted in his autobiography, an "idea came to me which might alleviate the hopelessness of the aged people of our community. I had not thought it through as anything else than that—just an idea which might restore hope!"[12]

Robert Earl Clements was born in Amarillo, Texas, in 1894. His father, a cattleman, moved the family to Long Beach in 1907 and began selling real estate. At age twenty, Robert Earl began a successful career in the same business. An enterprising individual could make a lot of money in real estate in Long Beach. The city's climate and proximity to the ocean made it an attractive place for retired midwesterners to settle. It soon acquired the nickname "Iowa by the sea." The *New York Times* said that the town was famous for a park "where retired farmers from Iowa and Kansas pitch horseshoes." In 1921 prospectors struck oil nearby, and in a short time the city became one of the world's leading producers of the black gold. In two decades Long Beach grew from a town of about 18,000 to a city of 140,000—the second largest in Los Angeles County.[13]

Clements never pretended that he joined Townsend for anything except the money. He reputedly told an early recruit to the movement that the "racket" was good for two years. In this respect, he was more honest than the good doctor, who at some point appeared to have convinced himself that he was the savior of the nation on a par with Lincoln or Washington. Under Clements's guidance, the two men set about getting the movement on a better footing. They rented office space, arranged to put out a good-quality pamphlet, hired a bookkeeper and a typist, and started a newspaper. On January 24, 1934, Townsend and Clements formed a nonprofit corporation called Old Age Revolving Pensions, Ltd. (OARP). There were three principal officers—California law required three incorporators—Townsend, Clements, and the doctor's younger brother, Walter, who worked as a porter at the Roosevelt Hotel in Hollywood. Townsend and Clements had full ownership and control of the new corporation.[14]

By early 1934, enough money was coming in from the sale of pamphlets and donations to allow the men to pay themselves a salary of $50 a week plus expenses (around $950 in 2019). This was quite a change for Townsend, who only two or three months previously could not pay his power bills. The number of new members grew rapidly, rivaling the explosive growth of the Utopian Society.[15]

The Townsend movement spread first to San Diego, where the percentage of the elderly in the population was about the same as Long Beach, and then to the rest of the state. In a short time it had spread beyond the state's boundaries. In May, Clements hired two men: Pierre Tomlinson, an acquaintance of Townsend from his South Dakota days, and Clyde E. Smith. He paid both on a commission basis. The men recruited new members and sold Townsend's pamphlet, the plan's newspaper, buttons, and windshield stickers as well as collecting donations. According to Tomlinson, Townsend promised a "hatful of money" if they went to work for him. As the movement expanded, the two men subcontracted the work to organizers in other parts of the state and other parts of the country. Eventually, they farmed out work to about three hundred subcontractors.[16]

Dr. Francis Townsend speaks to some of his followers at a meeting in the Olympic Auditorium in 1935. Los Angeles Daily News Negatives (Collection 1387), Library Special Collections, courtesy of Charles E. Young Research Library, UCLA.

Tomlinson explained that their job was to place Townsend on a pedestal and limit his public comments. "We tried to hold him in the background as much as possible, in order to build him as high as possible," he said. This was necessary "because of the tendency of Dr. Townsend to refute his own statements and make derogatory statements and contradict himself." At one point, Tomlinson and Smith tried unsuccessfully to send Townsend on a long vacation in the mountains at Lake Arrowhead.[17]

A river of money flowed into the Long Beach offices. Tomlinson said that, over the five or six months he and Smith worked for the organization, they brought in $30,000–$35,000 ($567,000–$660,000 in 2019). Nearly all of this money came in small amounts from the pocketbooks of elderly men and women. They were the kind of people who gathered on one rainy night in Covina, a small town east of Los Angeles, to listen silently to "an earnest young man" expound on the benefits of the Townsend Plan. The *Covina Argus* doubted that the approximately two hundred mostly elderly people in the audience cared whether or not the plan was realistic. They were "as drowning men" grasping at straws. Tomlinson told the story of a woman who resided in the Hollenbeck Home for the Aged in East Los Angeles who scrubbed floors in order to be able to contribute five dollars to the cause. Unsuccessful in convincing her to give a smaller amount, Tomlinson reluctantly accepted the donation. When he reported this story, Townsend shrugged it off, replying that if the movement did not take their money "these old fossils" would give it to someone else.[18]

Tomlinson and Smith remained with the OARP until November, when Townsend abruptly fired them. The two men were shown the door because they were making too much money, and after building a national network of organizers they were no longer necessary. Despite their connections dating back to the Dakota days, Townsend cut all ties with Tomlinson, denying that they were ever friends. "His parents are my friends," he said. "Pierre Tomlinson is not." Townsend and Clements found that OARP field agents working as subcontractors were hard to monitor. Because their livings depended on the size of their commissions, they were often very aggressive and there was no way of knowing if all of the money they collected made it to headquarters. In addition, there were independents not connected to the OARP at all, but merely piggybacking and selling their own materials.[19]

In the summer of 1934, Clements or Townsend, or both of them, hit upon the idea of creating clubs. These clubs gave structure to the movement, provided for the careful monitoring of collecting money, and kept the members busy and energized. "We decided that the best way to keep the people who were favorable to the Townsend plan informed as to the activities was to organize in some sort of a club," Clements recalled. The first, Club No. 1, in the working-class suburb of Huntington Park, was founded on August 23, 1934. Thereafter, the clubs spread rapidly across California and other parts of the country. In OARP publications, Townsend and Clements gave the impression that power in the movement resided with the members through the clubs. In reality, the clubs were completely independent of the OARP and had no voice at all in how the organization was run. All authority in the OARP continued to reside with the original incorporators.[20]

Anyone could start a club as long as they could find one hundred members. In sparsely populated rural areas, the required number was fifty. These were called "junior" clubs. In the beginning there was no upper limit on the size of a club. The largest in the country, Club No. 93, with a membership of 22,000, was in Los Angeles. At its head was George Highley, whose position made him a potential challenger to the doctor. The extraordinary size and influence of Club No. 93 is probably the reason for the introduction of a rule that limited new clubs to a maximum of one thousand members. All who joined a club paid a twenty-five cent per member fee (a little less than five dollars in 2019), or "contribution," as it was called. This went to the national headquarters. In exchange, everyone received a membership card, a copy of Townsend's pamphlet, weekly bulletins, petition forms, and a year's subscription to the newspaper. After October 1935, the clubs were asked to pay an additional annual "quota" of ten cents per member to the national office.[21]

The Townsend clubs spread across the country at a terrific rate. Although it is impossible to determine precisely how many clubs there were at any point in time, it is clear that there were a lot of them. By the end of 1934 there were about a thousand clubs nationally, with the greatest concentration in the West. Supposing that the average membership of clubs was about 150, this meant that the number of Townsend Plan supporters willing to pay the twenty-five cents membership fee was in the range of 150,000. The format of club meetings differed little from what one would expect to see at a Lions or Kiwanis club. Meetings began with the Pledge of Allegiance and a prayer. Without fail an American flag hung somewhere in the room, and there might also be a photograph of the revered doctor. An observer described the members as "just folks Methodist picnic people." Just as the divinity of Christ was not questioned at a Methodist meeting, no one questioned the OARP at a Townsend meeting. If critics appeared, they were quickly silenced. Merchants who refused to support the plan were liable to be boycotted. In Covina, the owner of the Citrus Belt music store closed his shop for a vacation and told his customers that he would not open again until the "Townsend old-age pension plan goes into effect."[22]

Most of Townsend's followers, like himself, probably were white Protestants of northern European extraction, but there were several African American clubs in Los Angeles. The OARP assigned low number designations to some of these clubs, which meant that they were among the earliest formed. Club No. 7 met on Thursday nights at a recreation room at 38th and Compton streets. Club No. 8 met every other Monday night at a Baptist church. In April 1936 the *Los Angeles Sentinel*, an African American newspaper, announced that a club was organizing a "monster Mother's Day mass meeting" at Central Baptist Church. "The Townsend Plan," the paper editorialized, "will not only cut down crime, it will provide work at a living wage for every boy and girl, man and woman in America who wants to work."[23]

In November 1934, with the election of John S. McGroarty, the OARP acquired a voice in the U.S. Congress. That fall, in a revolt against Hoover specifically and the Republican Party generally, Democrats swept all Los Angeles County seats in the House of Representatives. In the Eleventh District, McGroarty defeated the veteran Republican William E. Evans. McGroarty was one of Southern California's best-known personalities. He was the author of the *Mission Play*, an immensely popular three-hour dramatic production presented every year between 1912 and 1932 at the Mission Playhouse in the town of San Gabriel. The play presented a highly romanticized version of the history of the California missions from their founding to their secularization in the early nineteenth century. He was also the author of several books that presented a sentimental view of the state's Spanish and Mexican past. At the time of his election to Congress he wrote a regular column for the *Los Angeles Times* titled "Seen from the Green Verdugo Hills." In 1933, in recognition of his numerous writings on the state's history, the legislature named him poet laureate of California.[24]

McGroarty was born into an Irish Catholic family in Pennsylvania in 1862. He studied law and was admitted to the bar in 1894. He moved to Montana, where he worked as a legal advisor to Marcus Daley, owner of the Anaconda mine. He then tried his hand at mining in Mexico, went broke, and ended up in Los Angeles, where he called on Harrison Gray Otis and applied for a job at the *Los Angeles Times*. When he asked what he was supposed to do, the old general said, "Go upstairs and tell the city editor you're going to write for the paper." At the time of his election to Congress as a Democrat, thirty-one years later, he was still writing for the city's leading Republican newspaper.[25]

McGroarty never used his columns at the *Los Angeles Times* as forums for his political views. He wrote mostly about the bucolic life in his neighborhood nestled at the foot of the Verdugo Mountains. He related the adventures of his group of friends, dubbed the "Millionaires Club of Contentment and Happiness." Although he served two terms in Congress, McGroarty had little interest in the affairs of Washington or the life of a politician. After only two months in office, when a constituent criticized him for failing to reforest the Sierra Madre Mountains, he responded by telling him to "take two running jumps and go to hell." The *Los Angeles Times* professed affection for McGroarty but regretted that the poet replaced an experienced legislator. Asking "this gentle genius to lay aside his pen for the hurly-burly of Washington politics . . . would be like putting a Milton to building suspension bridges."[26]

On January 16, 1935, McGroarty introduced a bill in Congress to make the Townsend Plan the law of the land. His bill provided for a special Treasury grant of $2 billion (over $37 billion in 2019) to fund the program for its first month. Thereafter, a 2 percent transaction tax paid for the program. Originally, a national sales tax was to be the funding mechanism, but sometime in early 1934 Townsend and Clements awoke to the reality that such a tax would have to be set at an astronomical rate of 80–90 percent. Something called a "transaction sales tax" began to work its way quietly into OARP literature. This was a 2 percent tax, not on the final sale as with a sales tax but on every single financial transaction from a commodity's production to consumption. In the case of a loaf of bread, for example, taxes would be imposed on the farmer who raised the wheat, the miller, the retailer, and the consumer.[27]

McGroarty introduced his bill the day before Roosevelt's supporters submitted the administration's social security proposal. The president made his old-age insurance bill an administration priority partly in response to the strong popular support for Townsend's plan. Compared to the McGroarty proposal, the estimated monthly payment of $15 that the president's plan provided (less than $300 in 2019) seemed miserly. Furthermore, not everyone would be eligible. Only people who reached the age of sixty-five and who had been employed and making payroll tax contributions received benefits. The taxes would not even begin to be collected until 1937, and payments would not start until 1942 (later moved to 1940). Townsend condemned FDR's proposal and charged that all opposition to his own plan came from unspecified "high government authorities."[28]

McGroarty could count on formidable popular support. After all, the good doctor, no doubt exaggerating, claimed to have collected twenty million signatures supporting the plan. Politicians were reluctant to oppose a movement that claimed so many dedicated supporters. Edward Epstein, testifying on behalf of Roosevelt's plan, warned the Senate Finance Committee that Townsend's supporters "attack everybody who comes out against the Townsend plan, in a merciless way. I can warn you that any one of you that says anything against it will get these letters." Out of respect for the senators he added, "I do not think any Member of the Senate or any Member of Congress will allow himself to be intimidated." Senator Couzens of Michigan wryly responded, "You do not know Congress." Senator Gore of Oklahoma volunteered that he was "getting postal cards with my name printed on them." "So am I," said Senator Clark of Missouri. "So am I," added Senator King of Utah.[29]

Politicians around the country scrambled to endorse the Townsend Plan. Both Governor Frank Merriam and the California legislature did so. The legislatures of Arizona, Colorado, North Dakota, and Nevada did the same. City councils from Los Angeles to Minneapolis announced their support. These endorsements had little or nothing to do with the merits of the plan, much to do with the number of Townsend clubs within each political jurisdiction. The *Los Angeles Times* called McGroarty's bill "perfectly ridiculous" but admitted that it had immense public support.[30]

In January, the House Ways and Means Committee began hearings on the Roosevelt plan. Initially the committee had no interest in the Townsend bill, but ignoring it proved impossible. Several witnesses, including Townsend himself, appeared before the committee, but it might have been better for the plan if they had stayed home. The committee members asked many reasonable questions as to how the plan might work. Which financial transactions would be taxed and which would not be taxed? How would the $200 monthly pension be disbursed, how would fraud be avoided, how would the government know if the money was actually spent in the allotted time? Was the 2 percent tax adequate to raise the amount of money required? Witness after witness showed themselves unprepared and ignorant of basic facts. The bill itself was a sloppy piece of work, thrown together over a forty-eight-hour period. Townsend and a man named Frank Peterson, with the assistance of McGroarty and another member of Congress, did most of the work of drafting the measure.[31]

All of Townsend's witnesses—save one—had limited or no expertise on the subject of old-age pensions. Most admitted that they had not read McGroarty's bill or had given it only a cursory examination. Under the pressure of the members' relentless questioning, all admitted that the bill had flaws but argued that Congress could fix them. The last of Townsend's witnesses was Robert R. Doane, an economist. The committee extended the hearings one day to hear what he had to say. Doane came prepared with facts, figures, and charts. Under pressure, he reluctantly admitted to not having read the bill, and he conceded that based on what he saw in the newspapers he could not recommend its passage. Even Townsend, the man who claimed to be the sole author of the plan, could not answer the most basic questions. He seemed more concerned that Harry Hopkins, the New Deal relief administrator, called his plan "cockeyed" than with explaining how it would work. Townsend admitted that the bill would need to be revised to make it workable but refused to make specific recommendations. The House members who, to their credit, were simply trying to do their job seemed incredulous at the witnesses' inability to provide satisfactory answers. "Is it your idea," asked Representative Lewis of Maryland, "that you are merely submitting a suggestion to the lawmakers here about how the Committee on Ways and Means, if it took the time, might develop a bill that would be workable?" "Yes; I am," responded the doctor.[32]

Testimony against the McGroarty bill came from acknowledged experts on the subject. The most comprehensive critique came from Edwin Witte, a University of Wisconsin economist and executive director of the president's Committee on Economic Security. Witte pointed out that the annual cost of Townsend's plan, $24 billion, was more than all federal, state, and local taxes combined. If the OARP plan were adopted, half of the national income would go to benefit less than 9 percent of the population. Furthermore, a 2 percent tax on all of the transactions in the United States would not raise enough money to pay for the plan. According to Witte's calculations the rate would have to be at least 6 percent, an amount, in his opinion, "so heavy that it would stop all business and could not possibly be collected."[33]

The Townsend organization raised $22,500 for lobbying efforts but did very little lobbying. After four months, it spent only $2,404.96 of this fund. Even so, Townsend issued another appeal to the membership through a "Townsendgram" asking that each club contribute a minimum of fifteen cents per member. This brought in another $10,000. A supporter from Colorado Springs wondered why more had not been done to lobby for the bill. He asked, if "we don't do that, what are the old people of the country going to think of us, if we don't do something for them?" Clements's alleged reply is almost too hard to believe: "We don't give a damn about the old people."[34]

The Townsend bill died in committee. McGroarty introduced a new one that addressed some of the criticisms heard before the Ways and Means Committee. It added three taxes to supplement the transaction tax: a 10 percent increase in federal income tax, a 2 percent inheritance tax, and a tax of 2 percent on gifts over $500. The most important change, one that struck at the heart of the OARP, made $200 the maximum possible payment rather than the guaranteed payment. In McGroarty's revised bill, the actual pension could be as low as $50, depending on available tax revenue and the number of pensioners. OARP publicity glossed over the reduction in the size of the pension because $200 a month was the main reason for the plan's appeal. The bill went down to defeat in the House 206 to 56. The Senate never voted on the measure.[35]

The humiliation before the Ways and Means Committee and defeat in the House of Representatives only energized the rank and file. The number of Townsend clubs grew to more than five thousand. During the final quarter of 1935, the amount of money flowing into headquarters doubled. In October, seven thousand enthusiastic delegates met in Chicago at the first national convention of the Townsend clubs. In Los Angeles, a large crowd gave local delegates an enthusiastic sendoff. More than 175 delegates boarded a train at a downtown terminal. Another fifty joined at stations across the county as the train headed east. The convention had the appearance of a religious revival. Dr. Clinton Wunder, a former Baptist minister from Rochester, New York, gave the keynote address. "We believe God is on our side," he proclaimed, "and with God all things are possible." When the doctor spoke, the delegates crowded and shoved to get a better look at their leader. He told the crowd that "this is the greatest political convention ever held under the Stars and Stripes." He reassured the gathering that a 2 percent transaction tax would "produce an abundance of revenue" to fund "the retirement of 8,000,000 old folks on $200 a month."[36]

Clements understood that the McGroarty bill failed not because the hearings exposed its inadequacies but because not enough Townsend clubs existed outside of California and the Far West. For him, the lesson from the hearings was very clear. The plan's strongest supporters were members of Congress who had lots of clubs in their districts. Clements undertook a major reorganization of the movement. He divided the country into four regions with salaried directors at their head. In each region, state and local district organizers, paid on a commission basis, were to form at least one hundred clubs in every congressional district in the United States. At the national convention in Chicago, Townsend promised that, if "our drive is followed up in the East and the Midwest, we will eclipse our achievements in the West. In six months' time we shall have 80 per cent of the voting strength demanding enactment of the Townsend plan."[37]

In keeping with the national focus, Townsend and Clements moved headquarters to Washington, D.C., and established a radio division to make regular national broadcasts. To pay for all this, Clements squeezed the membership for more money. In addition to the twenty-five cents membership fee, the national headquarters assessed each club ten cents per member. Clements also created a special group called the Townsend National Legion, whose members paid one dollar per month for the privilege of getting a lapel pin and a subscription to the *Townsend Weekly*.[38]

Townsend should have been happy, but he was not. He deeply resented the fact that President Roosevelt refused to grant him a private audience. The House Ways and Means Committee and the Senate Finance Committee subjected him to humiliating interrogations. He felt that he had achieved the status of a player on the national stage and deserved more respect. Even though Clements's sensible strategy showed results, Townsend began thinking of going in a different direction altogether. The doctor's need to feed his ego undermined his already questionable judgment. He began using some of the movement's revenue to explore the possibility of a national political campaign. He hinted that he might launch a third party with himself as the presidential candidate and Senator Borah of Idaho for vice president. He also talked of disrupting the 1936 national elections by creating a situation where the voters elected a president and vice-president of different parties. In Michigan, he conferred with fiery radio priest Charles E. Coughlin. Townsend said that he and Coughlin shared a common interest in opposing the New Deal. "For a while we thought we could support President Roosevelt," he told the press, "but we have given up hope on him." In February 1936 he diverted the proceeds of a mass meeting of 12,000 people at the Olympic Auditorium in Los Angeles to further his ambitions of founding a political party.[39]

Townsend resented the widely held view that Clements was the brains behind the OARP. The doctor believed that his partner "was in the habit of doing things behind his back." Townsend also saw McGroarty as a rival. The congressman's age, celebrity, and skill with the written word made him a natural spokesman for the old people's crusade—and a possible challenger. When McGroarty introduced a new pension bill without Townsend's approval, his independence antagonized the doctor. Especially galling was the fact that the new bill gave up entirely on the idea of a $200 a month pension. (McGroarty's proposed legislation remained buried in the House Ways and Means Committee and never made it to the floor.)[40]

In addition to his worries about real or imagined challenges to his leadership, Townsend faced another troubling issue. There was a growing concern among people both inside and outside of Congress that the only purpose of the movement was to squeeze money out of the poor. Townsend brushed off these charges. "I am not a crook and this is not a racket," he said. In February 1935, Representative C. Jasper Bell, a Democrat from Missouri, announced the formation of a special congressional committee to investigate charges that the OARP was a "money-making scheme to defraud the elderly of their small earnings." At about this time, Townsend began taking advice from Sheridan Downey, an attorney who two years before had run for lieutenant governor on the End Poverty in California ticket (see chapter 9). Downey encouraged Townsend's ambitions to pursue the third-party strategy. He also convinced Townsend to agree to a plan to finance the pension fund through tax-exempt bonds rather than a transaction tax. According to the *Los Angeles Times*, the doctor fell under Downey's influence: "During the past several months, Clements has been talking into one of the doctor's ears and Downey has been whispering into the other, with the doctor following Downey's advice more frequently."[41]

Two days before the Bell hearings began, Clements resigned, taking $500,000 with him in compensation. At about the same time, the OARP board of directors accused George Highley, leader of the gigantic Los Angeles Townsend Club No. 93, of "disloyal conduct." Highley left the OARP, took a group of insurgents with him, and formed a rival pension group. Highley entered into an alliance with McGroarty. In December 1936 he sponsored a meeting of the "McGroarty Club No. 93" at which the congressman outlined the latest version of his pension bill. This one reduced the monthly pension to $100 a month and dropped the requirement that it be spent in any specified time frame. Funding through a 2 percent transaction tax was retained. McGroarty accused Townsend of duping old people and of "aiding and abetting a palpable fraud." Meanwhile, Clements formed a national network called "All-Americans, Inc." to build support for a $100 a month retirement pension.[42]

As others made for the exits, Townsend continued making a series of bad decisions. One of them was to organize a march of the elderly on the national capital similar to the 1932 Bonus March on Washington, D.C., by World War I veterans. A motor caravan starting in Los Angeles proceeded to the capital by way of San Antonio, Kansas City, and Columbus, Ohio. A crowd of "1,000 grayhaired men and women prayed, sang hymns and cheered" as the Southern California contingent left Townsend headquarters in downtown Los Angeles at 10 A.M. on May 5, 1936. The Los Angeles group consisted of two trucks made to look like covered wagons plus twenty automobiles. The travelers carried petitions allegedly bearing the names of ten million people endorsing the plan. The leader was Walter "Sparkplug" Warmbold, who shared his car with a Follies dancer and a cabaret singer. In Oklahoma, a crowd of six thousand Townsend Plan supporters attended a meeting featuring an Indian dance. Warmbold got involved in some kind of sexual indiscretion at the dance and had to leave the caravan. The marchers arrived in Washington, D.C., on May 17, where four members of Congress greeted them and received the petitions at the foot of Capitol Hill. Bell's committee later determined that the signed petitions had about 800,000 names rather than the promised ten million.[43]

From March to July 1936, Representative Bell's committee probed the workings of the plan, calling numerous witnesses, including Townsend and Clements. Committee members Gavagan of New York and Collins of California went to Los Angles to hear testimony, where, according to Ed J. Margett, northern California regional director, they were "as welcome as smallpox." At the Washington hearings, Clements testified that since its inception the OARP had taken in about $951,964.00 (over $9 million in 2019). He told the committee that for the year 1935 he received $12,585 in salary and dividends.[44]

During the Bell hearings Townsend's short temper and fragile ego were on full display. He accused the committee of being more interested in "besmirching the characters of people than in ascertaining anything of truth concerning the virtues of the movement." On more than one occasion, he lost his temper and jumped to his feet, requiring Chairman Bell to tell him to sit down. When pressured on an issue, he often contradicted himself, gave confusing replies, and passed the responsibility for some action on to someone else. In view of his position as head of a movement that he claimed was his sole creation, responses such as "that was not my idea" or "I did not write the article" did not go down well with the committee.[45]

Townsend claimed that after two and a half years of working in the movement he and his wife had only $500 to their names. This seems unlikely in view of his statement to the committee that between January 1934 and the end of March 1936 the OARP paid him, in salary and expenses, a total of $16,557.18 (over $300,000 in 2019). He also reported that during the same period he received substantial dividends from the *Townsend Weekly*. Fed up with the committee's questions, the doctor suddenly announced that he was going to leave. "In view of the apparent unfriendly attitude of this committee and the unfair attitude it has shown to me and the members of my organization," he said, "I deem it my duty to say that I shall no longer attend the committee meetings. . . . I do not propose to come back again except under arrest." He got up and walked out. The House cited Townsend for contempt of Congress. President Roosevelt later pardoned him, apparently deciding that sending an old man to jail was not worth the bad publicity.[46]

Contrary to the hopes of the investigators, the hearings failed to produce any sensational scandals, but they did publicize a number of uncomfortable facts. They revealed that a lot of people, especially Townsend and Clements, made a great deal of money from the movement. Some of the people associated with the plan were unsavory characters—the star in this regard was Margett, the northern California director, who had a criminal record that included pimping and bootlegging. The committee also concluded that the *Townsend Weekly* violated "minimum ethical standards" in some advertisements for patent medicines and "vitality" remedies aimed at the senior market. These exposés did little to shake the faith of most of Townsend's followers, who never questioned the doctor's intentions. The *Townsend Weekly* asked its readers to ignore the regular press and to believe only what they read in its pages—the paper "that dares and does tell the truth." According to the *New York Times*, the membership continued to "revere Dr. Townsend as a sort of a demi-god, a superman inspired by a divine revelation."[47]

After the hearings, Townsend pursued his desire to become a power in national politics more vigorously. He decided to support the third-party candidacy of Representative William Lemke of North Dakota, the nominee of the Union Party, and to join Rev. Gerald L. K. Smith, a reactionary racist and self-appointed successor to Huey Long, and the anti-Semitic radio priest Father Coughlin in an alliance backing Lemke's candidacy. Townsend went on a national tour with Smith and made speeches denouncing Roosevelt and the New Deal. At the foot of the monumental arch at Valley Forge, Pennsylvania, he and Smith pledged to stand "against the dictatorship in Washington."[48]

In July the OARP held its second national convention, this time in Cleveland. The *Times* reported that the elderly crowd, mostly from the West Coast and nearby Ohio towns, arrived at the convention hotel. A "goodly proportion" were African American, but the majority were "white, native-born Protestants." They paid a dollar registration fee, checked their baggage and immediately "made bee lines for tourist camps and boarding houses" where they could find cheaper lodgings. The opening program included the singing of "America" and "Onward Townsend Soldiers," the recitation of the Pledge of Allegiance, and a second pledge in support of the Townsend Plan, its principles, and its founder, "Dr. Francis E. Townsend."[49]

Townsend opened with a speech denouncing Roosevelt. Smith also gave a speech attacking the president and his programs. The next day, Coughlin spoke, and he also denounced Roosevelt. When Gomer Smith, the new vice president of the OARP, spoke in favor of the president, Townsend kicked him out of the convention. A Los Angeles African American newspaper, the *Los Angeles Sentinel*, expressed disappointment in Townsend's alliance with Smith. "Whether Townsend knows it or not, Smith is one of the worst possible allies, as far as Negroes are concerned." In addition, it pointed out that the platform of the Union Party was "strangely silent on the question of the ills of the Negro people—this in the face of the fact that the party pretends to be a genuine reform political party." Despite the fact that the convention voted to remain neutral in the presidential race, Townsend, Smith, and Coughlin had themselves photographed together and announced their support for the North Dakota representative. Lemke polled only 2 percent of the popular vote. The Union Party faded away rapidly.[50]

In September 1936, Townsend dissolved the OARP and formed a new nonprofit corporation, called the Townsend National Recovery Plan, Inc. (The three incorporators were Dr. Townsend, his son Robert, and a man named Young serving as the dummy.) In effect, the Townsend Plan became a family business. Robert was the doctor's anointed successor. "Captain Bob," as he was known, gradually assumed increased responsibilities and control of the movement. Dr. Townsend remained in charge for many years, giving up responsibility only reluctantly. He remained the movement's official leader until he died in 1960—a very old man.[51]

• • • •

In 1939, the *Los Angeles Times* wrote what amounted to an epitaph for the Townsend movement. In June of that year, the House of Representatives rejected the latest of "a long series of revisions of the $200-a-month scheme." The failure of the bill showed that politicians no longer feared Townsend and his elderly followers. Outside of California and other far western states, the movement was dead politically. The *Times* concluded that Townsend simply did not have the votes in the states where they were needed. The movement was "pitifully weak" in the "states which really count politically." No retiree ever received a penny in pension money from the Townsend Plan.[52]

9

END POVERTY IN CALIFORNIA

> Why not elect an honest man
> And inaugurate the Epic Plan?
> A plan poverty to obliterate
> Right here in our sunny state.
>
> Sinclair supporter

In 1916, Upton Sinclair and his wife, Craig, moved to Pasadena, a town about fifteen miles northeast of downtown Los Angeles. Not forty years old, Sinclair was already the author of a small library of novels, nonfiction works, plays, and articles. His greatest claim to fame was *The Jungle*, a novel published in 1906 that described horrific working conditions in the Chicago meatpacking industry. Sinclair wanted the book to expose the evils of the capitalist workplace, a kind of *Uncle Tom's Cabin* for wage slaves, but it was his descriptions of unsanitary conditions in the slaughterhouses that had the greatest impact. He later wrote, "I aimed at the public's heart and by accident hit it in the stomach." Although the book did not win many converts to socialism, he could claim at least partial responsibility for the passage of the Meat Inspection and Pure Food and Drug acts of 1906.[1]

The Jungle earned Sinclair the huge sum of $30,000 (about $800,000 in 2019). Rather than invest the money in some capitalist enterprise, Sinclair decided to found a cooperative colony as an experiment in communal living. He purchased a former boys' school in New Jersey called Helicon Hall and recruited about eighty people to live there. After a few months, the experiment collapsed when the school burned to the ground in a disastrous fire. The twenty-eight-year-old author quickly recovered and moved on to other enthusiasms.[2]

There is some truth to the criticism that Sinclair never met a cause he did not wholeheartedly embrace, but another way of saying this is that he was always open to new ideas, no matter how unconventional. Those who did not know him personally often dismissed him as a self-righteous crank, but those who did know him considered him thoughtful and congenial. He made friends from a variety of backgrounds ranging from Judd, a carpenter who worked on his house, to King Gillette, the razor tycoon, to Albert Einstein, the physicist. Sinclair genuinely liked people, valued their opinions, and was concerned for their welfare. Over the years he made a great deal money from his publications, but he promptly spent it on various causes. Craig, who had some business sense, took over the family finances.[3]

After moving to Pasadena, the Sinclairs bought a vacant lot in what a visitor called a "shabby workingmen's street." They moved a small house to the location. As their needs grew they added more buildings and joined them together to form an odd, hodgepodge structure. Inside, the rooms varied in size, color, style, and ceiling and floor heights. The living room was made from an old tailor shop—purchased for a hundred dollars—with the upper floor removed to create a cathedral ceiling. The couple furnished their home with purchases from junk shops.[4]

From this place, Sinclair churned out books and articles at a furious pace. He produced at least one book a year and became one of the world's most widely read authors. Notable works from this period include six nonfiction books that Sinclair called the "dead hand" series. The "dead hand" was Sinclair's answer to the "invisible hand," the term Adam Smith used to describe the impersonal forces that guided the actions of men and women in the marketplace. In his "dead hand" series Sinclair showed how capitalism corrupted important American institutions. *The Profits of Religion*

(1918) dealt with the church; *The Brass Check* (1920), the newspapers; *The Goose-Step* (1923), higher education; *The Goslings* (1924), elementary and secondary education; *Mammonart* (1925), art; and *Money Writes* (1927), literature. He also wrote several novels that depicted important economic and political events of the time. *King Coal* (1917) was about the Colorado coal wars of 1914; *Oil!* (1927), the petroleum industry in Southern California; *Boston* (1928), the Sacco-Vanzetti case; and *The Wet Parade* (1931), the evils of alcohol.

Sinclair was a socialist, but he was anything but an inflexible ideologue. "I do not call myself an orthodox Marxian," he wrote. "I do not call myself a complete orthodox anything." He was a member the Socialist Party of America but generally avoided becoming involved in its affairs. He did not feel obligated to follow official Socialist positions if he disagreed with them. He resigned from the party in July 1917, joining a handful of socialist intellectuals who supported President Woodrow Wilson's decision to ask Congress to declare war. The Socialist Party's official position was opposition to American entry in World War I. Several of its prominent leaders—notably Eugene V. Debs—went to jail for speaking out against U.S. involvement in the conflict.[5]

The Socialist Party could not afford to leave such a prominent figure as Sinclair out in the cold. In 1920 it welcomed him back. Several times over the next decade, he appeared as a speaker at party events. He agreed to be the party's candidate in several elections— U.S. Congress in 1920, U.S. Senate in 1922, and governor of California in 1926 and 1930. His candidacies were only symbolic; he never won more than a handful of votes. Sinclair was torn between the quiet life of a writer and the nagging feeling that he should be involved in public affairs. He claimed to want nothing more than to get up in the morning "and see the new sunshine on the wet grass, and on the scarlet hibiscus flowers and the pink oleanders and the purple and golden lilies; to stroll around in an old dressing-gown, with my mind full of my next chapter, and then presently bring a typewriter out into the sunshine, and sit there and pick away."[6]

From time to time, he left his typewriter and embarked on one of his "crusades." A notable one took place during a strike at Los Angeles Harbor in 1923. The Marine Transport Workers Industrial Union, an IWW affiliate, attempted to organize all workers on the waterfront. Approximately three thousand seamen, longshoremen, and lumber handlers walked off the job and closed down harbor operations. The response of the employers, orchestrated by the powerful Merchants and Manufacturers Association, was brutal. The police assaulted strikers and union sympathizers on the streets and broke up all strike meetings. They arrested anyone involved in picketing, leafleting, or any union activity. Even possessing an IWW membership card was a crime. Chartered Pacific Electric Railway cars loaded with strikers made regular trips between the harbor and the Lincoln Heights jail in Los Angeles. Strike organizers moved their rallies to a privately owned lot called Liberty Hill, but Los Angeles chief of police Louis D. Oaks, in this case ignoring the sanctity of private property, ordered his men to break up even these meetings. The message was clear: there was no freedom of speech anywhere in the harbor area.

Sinclair decided to see if the police dared to prevent a prominent individual, such as himself, from making a speech at the harbor. He obtained the permission of the property owner to speak on Liberty Hill and recruited a small group of supporters to accompany him. He confronted Chief Oaks and told him that he intended to assert his First Amendment rights. The chief responded with the remark that "Constitution or no Constitution, if you try to speak at the harbor you will be arrested." Sinclair and a few brave souls made their way to the hill, where he started reading the First Amendment. He had barely begun when the police arrested him and dragged him off. One by one, the men with Sinclair were arrested the moment they began speaking. The police did not arrest one member of the group, Kate Crane Gartz, because she was a woman.[7]

Sinclair and his party were then spirited off to an unknown location, where they were held incognito for eighteen hours. Sinclair's attempted speech and arrest earned worldwide newspaper coverage. The LAPD, uncomfortable with the attention from the press, ended the ban on public speaking and allowed Sinclair to return to Liberty Hill, where he read the Constitution. Yet Sinclair's efforts had no effect on the outcome of the strike. By the time he made his second speech, the port had resumed normal operations. The most lasting consequence of Sinclair's fight for free speech at the harbor was the founding of the Southern California branch of the ACLU, for many years a lonely voice for the First Amendment in Southern California.[8]

Early in 1933, when A. L. Wirin, a local civil rights attorney, asked him to speak at an event, Sinclair declined. "I am going to stick to writing and publishing books for the rest of my life," he explained. "My crusading days are over." In less than a month after turning down Wirin, Sinclair accepted another invitation, this time before the members of the Men's Club of Beverly Hills, to speak on the Depression and what was to be done about it.[9]

Sinclair had plenty of things to say about the Depression and what needed to be done about it. He was finishing up a small book in the form of letters to a fictional businessman named Perry titled *The Way Out: What Lies Ahead for America.* The epistolary form was not new to Sinclair. In 1926 he had published a booklet, *Letters to Judd: An American Workingman*, in which he explained the economic facts of life to a member of the working class. His message was simple: the economy was rigged against the worker and the only salvation was socialism. The view point of *The Way Out* was basically the same, but directed at the "captains and managers of industry" rather than workers.

The Way Out, which appeared in May, is revealing because of what it tells us about Sinclair's understanding of how the economy worked. Central to his thinking was a concept similar to the "iron law of wages," an idea that dated back to the writings of two eighteenth-century Englishmen, Thomas Malthus and David Ricardo. It held that, regardless of economic conditions, wages always fell to the bare minimum level that workers needed to survive. Sinclair believed a permanent reservoir of unemployed workers prevented wages from rising. "The private owners pay to each worker a competitive wage," Sinclair explained, "that is, the lowest price for which any one can be found to do the work. Since under our system there is always a superfluity of workers, a competitive wage means that each worker gets what it costs him to exist."[10]

His criticisms of the New Deal suggest that he believed there was only so much of the world's wealth to go around, and if some was taken from one person or class and given to another, one would be poorer and the other richer. Poverty existed not because there was not enough of this wealth to go around but because the capitalist class monopolized most of it and refused to give the laboring class its fair share. Eliminating capitalism and replacing it with production for consumption, not for profit, would open the world's wealth to everyone equally and wipe poverty from the earth. Sinclair believed that New Deal programs simply borrowed money from one part of the economy and spent it on another. He liked to say that they moved money from one pocket to another. As an example, he pointed to the farm subsidy program designed to shore up the prices of agricultural commodities. Farmers may have benefited, he thought, but consumers paid for the subsidies through higher prices. This was "getting rich by picking one another's pockets."[11]

Sinclair was an economic nationalist. He believed that there was no point in looking for international markets to bring in money. He argued that the United States did not need the rest of the world for most of its needs, because it could produce almost everything it needed. The only reason capitalists bought foreign goods was that workers in some other countries were willing to accept less pay. "So it appears that the purpose of international trade is to bring the advanced people down to the coolie standard."[12]

For Sinclair, there was only one way out—government ownership of the means of production. "Every time the government is spending a dollar, ask whether it is spending the dollar for goods or for the means to produce goods. If the former is the case, the money is wasted. If the latter is the case, the money is saved. I make this statement without qualification. I don't care what it is that the government needs, the government should make it." If the government sends out young men to plant trees—as the Civilian Conservation Corps did—he thought this a good thing. "But when the government buys shoes and khaki uniforms for these men, it is a socially wasteful action, because the government should buy clothing factories and shoe factories, and never again pay a profit to a private contractor for such a service." Sinclair did not believe that government spending would stimulate the economy. Instead, he predicted disaster: "The billions which our government has ladled out to bankers and railroads and manufacturers and farmers and veterans and unemployed—all these sums will be gone, and the effort to restore purchasing power will have failed."[13]

The Way Out reached a receptive audience. Many of Sinclair's readers may not have shared his vision of a socialist future, but the idea of self-help—rather than relief—fit well with American ideas of self-reliance. The popularity of the book pushed Sinclair in the direction of another "crusade," but he faced a strong headwind from Craig, who was not eager to see her husband drawn into another cause. Sinclair was profoundly worried about the state of the country and wondered if writing books was enough to make a difference. If "Big Business wins this fight," he wrote, if "Fascism comes to America as we have seen it come to Italy and to Germany, what place will there be for an author? What is the use of writing books, and printing and distributing them, only to see them burned by a Hitler?"[14]

In mid-August, Sinclair received a letter from a man named Gilbert Stevenson, the chairman of the Democratic central committee of the 60th Assembly District of California. Stevenson urged Sinclair to declare himself a candidate for governor on the Democratic ticket. This was an unusual request to make of a Socialist Party member, but Sinclair agreed to meet with Stevenson and a group of Democrats on August 31. "That was how I fell into the trap," he explained, "and ceased to be an author and became a politician for fourteen months."[15]

Sinclair told the group that he would write up a program explaining what he would do as governor. The document that he produced, *I, Governor of California and How I Ended Poverty: A True Story of the Future*, became his central campaign document. Sinclair understood that a Socialist Party candidate could never win a statewide election. "So long as I was a Socialist I was just one more crank," he said. On September 1, Sinclair changed his party registration. His secretary wrote that most "of the mail these days consists of letters of protest and denouncement." Even his son, David, was shocked at the news. Sinclair tried to smooth it over. "As you know, I have never been much of a party man—I am more interested in spreading the ideas, and this seemed to me an especially good opportunity for that." On September 20, the Socialist Party state executive committee expelled Sinclair. It also warned other party members who might follow Sinclair that the same could happen to them. These were empty threats. Sinclair's departure was a serious blow to the party. Most rank-and-file members, and many of its younger leaders, such as the future congressman Jerry Voorhis, left to follow Sinclair. The party that had showed some glimmerings of life in 1930 was dead in California once and for all.[16]

Some longtime friends warned Sinclair that he had made a mistake in deciding to run for office. Fulton Oursler, editor of *Liberty* magazine, told him that the real danger was that he might be elected. "You are a dreamer, a reformer, a novelist, and your field is that of exhorter.... I am against this ... one hundred percent." Sinclair's response to Oursler's letter suggested that he did not fully understand the consequences of his decision. He appeared to believe that he could walk away from the political life and return to his writing anytime he wanted. He told Oursler, "I probably cannot get the nomination, and if I did, I would not get elected.... later on if I find that the fight is getting too hot and it is wearing me out, I can withdraw in favor of some younger person." Even as he finished up the draft of the *I, Governor* manuscript, Sinclair debated inserting a paragraph explaining that the book was to be taken "as fiction," and that he was not actually going to give up the writing life and run for governor. According to his own account, Craig, who opposed the whole thing from the start, told him, "You have publicly committed yourself! Terrible as it all seems, you must go on with it."[17]

At the time that Sinclair decided to run for governor on the Democratic ticket, California, including the city and county of Los Angeles, was solidly Republican. The last Democratic governor was James Budd, elected in 1895. During the decade of the 1920s, the Democrats failed to elect a single U.S. senator and sent only one member to the House of Representatives. In 1930 the Republicans held ten of the eleven congressional seats from California and seventy-four of the eighty seats in the state assembly. Registered Republicans outnumbered Democrats by a three-to-one margin. The Democrats, shut out of power, had little to do but fight among themselves. The party was torn between northern and southern California factions. William Gibbs McAdoo, a Protestant in favor of Prohibition and rumored to have the support of the Ku Klux Klan, led those to the south. He served as Woodrow Wilson's secretary of the treasury. His name was known to almost everyone in the country because his signature appeared on every war bond issued during World War I. In 1932 he attempted to secure the party's presidential nomination. When he realized that he could not win, he threw California's support to Franklin Roosevelt. The new president showed his gratitude by giving McAdoo control of nearly all patronage in the state. Justus Wardell, a San Francisco stockbroker, was the leader of the northern faction of the Democratic Party. Wardell was a Catholic, anti-Prohibition, and by definition anti-Klan. Isidore E. Dockweiler, also a Catholic, was the leader of this faction in Los Angeles.[18]

Nineteen thirty-four was shaping up to be a good year for the Democrats. Roosevelt swept the state in 1932 with 1,324,157 votes; Herbert Hoover trailed far behind with 847,902. The new president carried Los Angeles County with over 57 percent of the vote. This was the first time the county had voted for a Democratic presidential candidate since Samuel Tilden in 1876. McAdoo won a U.S. senatorial election and became California's first Democratic senator since James D. Phelan in 1914. The size of the party's delegation in the House of Representatives jumped from one seat to eleven.

Sinclair's campaign slogan, End Poverty in California (EPIC), became the name of the movement he created. He assured his readers that, when he said he was going to end poverty in the state, he really meant it. "I know exactly how to do it, and if you elect me Governor, with a Legislature to support me, I will put the job through—and it won't take more than one or two of my four years." The heart of Sinclair's program was to put the unemployed to work in state-owned agricultural and industrial colonies. A new agency called the California Authority for the Land (CAL) would operate the cooperative colonies. The farms were to provide housing and facilities for cafeterias, retail stores, and recreational facilities. "Every land colony will become a cultural center, with a branch library, a motion picture theatre, a lecture hall where we can explain the principles of co-operation," he explained. The colonies would provide meaningful work and enable the unemployed to become proud self-supporting citizens. His plan also provided for a California Authority for Production (CAP) to acquire and operate factories. Like the agricultural colonies, factories would have their own kitchens, stores, and recreational and cultural facilities.[19]

These colonies were to operate separately from the California economy. "Let us construct a complete industrial system, a new and self-maintaining world for our unemployed, in which they will live, having as few dealings as possible with our present world of speculators and exploiters," Sinclair explained. Only members of the colonies would be allowed to purchase the crops and manufactured goods the cooperatives produced. They would use scrip,

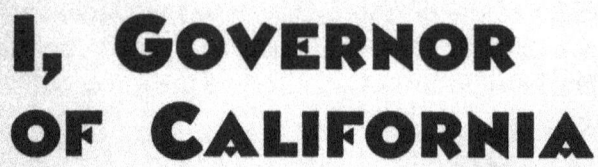

Upton Sinclair's pamphlet describing his EPIC plan to rescue Californians was a best seller at 20 cents. Courtesy of the Lilly Library, Indiana University, Bloomington, Indiana.

issued by a California Authority for Money (CAM), rather than U.S. dollars to make these purchases. CAM would be empowered to issue $300 million (almost $6 billion in 2019) worth of bonds to be sold directly to the people of the state without paying commissions to middlemen such as bankers.[20]

What would EPIC offer the majority of Californians who were not members of one of the cooperatives? It would lighten the burden on taxpayers because those who joined a colony would no longer be on relief. It would strike a blow at the welfare racket "by withdrawing the hundred million dollars a year which the State is now paying the unemployed, and which they are spending for goods." Sinclair promised to eliminate the 2.5 percent sales tax that Governor James Rolph had signed into law the previous year. The tax, called "a penny for Jimmy," was unpopular among low-income consumers. Rolph compounded this sin when he vetoed a modest state income tax that fell on those with higher incomes. Sinclair proposed eliminating the sales tax and substituting a graduated income tax beginning at $5,000 per year (about $95,000 in 2019) and imposing a rate of 30 percent on incomes over $50,000 per year. "They take that much in England," he explained. He also called for an increase in the state inheritance tax. He promised to eliminate property taxes on all homes assessed at $3,000 or less, prompting the appearance of signs in front of houses reading, "This Home Will Be Tax Exempt Under the EPIC Plan." He also wanted a 10 percent tax on all unimproved land, a measure aimed at speculators.[21]

The EPIC program provided for a pension of $50 a month (about $955 in 2019) for every California resident who was sixty years or older and had lived in the state for three years. The pension may have been the part of the EPIC platform with the greatest appeal to voters. One supporter, who called himself "Nuggets, the Poetical Prospector," sent Sinclair a short composition that concluded with this stanza:

I'm fifty two, and I'm out.
Yet I'm strong, and healthy, and stout
But my hair has turned gray,
And they say nay, nay—
You're too old, so I guess, I ought to be shot.[22]

Sinclair chose Richard S. Otto, a thirty-five-year-old real estate developer, as his campaign manager. His chief qualification for the job appeared to be that Sinclair thought him "one of the finest fellows I have ever known." Sinclair set up headquarters in the front room of his secretary's house. "There my new friend Richard S. Otto and I answered letters, filled orders for the book, and received the visitors who came in a constantly widening stream." The secretary left, complaining of all the "coming and going." The campaign soon moved into a thirty-two-room office building. Reuben Borough, a veteran Los Angeles reporter and progressive activist, became the editor of a weekly called *EPIC News*. The initial press run was 20,000 copies. By the time of the general election in November, two special editions had almost two million copies each.[23]

Sinclair's campaign had no wealthy donors or experienced politicos behind it. In mid-May he reported to a correspondent that the total contributions to the campaign fund amounted to only $1,500, and that the largest by "any one person is $150.00." Sinclair's primary campaign transportation was a 1928 automobile that broke down "now and then," forcing the gubernatorial candidate to hitchhike to the next event. Sales of *I, Governor of California*, which Sinclair claimed was the "bestselling book in the history of California," paid for some expenses. By February 1934, 120,000 thousand copies were in print.[24]

As with the Utopian Society and the Townsend movement, Sinclair's supporters felt the need to have a place to come together. Otto supervised the formation of clubs. They proved to be an effective means of selling literature and collecting donations. By the end of 1933 there were 103 EPIC clubs; two months later there were three hundred. By the time of the primary election there were approximately one thousand, and just before the general election in November about two thousand. Along with the growth of EPIC clubs there was an increase in registered Democrats. By the time of the primary election, the party had added 350,000 new members in California. In Los Angeles County, Democratic registrations led those of Republicans by 138,000.[25]

EPIC supporters raised money as they might have done for the construction of a new church or sending a high school band to Washington, D.C. They organized choruses that sang campaign songs such as "The Coming Day" to the tune of "The Battle Hymn of the Republic." There were EPIC softball teams, bake sales, rummage sales, picnics, and merchandise auction sales. As the day of the primary election approached, big offers of cash came in from gamblers, insurance interests, companies that hoped to do business with the

EPIC campaign signs placed on a street corner location in 1934. Harry Quillen, photographer. Los Angeles Photographers Photo Collection, courtesy of the Los Angeles Public Library.

state, and individuals who wanted to be appointed to offices. Sinclair claimed to have refused more than $250,000 of such donations.[26]

It is unlikely that most of those who flocked to the EPIC movement were converts to socialism. Sinclair's message of self-sufficiency, of work rather than relief, fit well with traditional American values. Many of his supporters saw no contradiction in supporting both EPIC and the New Deal. Sinclair found it politically wise to deny that EPIC conflicted with the New Deal. "I have most emphatically and on every possible occasion asserted the claim that the Plan does conform *exactly* to President Roosevelt's policy."[27]

Sinclair's speaking style appealed to the plain people in his audiences. Walter Davenport, a reporter for *Collier's* magazine, reported that he was "noticeably devoid of platform mannerisms, of posturing, of studied declamatory arts." The audience hung on every word as if it was "as new and fresh as tomorrow morning's dew."

A South Gate resident told his friends, "I don't care if Mr. Sinclair advocated catching the sunshine in buckets and spreading it over the soil by hand, I would still be for him because I know he has vision, courage, and wisdom and cannot be touched by the slimy hands of graft."[28]

Even seasoned reporters did not quite know what to make of Sinclair. Webb Waldron, a correspondent for *Today* magazine, visited the author at his home in Pasadena, where he was met by Sinclair in pajamas and bathrobe peeking out at him through a crack in the door. He "seemed to me not quite real," Waldron recalled, "something like an elf." He had been campaigning for weeks and up all night, yet he answered Waldron's questions "sharply and concisely" in his "soft voice and charming manner with no sign of exhaustion." "How does he do it?" he asked himself. "What a dynamo! Yet, that impression of the elf, the creature not quite of this earth, remained with me, and I went away wondering whether this gentle fellow really was the bogey man who had thrown such a scare into California."[29]

Sinclair's rallies resembled revival meetings. Davenport described an EPIC event at the Hollywood Bowl. Those who waited for Sinclair were "an arm-flinging, camp-meeting crowd" that sang hymns and waved little American flags. Davenport noted that in San Francisco the crowds would have "raised cries of violence, of taking, of burning, of lynching. But here in Los Angeles it was Yea, brother, and Amen." Southern California supporters were a "pamphlet-hawking and tract-distributing horde which, to our mild surprise, seemed to consist chiefly of middle-aged people with a pronounced leaning toward the evening side." At Sinclair rallies, campaign workers asked for donations in addition to the admission charge. Many who reached into their pockets "look as if twenty-five cents was no trifling matter with them." Davenport asked his readers, "How much would you pay, let's say, to hear the run-of-the-mill office-seeker?"[30]

Democratic regulars had difficulty coming to terms with Sinclair's grassroots insurgency. Isidore Dockweiler announced that, if Sinclair secured the nomination, all "good Democrats" should support the Republican nominee. *EPIC News* reported that he was heard to say that, if Jesus could not end poverty, then how could Upton Sinclair? George Creel, a Bay Area resident and regional director of the

National Recovery Administration, emerged as Sinclair's leading opponent in the primary election. He sold himself as an alternative to reactionary conservatism and social experimentation.[31]

Sinclair campaigned almost continuously from November 1933 to August 1934, taking a short break in April. A slate of candidates joined him on an EPIC-approved ticket. Sheridan Downey, who initially wanted to run for governor, was the candidate for lieutenant governor. Critics called them Uppie and Downey. Downey, from northern California, gave balance to a ticket dominated by Southern Californians. Patrick J. Cooney and William Kindig, two Southern Californians, ran for attorney general and controller. There were also EPIC candidates running for the legislature.

Sinclair spent most of his time campaigning in Southern California, where 40 percent of the state's registered Democrats lived. Creel thought the region was like a foreign country. When "I crossed the Tehachapi into Southern California," he later recalled, "it was like plunging into darkest Africa without gun bearers. Epics, Utopians, and Townsendites might have their points of difference, but all turned faces of hatred to me when I attacked the validity of their creeds." He thought that Sinclair's plan made no economic sense. He claimed that his pension plan was too expensive and that the EPIC provision to exempt some homes from property taxes would starve counties of revenue. He accused Sinclair of simple mathematical errors in some of his calculations. Despite his apparent lack of sympathy for Sinclair's supporters, who, after all, were victims of the Depression, Creel's arguments were not wrong-headed. There were many unanswered questions about Sinclair's program. How much agricultural land and how many operable factories were actually available for cooperative use? How much would it cost to acquire them? Who would buy the bonds that Sinclair hoped to market to finance his plans? Just how realistic was it that the unemployed would flock to his cooperatives? And did Sinclair really understand that his plans required an enormous administrative apparatus?[32]

Creel's criticisms failed to convince Sinclair's voters to abandon him. Sinclair was so confident that he would win the primary that he wrote Eleanor Roosevelt and told her that he wanted to come to Washington after the election and meet with the president. "I should like to know if the President will give me half an hour of his time." He received a reply from the White House executive office, reminding him that the president would take no part in local politics. "If however you are coming east and would like to see the president I will be glad to arrange for that with the very distinct understanding that there is to be no discussion of your campaign or politics in your state."[33]

Sinclair defeated Creel by 51.7 percent to 34.1 percent of the total cast. He won the most votes in a Democratic primary in the history of the state. Sinclair owed his victory to Southern California, carrying nine of the region's ten counties. Downey won the lieutenant governor's race but trailed Sinclair by almost 100,000 votes. All other statewide EPIC candidates lost. Three EPIC-endorsed candidates won seats in the state senate. For the state assembly, thirty EPIC candidates were victorious, twenty-seven of them from Los Angeles County.[34]

Acting governor Frank F. Merriam won the Republican primary. He was an Iowa-born resident of Long Beach, seventy years old, best described as "colorless," and a died-in-the-wool reactionary. Merriam had assumed the office of governor when James Rolph died of a heart attack the previous June. His position as acting governor and his use of troops to quell the 1934 harbor strike in San Francisco gave him the leverage to outmaneuver his rivals to become the Republican nominee. Raymond Haight, a liberal Republican, joined Sinclair and Merriam in the general election when he announced that he was a candidate for governor on the Commonwealth Party ticket.

Sinclair, carrying a gift box of California fruit, got on a train and headed east to meet with the president. He did not take seriously Roosevelt's insistence that he would not discuss politics. He met with the president on September 5, at Roosevelt's country residence at Hyde Park in New York. The two had a congenial conversation that lasted a full two hours. Sinclair said that Roosevelt told him he was familiar with the EPIC plan and discussed the financial burdens of the welfare system. He claimed that Roosevelt told him he was going to come out in favor of production for use and would do so on the radio sometime around October 25.[35]

On that date, Sinclair and a few friends gathered around a radio to hear what Roosevelt would say. "Somewhere around six o'clock the President gave his speech," Sinclair recalled. "The President spoke in connection with some drive for charity funds, and read a five-minute sermon on the beauty of giving and the sacredness of the emotion of pity." There was no mention of production for use. This was disappointing, and Sinclair made the situation worse when he told some supporters that the president might support EPIC in a speech that evening. Everyone, then, knew that the candidate spent the night listening to the radio to hear Roosevelt's announcement of the endorsement of his candidacy.[36]

Democratic regulars were in a state of shock after the primary election. Wardell and Dockweiler refused to endorse Sinclair. Creel and McAdoo held off from declaring their support one way or another. McAdoo finally endorsed Sinclair and had his picture taken with him. He then went on a trip and stayed away from California until after the election. While Sinclair was in the East, Downey and Culbert Olson met with Creel and agreed to a compromise platform that appeared to strip away most of the EPIC program, but Sinclair had no intention of dropping the EPIC plan. He wrote yet another pamphlet, *Immediate EPIC: The Final Statement of the Plan*, which retained basic features of EPIC. Creel considered *Immediate EPIC* "at utter variance with our understandings"—in other words, a double cross. In mid-September the Democratic state convention adopted a revised EPIC platform that downplayed the radicalism of Sinclair's program. Sinclair interpreted it to mean that he could still campaign on the EPIC program, even though its specifics were not spelled out in the platform. Creel believed that the platform meant that the party had abandoned EPIC altogether. He told the *New York Times* that at "the convention we threw out almost every one of his EPIC planks." This disagreement eventually led Creel to disavow Sinclair's candidacy altogether.[37]

The platform declared that the Democratic Party opposed communism, fascism, and Nazism and defended the home, private property, freedom of religion, and the American way of life. There was no mention of the agricultural and industrial colonies that were the central feature of the EPIC program. The platform called for the repeal of the sales tax, the passage of a state income tax on corporations and individuals, and a small increase in bank and inheritance taxes. It backed away from the tax exemption on real estate assessed at $3,000 or less but called for a constitutional amendment that provided for a tax exemption on property assessed at $1,000 or less and gave the legislature the authority to exempt property assessed at $3,000 or less when state finances permitted. It dropped the demand for a 10 percent tax on unimproved land and replaced it with the vague statement that holdings should yield a fair tax.

In what may have been a fatal mistake, according to the historian Jackson K. Putnam, the platform dropped the old-age pension plank and, instead, pledged to support whatever program for "societal insurance" President Roosevelt presented to Congress. Sinclair failed to understand the importance of the old-age assistance provision in the EPIC program to the state's elderly population. Its elimination handed Merriam an unexpected gift. The governor asked the California legislature to pass a resolution urging Congress to pass an old-age pension law. This was an empty gesture, but the state's elderly population took notice. When Dr. Townsend spoke to almost ten thousand people at the Hollywood Bowl in September, Merriam sent a telegram declaring that he was "heartily in favor of old-age pensions." For his part, Sinclair made it clear that he thought that Townsend's plan was "no good."[38]

At the beginning of September, Sinclair led Merriam by a substantial margin. Haight had no chance of winning but was likely to take votes from Sinclair. The Republicans and dissident Democrats, well organized and well financed, commanded considerable resources for their campaign to defeat Sinclair. The *Los Angeles Times* announced that the "indifference of former days to political questions has been dropped and business concerns are out aggressively to defeat Sinclair and the policies for which he stands." Thomas J. Murphy, Republican, announced to a gathering of fellow real estate dealers, "We've now got to sacrifice some of our time to save our homes, our State, our constitution and our business. We are facing a real menace in Socialism and radicalism." Southern California business leaders formed a group called United for California to coordinate the campaign. Commanding nearly unlimited resources, Asa Call, vice president of Pacific Mutual Life Insurance Company, assumed command. Disaffected Los Angeles Democrats formed the American Democracy of California and called on all Democrats to join them.[39]

Arthur M. Schlesinger Jr. called the anti-Sinclair campaign "the first all-out public relations *Blitzkrieg* in American politics." It was one of the dirtiest campaigns in California history. The campaign also saw the appearance of something new in American politics—the professional political consultant. Clem Whitaker and his associate Leone Baxter founded Campaigns, Inc., a firm that managed all aspects of a political campaign—packaging and selling a candidate like any other product. Whitaker and Baxter signed on to work for George Hatfield, the Republican candidate for lieutenant governor. They also mined Sinclair's voluminous writings in search of anything radical, anti-Christian, anti-marriage, or anti-American. They found plenty, even though they had to stretch things a bit and take some material out of context. From the end of September until just before election day, the front page of the *Los Angeles Times* featured a quote from one of Sinclair's writings that the paper thought exposed his radical and anti-Christian beliefs. "Verily, out of his own mouth shall he be judged" was the paper's slogan during the campaign.[40]

The anti-Sinclair strategy did not tout the virtues of the uninspiring Merriam or expose the defects of the EPIC program. Instead, it attacked the candidate himself. The *Los Angeles Times* blasted Sinclair for his lack of qualifications. The paper pointed out that the Helicon Hall cooperative that burned down four months after its founding was his only management experience. The *Times* delighted in advertising Sinclair's admission that his wife handled the practical side of his affairs. The paper asked, "Does this mean that Mrs. Sinclair would be the real Governor of California should Sinclair be elected?[41]

The motion picture industry, led by MGM reactionaries such as Louis B. Mayer and Irving Thalberg, came out strongly against EPIC. These movie moguls worried that Sinclair's election might mean higher taxes on their industry. Joseph M. Schenck, president of United Artists, announced that if Sinclair were elected the motion picture industry would have to leave California. He believed that a Governor Sinclair would "soak the movies between 40 and 60 percent in taxes." The seven major studios in Southern California assessed their higher-paid employees one day's pay for the Merriam campaign. All employees were "advised" as to how they should vote in the election. Thalberg arranged for the shooting of fake newsreels that depicted bums flooding into California in anticipation of Sinclair's victory. A *New York Times* reporter spotted movie equipment and "some second-rate players" around the city filming scenes for the bogus newsreels. He also heard that a "leading newspaper of Los Angeles" asked one of the studios for a still photograph of bums entering California. The studio supplied it and the paper published it as authentic.[42]

Sinclair, in a huge gaff, said that if he were elected "about one-half of the unemployed of the whole country" would flood into California. Republican state senator Ralph E. Swing painted a horror picture of the state's borders. "Never in the history of California has there been such an influx of socialistically inclined and poverty-stricken people as have flowed through our entrance gates since the nomination of Sinclair." A *Los Angeles Times* correspondent wrote a story about an alleged encounter at the California border with a group of migrants arriving from Texas. He asked the driver of one of the vehicles where he was headed. "We're comin' to Californey," he replied, "to git some of that free land when this feller Sinclair is elected Governor."[43]

Creel, angry that Sinclair did not abandon his original EPIC plan as he thought they had agreed, announced that he was withdrawing his offer to campaign on Sinclair's behalf. "We knew you for a Socialist, and we rejected your Epic plan as an unconscionable vote-catching device, but due to our dislike and distrust of the Republican candidate, we agreed to swallow you if too large a stain was not put on our gullets." The EPIC campaign still hoped that Senator McAdoo would endorse Sinclair. When asked if he could speak at rallies or on the radio in support of Sinclair, he replied, "I don't see how I can assume any additional burdens just now."[44]

The Democratic turnout on November 6 exceeded even the size of the 1932 Roosevelt landslide. Sinclair won more votes than any Democratic candidate for governor in the history of the state. These were impressive numbers, but they were not enough. Merriam easily won, 1,138,620 to 795,537. He carried Los Angeles County by almost 50,000 votes, though Sinclair won majorities in the industrial belt that stretched from downtown to the harbor area. In Belvedere Township (East Los Angeles), he won 70 percent of the vote. In the towns of Hawthorne, Maywood, Lynwood, South Gate, Bell, El Cerrito, and Compton, where blue-collar workers lived, he won from 50 to 64 percent of votes cast. In the affluent suburbs of South Pasadena, San Marino, and Beverly Hills, his percentages fell well below 20 percent. Surprisingly, he did poorly among women, even those from working-class families. Not so surprisingly, he did not do well with African Americans, for whom he appeared to have little interest or sympathy. Sinclair also did poorly among voters over the age of fifty-five—an indication that dropping the pension plan from the party platform was a mistake.[45]

The election returns were not all bad news. The voters elected twenty-four EPIC-endorsed candidates to the state assembly, fifteen of them from Los Angeles County. Three EPIC state senatorial candidates won as well. One of these was Culbert Olson, who represented Los Angeles County. As its titular head, Sinclair had the power to name Olson chairman of the California Democratic Party. Four years later, Olson won the 1938 gubernatorial election, succeeding where Sinclair had failed.

Sinclair told his supporters that losing the election did not mean the end of the EPIC movement. Jerry Voorhis, who lost his race for the legislature, wrote Sinclair the morning after the election, "All I want to know is—'where do we go from here?'" A newly incorporated organization, the End Poverty League, with Otto as president, carried on the work. Sinclair believed that the new EPIC legislators should push for programs such as the thirty-hour work week, the repeal of the sales tax on the necessities of life, a state income tax equivalent to the federal income tax, and state appropriations for the purchase of land and factories to enable the unemployed to produce goods for their own consumption.[46]

At this crucial moment, Sinclair stepped back from his role as the leader of EPIC. His first duty, he believed, was to write a book, *I, Candidate for Governor: And How I Got Licked.* With characteristic concentration, he feverishly worked on the book, to be published serially in newspapers across the country. He handed the leadership of the movement to Otto and the directors of the End Poverty League. He stopped making public appearances, receiving visitors, and answering his mail. He limited his contact with his former followers to a weekly column in *EPIC News.* His friend Oursler was right when he warned Sinclair that he was at heart a writer and made a poor politician.[47]

Almost immediately, divisions emerged within the movement that Sinclair dismissed as clashes between personalities. "Everybody was under terrific tension during the campaign and all the little disagreements had to wait and blow up when the pressure was relieved." If this was the case, he might have been able to resolve problems had he appeared to discuss the issues in person. Instead he sent a curt message: "I request all persons who are not satisfied with decisions of the Board of Directors of the End Poverty League to leave headquarters and go about other affairs. . . . I am writing a book for the movement to End Poverty and will do nothing else at present."[48]

Olson warned Sinclair that EPIC leaders were "unable to work with Mr. Otto." Sinclair's reply—when he did reply—was "Why don't you go down and help them?" He insisted, "The only course I could follow was to let the movement settle their own problems for themselves. Certainly it is impossible for me to try to do it while I am giving all my energies to the new book." As president of the End Poverty League, Otto considered himself the leader of the EPIC organization and its network of clubs. Olson believed that the clubs were most effective as the political arm of the movement. He wanted to integrate the clubs into the California Democratic Party, even dropping the name EPIC from their titles. He thought the End Poverty League should serve an educational function and provide support for the Democratic Party. Otto was not pleased with the idea of reducing the League to nothing more than a subsidiary of the Democratic Party. He blasted Olson in an editorial in the *EPIC News:* "I deeply regret the mistake we very obviously made in placing Olson in office as state senator and as chairman of the Democratic State Central Committee." His "present actions indicate all too clearly that he places personal ambitions ahead of Upton Sinclair and EPIC principles." Olson countered that Otto acted as if he were dictator of the End Poverty League. Sinclair stood by his friend Otto. In an editorial in the *EPIC News,* he wrote that from the very first hour Otto was his right hand. "At a time when Senator Olson was unwilling to take his stand as an EPIC man, and sought my approval to run in the Democratic primaries with EPIC support, but without being avowedly an EPIC man, Richard S. Otto was coming every day to our little one-room EPIC headquarters at eight o'clock in the morning and working there until late at night." In an angry letter, Sinclair made his position clear to Olson. The End Poverty League and its board of directors were to remain intact, with Otto as president, and the clubs would continue as EPIC clubs. "This should be easy for anyone to understand," Sinclair wrote.[49]

At the end of December, Sinclair finished the book. He wrote 70,000 words in five weeks, an impressive feat of self-discipline. Finishing the book did not, however, mean returning to the fray. Sinclair said that he received an offer to make a motion picture about EPIC. "If I am able to do this it will be the greatest service I have ever rendered to the cause," he explained to a friend, "but it will mean that again I shall not be available to answer all the enormous mail and to comply with all the requests which pour in upon me from all over the world." He never made the movie, but other projects appeared. At the beginning of January, he wrote the board of directors of the End Poverty League that he was "at home occupying my mind with the first chapters of a long novel." He assured the directors that they were fully capable of doing their work. "Keep flying the flag," he wrote.[50]

• • • •

EPIC began to slowly disintegrate. In April, Otto and the entire board of directors of the End Poverty League resigned. Otto bought an 85-foot yacht and sailed off for the next four years. Kate Richards O'Hare, a veteran socialist activist, became the new executive secretary. Sinclair informed her that he was too busy to be involved in the affairs of the League and that they were in the "hands of the new board of directors." After six months on the job as executive secretary, O'Hare filed a depressing report. She believed that EPIC was a "real mass uprising of the people" and that Sinclair had betrayed it by walking away from his responsibilities as leader. "It is an established axiom of human movements that a leader must lead three hundred and sixty-five days a year and twenty-four hours a day, and the final test of all leadership is to lead in time of defeat." Leaderless, EPIC soon disappeared from California's political scene.[51]

10

HAM AND EGGS

> You can't dismiss it [Ham and Eggs] by simply calling it crazy. There is more to it than an ignoble desire to live on somebody else. Underneath it runs a very real and widespread feeling of desperation.
>
> *Whittier News*, October 2, 1938

George Creel, who lost the race for the 1934 Democratic California gubernatorial nomination to Upton Sinclair, nursed a lifelong contempt for Southern California and everything that came out of it. He thought that stupidity and greed motivated the elderly who flocked to movements such as the Townsend Plan. In his 1947 memoir, he wrote that a "vast happiness permeated all of Southern California with elderly people crowding stores, real-estate offices, and automobile agencies, joyfully picking out furniture, homes, and cars in full confidence that the national treasury would soon gush forth a golden stream." It is shocking that Creel, a prominent New Deal figure on the West Coast, should have so little sympathy for the victims of the Depression. Joy was certainly not the prevalent mood of California's aged. In 1934 the Los Angeles County department of charities reported that 29,295 people age sixty years or older were on the welfare rolls. This was about 20 percent of the county's elderly population. The department's figures included only those persons on welfare. The actual percentage of the elderly living in poverty is difficult to calculate, but it was certainly much higher than 20 percent. Many of the aged poor did not qualify for welfare because they did not meet the county residency requirement or they tenaciously held on to their homes, making them ineligible for aid. Too old to work and too young to die, they faced a grim future.[1]

The historian Jackson K. Putnam noted that "there were probably at least eighty different old-age welfare schemes bidding for political support in the state during 1937 and 1938." One of these, officially titled Retirement Life Payments, appeared as Proposition 25 on the 1938 general election ballot. It won a place on the ballot after a petition campaign that collected 789,104 signatures. This was the largest number ever collected for a state proposition up to that time. Carey McWilliams called it "by all odds, the most fantastic, incredible, and dangerous" political movement in Southern California history.[2]

If a majority of California voters supported the proposition, the state constitution would be amended to permit the government to issue thirty one-dollar warrants every Thursday to unemployed residents of California fifty years of age or older. The framers of the proposition expected that the warrants, which could be spent like U.S. dollars, would accelerate the circulation of money, stimulate the economy, and open up jobs for people under fifty. Each warrant would be negotiable for one year, provided that once a week the current bearer purchased a special two-cent stamp and affixed it to the back. At the end of the year, if fifty-two two-cent stamps, one for each week of circulation, were attached, the state redeemed each warrant for one dollar in U.S. currency. The observant reader will note that fifty-two two-cent stamps added up to $1.04, giving the state of California four cents on each warrant to pay for the cost of the program. Sponsors of the proposition expected businesses to accept the warrants the same as money. The proposition required the governor to appoint the program's administrator from a list limited to three men: Roy G. Owens, Will Kindig, or John B. Elliot. This administrator would receive a salary of $7,800 a year (over $140,000 in 2019) and had the power to appoint four assistant managers at $7,280 a year each. He was also empowered to request up to $700,000 (over $12 million in 2019) from the state to set up the program. In addition, the proposition called for a 3 percent income tax on all Californians and corporations.[3]

The origins of Proposition 25 are complicated but can be traced to Robert Noble—a Pennsylvania native who moved to Los Angeles in the 1920s. It is likely that Noble saw Southern California as a place where he could reinvent himself and start a new life. His birth name was Robert L. Coker, which he probably changed to cover up his past. This past included time in Portsmouth Naval Prison for desertion, a dishonorable discharge for refusing to serve in Europe during the war, and a conviction for robbery. He also may have spent time in a sanitarium because of a delusion that he was Jesus Christ. For all this, Noble was an articulate charmer who possessed what the writers Winston and Marian Moore called a "superbly developed ego." He was the very epitome of a smooth operator—poised and self-confident. In Los Angeles, he acquired some fame delivering inspirational radio talks and making the rounds as a well-paid speaker at service clubs where wealthy and well-connected members, mostly women, found him irresistible. His promotional skills led him to the real estate business, where he sold property and gave pep talks to sales people.[4]

The Depression put an end to Noble's real estate career. He sought new sources of income in reform movements. He joined Upton Sinclair's campaign for governor—a move that put an end to his popularity with the moneyed class. The invitations to speak at service clubs stopped coming. After Sinclair's defeat in November 1934, he fell out with the former candidate regarding the direction of the movement. Opinions about Noble among EPIC supporters varied. One Los Angeles woman admonished Sinclair, hoping that someday he might "have an opportunity and will to use it—to make amends to a grand leader and *doer*—Bob Noble." Another, Olive Cushing Dwinell, chairman of the Inglewood EPIC-Democratic Club, was of the opinion that Noble was not "able to withstand the pressure and lure of money and power he has been offered. And I happen to know something of his weakness for booze." Noble dabbled in the Townsend Plan and then migrated to Huey Long's Share the Wealth movement, calling himself Long's representative in Southern California. After the Louisiana senator's assassination, Noble went to New Orleans for the funeral and created a scene when he threw himself on Long's grave.[5]

Somewhere along the way, Noble read or heard about the economist Irving Fisher's idea that a stamped scrip might help stimulate the economy. Fisher was a respected Yale professor and considered the leading American economist of his day. He thought if local governments issued scrip in limited quantities and for short periods of time, it might "prime the pump" and help unlock the stagnant local economies. Noble took Fisher's idea and turned it into a program aimed at the older population. His California Pension Plan proposed that all unemployed Californians over the age of fifty receive $25 a week (a little more than $450 in 2019) in scrip issued every Monday. To remain negotiable, each note required that a stamp be affixed every week for a year. He adopted the slogan "Twenty-Five Dollars Every Monday Morning," formed an organization, and asked his followers to pay dues of one cent a day, collected monthly. Noble understood that small donations from large numbers of people added up to big money. All received a membership card, making it appear that they belonged to a real organization, which in reality existed only on paper. In addition to his radio broadcasts, Noble spoke to increasingly larger crowds of the same desperate people who filled auditoriums for Francis Townsend and Upton Sinclair. He began publication of his own newspaper, the *Noble News*.

A turning point in Noble's scheme came when he made the acquaintance of the brothers Willis and Lawrence Allen. Willis recently had some bad luck when a federal court fined him $100 and sentenced him to two years' probation for mail fraud involving deceptive advertising for a men's hair tonic called Grey Goose. When they met Noble, the brothers were promoting a scheme called the Cinema Advertising Agency, which was to sell radio air time to reform groups. They rented an office building in Hollywood and sublet space to other tenants. One of these was Noble, who occupied an office in the rear of the building. The Allens' plan for the Cinema Advertising Agency hit a wall when they could not find a local station that would give them air time. They tried to work around this problem by persuading George W. Berger, head of the Federal Radio and Television Corporation (not a government agency), to build a radio station in Mexico with a transmitter powerful enough to be heard in Southern California. A Mexican businessman, M. P. Barbashano, served as the liaison with the Mexican government to obtain the appropriate licensing. All the Allen brothers needed to complete the deal was money. They noted that one of their tenants, Mr. Noble, was bringing in a lot of cash with his stamped warrant scheme.[6]

Billboard advertising Robert Noble's radio program to promote his pension scheme in 1937. Herman J. Schulfeis, photographer. Los Angeles Photographers Photo Collection, courtesy of the Los Angeles Public Library.

Lawrence Allen already worked as Noble's attorney for a small stipend. He also persuaded Noble to use the Cinema Advertising Agency as his agent for arranging radio time. The brothers asked Noble for help with their financing problems, and he handed over about $2,000. The brothers still needed more money. Barbashano, meanwhile, asked for assurances that the Allens had the financial wherewithal to proceed with the construction of the radio station. The brothers sent the Mexican businessman a document on Federal Radio and Television Corporation stationery. This was a receipt for $30,000 for equipment that they claimed to have purchased (but actually had not) for the station. They forged Berger's signature. This soon came to Berger's attention, and he went to the police. The department referred him to acting captain Earle Kynette, head of a departmental unit known informally as the "spy squad."

It so happened that Noble was well known around city hall. In addition to promoting his stamped warrant scheme, he used his radio time to attack corruption in Mayor Frank Shaw's administration. Kynette had the unofficial assignment of dealing with Noble. He saw the Allen brothers as a way to do this and possibly make a few bucks of his own. Using the fraudulent documents as a threat, he encouraged the two men to hijack Noble's California Pension Plan. He even loaned them money to help carry out the scheme. Without bothering to tell Noble, the brothers arranged a meeting of California Pension Plan members at Clifton's Cafeteria. The Allens persuaded the group that the movement was going nowhere under Noble and that they should elect a new board of directors that included the Allen brothers and several of their friends. There was opposition from loyal members, but in the end the takeover was successful. The brothers shut down Noble's radio program—the Cinema Advertising Agency held the contract with the station—and began opening all mail addressed to the California Pension Plan. The brothers diverted all dues into their own pockets. Noble found himself in a difficult situation. He had no money, was shut out from the radio station, and found no others willing to accommodate him. Kynette allegedly put the word out to radio stations that it was not wise to cooperate with the deposed leader. When Noble gathered together his loyalists, the spy squad used stink bombs to break up the meetings.[7]

Noble assembled what remained of his elderly followers and organized a protest march on KMTR, the station that in the past had broadcast his radio programs. Kynette broke up the marchers with a tear gas bomb and destroyed a participant's camera on the grounds that it might have contained a gun. "We were told they were coming with thirty-thirty rifles," he later testified in court. The police beat and dragged Noble off to jail on the charge of parading without a permit and blocking the sidewalks. The newspapers reported other charges, but they do not seem to have been pursued in court. They included "grand theft bunko" for swindling elderly people out of their savings and for attempting to extort radio time from station KMTR. Despite credible evidence that Kynette and his men had attacked the march of elderly men and women without provocation, a jury found Noble guilty. The judge fined him $50. A jury also found two codefendants guilty, sixty-eight-year-old Viola

Robert Noble (on the right) at his trial for running the pension scheme that eventually became Ham and Eggs. Los Angeles Daily News Negatives (Collection 1387), Library Special Collections, courtesy of Charles E. Young Research Library, UCLA.

Moore and Maggie Dee, a fifty-year-old school teacher, but they received suspended sentences.[8]

Stories about Noble and his past suddenly began appearing in the newspapers. Kynette reported that he had found "piteous letters" in Noble's files begging for the return of money he had borrowed. A story appeared about the pension leader's former identity and a 1918 burglary conviction. Then there was the sudden and highly publicized appearance in the city of a woman who claimed to be Noble's ex-wife, whom he had abandoned along with their two children when he moved to Los Angeles. Still, Noble managed to command the loyalty of a handful of devoted followers. He continued publication of *Noble News* and used every opportunity available to keep himself in the public eye. In November 1938 he appeared on the ballot as a candidate for governor of California on the Commonwealth Party ticket; he won 23,787 votes, less than 1 percent of the total cast.[9]

The remaining obstacle to the Allen brothers' full control of the pension movement was Captain Kynette, who in exchange for services rendered expected to receive a share of the pension plan profits. This problem resolved itself without any effort on the part of the Allens. In June, a jury found Kynette guilty of the attempted murder of Harry Raymond, a private detective who worked for Clifford Clinton, another of Mayor Shaw's enemies. Kynette placed a bomb in Raymond's car that destroyed the automobile but failed to kill his target. In his new residence in San Quentin Penitentiary, Kynette was no longer, at least for the time being, a threat to the Allen brothers. With this problem behind them, Willis and Lawrence began putting together a group of people to promote their plan.[10]

Their most important recruit was the former silent screen actor and real estate salesman, Sherman J. Bainbridge, who signed on for a salary of $25 a week. Bainbridge's film credits include *In the Coils of the Python* (1914), *Custer's Last Scout* (1915), and *The Circus Girl's Romance* (1915). The former actor had a history of involvement with reform groups. At the age of twenty-six, he ran for Congress in the 1916 primary election on the Progressive ticket and won fifty-two votes. He served on the board of directors of the EPIC movement and in that capacity advocated a $200 pension for all Californians over the age of sixty. Winston and Marian Moore described him as a "strange bird" because he was not "a high-powered opportunist, not a parlor pink, not an agitator, but a real economic reformer, one of those strange people who, for absolutely no personal reason, want to make the world a better place." Bainbridge was a dynamic speaker and attracted large audiences at his rallies. It was at one of these that he gave the movement the name for which it is most commonly known. Swept away by the enthusiasm of the crowd, he shouted to his audience, "We want our ham and eggs!"[11]

Bainbridge brought in his friend Roy G. Owens as his assistant on a salary of $10 a week. Born in Indiana in 1896, Owens attended school in Shreveport, Louisiana, dropped out after the ninth grade, and took a job in a hardware store and then as an equipment salesman. In 1923 he became the executive secretary of the American Manufacturers Export Association. He relocated to California in 1929 and worked as a salesman until he joined the ranks of the unemployed. For a time he held a WPA job on the Federal Writers

Project. Owens considered himself an authority on economic matters and gave himself the title of engineer-economist. People who knew him said that he had a "Jehovah complex"—that he was absolutely convinced of the correctness of his views and that those who opposed him were not only wrong but evil. Drawn to the Utopian Society like a fly to honey, he served briefly as a director. In those days he was an advocate of something called the Utopian National Dated Money, similar to the Technocratic energy dollar. After the Utopian Society faded, he became involved in the Father Divine cult. Divine, an African American preacher, claimed to be the incarnation of God. The leader of the movement in Los Angeles was a man named John W. Hunt, otherwise known as John the Revelator or John the Baptist, who lived in a mansion in Beverly Hills. Owens spent his time with the cult writing a bill called the "Righteous Government Act of 1936." This bill proposed to create the Money Issue and Regulating Authority of the United States of America. The agency would have at its head a chief engineer economist who would be in charge of the nation's tax and monetary programs. Its manager would have extraordinary powers including the ability to nullify all laws in conflict with the act. A feature of the proposed law was that anyone age fifty or older would be classified as retired and would not be required to work. The document concluded with the statement that the "whole capitalistic conception of interest and taxes, wages, debt, and profit and loss shall be discontinued and forgotten." Father Divine was not interested in such sweeping political or economic measures and dropped Owens and the proposed law. After his flirtation with the cult, Owens was at loose ends until Bainbridge brought him into Ham and Eggs.[12]

The Allen brothers may have been satisfied with nothing more than pocketing the membership dues that flowed into their offices. It was probably Owens who suggested that the dated scrip idea needed to become California law. For this to happen it was necessary to amend the California constitution to make it legal for the state to issue the stamped warrants. A small obstacle stood in the way. It was necessary to abandon the name California Pension Plan and the slogan "Twenty-Five Dollars Every Monday Morning," because Noble was the legal owner of both. The fix was easy. The brothers changed the name of the plan to Retirement Life Payments and the slogan to "$30 Every Thursday." This freed them from any tie to Noble, and the addition of five dollars to the weekly benefit made their plan more attractive. The official explanation for the change was that $30 a week was the amount "necessary for an American standard of living on the Pacific Coast," and issuing scrip on Thursday made it possible for employers who might pay wages in stamped warrants to meet Saturday payrolls.[13]

Bainbridge's crowning achievement as a publicist for Ham and Eggs came about as a result of the death of a San Diego man named Archie Price. Price was a sixty-four-year-old with no hope of ever finding a job. One day he walked into a newspaper office and announced that his life was hopeless and that he saw no alternative but to commit suicide. The next day he swallowed a dose of poison and left a note that said, "Too young to receive an old-age pension and too old to work." In death Archie Price became a symbol of the plight of the elderly during the Depression. Bainbridge immediately saw the possibilities of the situation and organized a funeral cortege of hundreds of automobiles that drove from Los Angeles to San Diego. He arranged to have Price's body exhumed from a pauper's grave and reburied in the prestigious Glen Abbey cemetery. The event included music, flowers, and speeches. Sheridan Downey, a senatorial candidate, and Culbert Olson, candidate for governor, made appearances. Willis and Lawrence produced a one-reel motion picture called "Marching On," shown in theaters across the state. Price's funeral was a triumph, but it ended badly for its organizer. Returning to Los Angeles, Bainbridge was injured in an automobile accident and spent several months recovering in the hospital.[14]

Owens wrote the document that became Proposition 25. From his hospital bed, Bainbridge wrote the text of a twenty-eight-page pamphlet that contained a summary of the plan, with answers to almost every possible question about it and its implementation. He included the full text of the proposed amendment. The booklet appeared under the title "Ham and Eggs for Californians: Life Begins at Fifty, $30 a Week for Life, Questions and Answers." A color picture of a plate containing two fried eggs (sunny side up), an enormous slice of ham, french fries, and a few sprigs of parsley graced its cover. The document was a brilliant work of salesmanship. Anyone reading it, especially if they were unsophisticated about economic issues and predisposed to believe it anyway, must have found the document persuasive.[15]

As the Proposition 25 campaign moved forward, Owens assumed an increasingly larger role as theoretician. The *Beverly Hills Citizen* called him "more or less the real leader of the movement." The Allen brothers focused on the organizational aspects of the campaign. Attention to detail was the hallmark of their work. They followed Noble's lead and kept dues at one cent a day, collected every month. They established branch offices up and down the state on the assumption that contributors would be more inclined to send money to a local address than to Southern California. These offices, which forwarded correspondence unopened to headquarters, were nothing more than mail drops. All members received passbooks and envelopes for sending in dues. Dues-paying members received stamps to be affixed to the passbooks. Special stamps recognized extra monetary contributions.[16]

The Allen brothers needed to collect 187,000 signatures to get the proposition on the ballot. They had an invaluable asset at their disposal—a highly motivated force of volunteers willing to work for free. The campaign printed 100,000 copies of the Ham and Eggs pamphlet and sold them for twenty-five cents each. When this supply was exhausted, it ordered another 100,000. It also published a weekly newspaper called *Ham and Eggs for Californians*. Radio programs broadcast over eight stations; newspaper advertising, mass meetings, and attention-getting events such as the Archie Price funeral were the primary means of promoting the plan. Sound trucks proved useful in rural communities; one was dressed up to look like a locomotive and another like a giant box of mint candies. Willis, a former University of Southern California cheerleader, started meetings with a cheer: "Five! Ten! Fifteen! Twenty! Twenty-five! Thirty! Ham and Eggs!" The membership grew rapidly, as did the flow of money. By October 1938 there were 250,000 members statewide. Income amounted to about $2,000 a day. The headquarters in Hollywood employed three hundred mostly young, female clerks working three shifts, twenty-four hours a day. "In a section of the country well used to the new, the different, the super-colossal," wrote the reporter for the *Beverly Hills Citizen*, "this business is outstanding for its sheer 'super-colossalness.'"[17]

The Allen brothers were well aware that both the Utopian Society and the Townsend movement floundered in part because of the loose control and misuse of money. Ham and Eggs adopted strict policies in the handling of membership dues and contributions. The Hollywood office kept a master file in which workers recorded incoming funds and immediately deposited them in the bank. All donors received receipts so that they could keep track of how much money they contributed. The organization did not maintain large bank balances because the money quickly went out to pay expenses. Raymond D. Fritz, CPA, efficiently managed the organization's business office. He maintained a low profile, working behind the scenes and making no public appearances. (That was just as well; Fritz was a Nazi sympathizer who refused to allow Jews into the organization.) The firm of Wright and Frost, certified public accountants, regularly audited the books and reported no problems. Ham and Eggs appeared to be an honest operation that accounted for every penny—incoming and outgoing.[18]

The brothers were quite pleased with themselves and the organization they had created. According to Winston and Marian Moore, Lawrence Allen "went around smiling to himself like the proverbial canary-eating cat, while Willis . . . paced up and down the hall, beating his fist against his open palm and chortling, 'Is she sweet or is she sweet? Wowie!'" It seems unlikely that the Allen brothers would be pleased with a movement that netted them each a salary of $30 a week—the official top pay at headquarters. Why did the brothers act as if they were sitting on a gold mine? The reader will recall the Cinema Advertising Agency that Lawrence and Willis formed to book radio time for reform groups. The agency, which the Allen brothers exclusively owned and operated, acted as the agent for all Retirement Life Payments expenditures. The agency charged a 15 percent commission and, because it had no employees other than its owners, all the money went to Lawrence and Willis Allen. The beauty of this arrangement was that the bigger the expense, the bigger the commission. There was no need to economize, to take bids, or to negotiate the cheapest price for any service. Everything was perfectly legal and all financial arrangements completely transparent. The 15 percent commission, paid to an organization that amounted to nothing more than a desk in the corner of the Hollywood office, kept the brothers rolling in cash.[19]

Ham and Eggs quickly became a major political organization in the state. Its force of volunteers collected 789,000 signatures—far in excess of the 187,000 needed. This number was a quarter of the state's registered voters and the largest number of signatures collected for any proposition up to that time. Politicians suddenly awoke to the power of Ham and Eggs. They learned that opposing the movement was dangerous. This lesson was made painfully clear when the formidable political veteran Senator William Gibbs McAdoo, who opposed Ham and Eggs, lost the August Democratic primary to Sheridan Downey, an enthusiastic supporter. Two Los Angeles residents, state senator Culbert Olson and Representative John Dockweiler, a Ham and Eggs supporter, competed for the gubernatorial nomination. Olson managed to win by not overtly opposing the pension plan, but at the same time not endorsing it. Assemblyman Ellis Patterson, who endorsed Ham and Eggs, won the nomination for lieutenant governor.[20]

The *New York Times* believed that the broad support of the plan was

> another indication of how fertile the soil of Southern California is for the growth of unusual ideas as well as for oranges, dates, and palm trees. This part of the state is full of old people, retired or semi-retired, largely from the Midwest. ... One is struck by the resemblance of many of these old people to the kind of folk one used to see at country fairs, trying to get something for nothing by guessing which shell the little pea was under or eagerly handing over their hard-won dollars to the medicine man with the Indian root cure-all and his slick talk from the back end of a buggy.[21]

These views were nothing more than expressions of regional prejudice. The reason Ham and Eggs was so popular despite its obvious flaws was that it offered generous benefits to a segment of the population that had few alternatives. Those who supported the proposition did not need to be convinced of the accuracy of its arguments or the viability of the program. The *Culver City Citizen* drew a more accurate portrait than the *New York Times* of the kind of people who supported the measure:

> There are young people, who are aiding their parents, or relatives, who have fallen upon evil times. ... There are the

physically fit men and women who are gradually losing the spirit to go out and fight for a job, because they know that many employers have set up arbitrary age limits which bar them out. These people have to have some hope for the future and they find this in the pension plans, with a maximum of hope in the present one, on which they may at least vote.[22]

In October, an organization called the Research Institute conducted a postcard survey that asked for the opinions of Los Angeles voters on current issues. All of the questions—except for the first one that asked if the recipients approved of Hitler's dismemberment of Czechoslovakia—were about the federal social security program, the California old-age assistance law, and the proposed California Life Payments initiative. The surviving 141 cards show that in the month before the election many potential voters—even those who would benefit from it—opposed Ham and Eggs. Based on the comments written on the cards, those who did support it did not necessarily do so because they believed that it was a good idea. Some respondents said that they supported the measure because, if it passed, the government would be forced to come forward with a strong pension law. One respondent wrote that the "Life Payments Act sounds a little impractical, but you never can tell, maybe it's the very thing to get us out of the present mess—commonly known as depression, recession, unemployment, lousy distribution of capital, etc."[23]

When Proposition 25 qualified for the ballot, California businesspeople awoke to the realization that a measure that many of them had not taken seriously could become law. Their reaction might be compared to a man walking across a trestle who suddenly realized that a train was coming. The bankers led the opposition with the announcement that California financial organizations would not accept the warrants for deposits, exchange them for cash, use them as collateral, or handle them at all. The *Los Angeles Times* believed that the banks' refusal to take the stamped scrip was a "mortal blow" for the plan. The California Manufacturers Association, Southern California Wholesale Grocery Distributors Association, Southern California Retail Council, California Retailers Association, Los Angeles Credit Men's Association, Associated Produce Dealers and Brokers, Southern California Restaurant Association, and others announced that their members would not accept warrants. If the proposition passed, businesspeople believed, they might be forced to buy products out of state and sell them in state for warrants of uncertain value.[24]

The *Los Angeles Times* published a fourteen-part series titled "?30 Dollars Every Thursday?" that painted a picture of a California in which hardworking citizens ended up supporting an idle class that lived on state-issued scrip. The series argued that if the proposition passed it was "going to be very, very juicy" for its organizers. It spotlighted the provision in the proposed constitutional amendment that required the governor to appoint a well-paid administrator from a list of three Ham and Eggs organizers. This administrator was empowered to recruit agents who received a commission of ten cents a head per week for each retired person who signed up and a 2 percent commission on stamps sold. The *Times* calculated that if there were a million participants it would amount to "$100,000 a week [more than $1,800,000 in 2019] for the administrator's palsy-walsy agents PLUS 2 percent of stamp sales" that would total about $60,000 a week. The newspaper pointed out that public employees would be the "goats" of the proposed amendment because they would be required to accept half of their pay in warrants. State and local government would suffer because the law specified that the scrip could be used to pay taxes. The *Times* envisioned businesses and wealthy individuals hoarding scrip so that they could pay taxes in depreciated paper.[25]

Other newspapers joined the chorus against the plan. The *Los Angeles Examiner* declared the measure impractical and probably unconstitutional. The *Inglewood News* pointed out that the owner of a typical home in Inglewood paid property taxes of $122.14 a year. "It would take the taxes of thirteen such homes to pay one pensioner $30 every Thursday." Opposition to the proposition extended beyond the business community and its allies. Los Angeles city attorney Ray L. Chesebro advised the city treasurer to refuse to accept warrants until the courts ruled on their legality. President Roosevelt, in an unsuccessful attempt to support his ally Senator McAdoo in his run for the Democratic senatorial nomination, announced his opposition to Ham and Eggs, as did Henry Morgenthau, the secretary of the treasury. The official position of the federal government was that Ham and Eggs was unconstitutional because

Article I, Section 10, of the Constitution gives Congress the exclusive right to "coin money." All banks in California under federal supervision were therefore forbidden to accept warrants.[26]

Ham and Eggs was an easy target for lampoons. "If We Had Some Ham, We Could Have Ham and Eggs, If We Had Some Eggs," proclaimed a headline in the *Los Angeles Daily Journal*. Upton Sinclair, in an article in *Liberty* magazine, wrote that if slightly more than 800,000 people qualified for the warrants it would be necessary to issue well over a billion each year along with an estimated 65,788,320,000 two-cent stamps. "I don't know how it strikes you, but to me the most horrifying feature of this plan is that it will require the people of California to lick sixty-five billion stamps in the course of a year, close to 200 million stamps every day, eight million per hour." James Frisbie, of El Monte, announced his own plan. "Forty dollars every Friday for fatties under Forty." No one "has yet conceived of revenue for the weekly payments," but he hoped that someone "would think of something soon. Bob Schiller and Bill Brown, two students at UCLA, announced the "Fifty dollars every Friday for folks under Fifty" plan. The students maintained that "life begins at zero" and that younger people had more opportunities to spend money than older people. Bob and Bill explained that their proposal "will give, to those under fifty, something to do while waiting to become fifty years of age. It might be called a dress rehearsal." Under their plan, the warrants would take the form of milk bottle caps. Each time a bearer used a warrant, he or she would pay a penny to the receiver, who punched a hole in it. After it was used one hundred times, there would no longer be room for any more holes, thus making the warrants "self-liquidating."[27]

Ham and Eggs organizers cautioned their supporters to ignore the campaign against the movement. "False pictures of the distress to be wreaked on California businessmen are painted by shrewd publicity agents and fast-talking sales experts, in order to secure donations to fight the people's pension movement around the Retirement Life Payments Act." The Retirement Life Payments official newspaper, *Ham and Eggs for Californians*, claimed that in Los Angeles County 26,534 merchants placed signs in their windows indicating that they would accept California Life Payments. In the working-class neighborhood of East Los Angeles, thirty-eight merchants declared their support. Many of these businesses may have done so out of fear that Ham and Eggs supporters would boycott them. Merchants in poorer neighborhoods may well have concluded that scrip was better than nothing. Engineer-economist Owens brushed aside the *Times* assertion that the bankers had dealt their movement a death blow. He announced that, if the banks failed to take "advantage of the opportunity facing them ... plans for establishment of a vast network of fiscal agencies to handle Ham and Eggs warrants throughout California" were being finalized.[28]

As election day approached, the prospects for Proposition 25 looked good. It is possible that Lawrence and Willis Allen were actually not eager to see their measure become law. If it did, the flow of money into headquarters would stop. The historian Jackson K. Putnam believed that this was the only explanation for the brothers' erratic behavior during the campaign. At the California Democratic convention, Willis asked party leaders to drop the question of endorsing Ham and Eggs. For a time the brothers considered backing Merriam for governor, even though he opposed Proposition 25. Bainbridge urged the two men to increase campaign spending, but they held back, claiming that they were saving cash for postelection activities.[29]

Proposition 25 went down in defeat, 1,398,999 to 1,143,670. This was a relief to business interests—and possibly to the Allen brothers as well. They immediately began raising money for another campaign. Less than a week after the election, the brothers held a rally at Shrine Auditorium where eight thousand supporters contributed $1,700 (about $30,000 in 2019) to continue the struggle for the pension movement. The new strategy was not to wait until the 1940 election to put another proposition on the ballot but to demand that the newly elected Governor Culbert Olson call a special election as soon as possible. The brothers feared that the longer the wait, the greater the risk that enthusiasm for the movement would decline.

One reason for the urgency may have been the unwelcome publicity that piled up during the early months of 1939. From his cell, Earle Kynette brought a lawsuit against the brothers charging that they promised him a third of the revenues from the pension plan in exchange for a loan of $130 and police protection from Noble and his followers. During these proceedings, the Allens were forced to reveal, contrary to previous statements that they received salaries of no more than $30 a month, that they actually collected $7,000 a year each (about $128,000 in 2019). Public admissions such as this embarrassed Bainbridge, who came to feel that the brothers were a liability to the movement. He demanded that they give up their interest in the Cinema Advertising Company. When they refused, he resigned. Carl Kegley, the attorney for Ham and Eggs, also left when Lawrence and Willis ignored his demand that they resign from the board of directors because they had "become a burden to the pension movement." Owens, apparently not willing to give up the generous compensation for his role as engineer-economist, did not follow his friend Bainbridge out of Ham and Eggs.[30]

In April four women, former employees, filed a complaint with the California Department of Industrial Relations claiming that the brothers owned them $899 in unpaid wages. They said that they were paid an average of only a dollar a day. An affidavit, filed in support of their claim by a man named Foghorn Murphy, asked Willis why he paid the women so little. "Well, Murph," he reportedly said, "what's stopping the good-looking gals from getting a good 'John' on the side?'" The women offered up some interesting information about the Allens: they pocketed about $100,000 in Ham and Egg funds, paid Kynette to stinkbomb Noble's meetings, and formed alliances with local communists, fascists, and Japanese nationals. At the end of April, the Internal Revenue Service placed a lien of $7,629.04 against Ham and Eggs for failure to pay Social Security payroll taxes.[31]

Meanwhile, Noble had not gone away. An expert at creating publicity, he looked for ways to keep himself in the news. In December he picked up a traffic sign and smashed two windows of Dalton Auto Loan on Wilshire Boulevard. He told reporters that he was angry because the company, which owned KMTR radio, had canceled his contract. After a trial attended by some two hundred of his supporters, a judge sentenced him to ten days in jail. A photograph in the *Times* shows the pension reformer passionately kissing his wife as he is led off to his cell. In fact, his sentence was not to begin for another five days. Before serving his time, Noble attended newly elected Governor Olson's inauguration in Sacramento. While his supporters demonstrated outside the capitol building, Noble got a seat in the balcony in the assembly chamber. When the ceremony began, Noble shouted, "I demand to be heard!" As the audience turned their heads toward the noise, they caught a glimpse of capitol police hustling Noble out of the chamber.[32]

By May 1939, Retirement Life Payments had gathered over 500,000 signatures asking Governor Olson to call a special election. It organized a march of thousands of supporters to carry an additional 590,580 petitions to the state capital. The largest contingent, about 30,000, was from Los Angeles County. That evening Olson met the Ham and Eggs demonstrators at the state fairgrounds, where he announced that he would call a special election but refused to set a date. Olson also said for the first time that he did not consider Ham and Eggs a workable plan. A few weeks later the governor set November 7 for the special election. This displeased the Allen brothers, who wanted an immediate vote. "I feel glad, I feel sad, and I certainly feel mad," Willis said over the radio. For the next few months the brothers faced the task of maintaining their followers' enthusiasm.[33]

The second Ham and Eggs initiative appeared on the ballot as Proposition 1. Engineer-economist Owens was its author. The new measure differed in significant ways from the first. In addition to writing the 3 percent sales tax into the constitution, it added a 3 percent tax on the gross revenues of a company—similar to a sales tax but levied on the seller of the goods rather than the purchasers. Stamped scrip was exempt from the tax. The list from which the governor was required to choose the administrator was shortened to two—Owens and Will Kindig, a former Los Angeles city councilman. The administrator had extraordinary powers, including the right to call special elections in which the voters could decide by initiative referendum changes to the Life Payments law. The administrator was also to head a new banking system. "We are setting up a new banking structure in this country, and the J. P. Morgans are shuddering in their boots this afternoon," Owens said.[34]

California Citizens Against 30 Thursday (with Northern and Southern California branches) orchestrated the campaign against Proposition 1. Between August and November the group spent $306,655.68 (over $5,500,000 in 2019). On radio stations they made 1,877 spot announcements, 1,170 fifteen-minute news broadcasts, 335 fifteen-minute speech broadcasts on local stations, and fifty-one statewide. The organization placed 777 advertisements in metropolitan and weekly newspapers. Two hundred fifty-two paid speakers addressed 2,564 anti–Ham and Eggs meetings. Salaried workers were in charge of each of the Los Angeles City Council districts, and outside the city there were headquarters in every town. By the end of the campaign, California Citizens Against 30 Thursday had seven thousand volunteers and one thousand paid workers in Los Angeles County.[35]

The Allens countered with regular radio appearances. Charles F. Wright, the author of a Ham and Eggs opposition manual, warned his readers that Lawrence Allen had a "sweetly pious quality in his voice that literally wrings a shower of copper, silver and greenbacks from the trembling hands of the aged, Yea, verily, Brother Allen has a way with the elderly, especially the elderly women." On the fourth of July, Ham and Eggs held a large rally in Zoo Park in Los Angeles. Lawrence Allen said that it was the largest "that any organization has ever held in this state at any time." At the end of August, Lawrence announced the creation of the Honor Medal Award, a bronze medal that would go to every member who recruited five new members or obtained five new subscriptions to *National Ham and Eggs*. Engraved on the medal were the words "Honor Medal Award for Special Campaign Service." "There, fellow members," Lawrence announced, "is a history making medal that will be renowned around the world." In Southern California, Ham and Eggs sponsored a touring three-ring big top circus. The brothers sweetened their plan to make it more appealing. They said that it would be possible for recipients to cash in their warrants for U.S. dollars after only thirty days and with only five stamps attached. Critics immediately blasted the idea as economically impossible.[36]

California Citizens Against 30 Thursday hired political consultant Clem Whitaker to poll potential voters on whether or not they approved of Ham and Eggs. At the end of July, Whitaker mailed out 100,000 postcards to Southern California counties asking voters if they supported the plan. In Los Angeles County, 55 percent of those who responded supported the proposition. In September and October, Whitaker conducted door-to-door interviews of over four thousand potential Ham and Eggs voters in the ten counties of Southern California. The first survey was during the week of September 17, the second October 14–18. The surveys showed that support for Ham and Eggs declined as election day approached. In September, 47 percent of those interviewed were against Ham and

Eggs and 33 percent supported it; 14 percent were undecided. A month later, the percentage against the proposition had increased to 56.8 and the percentage supporting it fell to 27.8.[37]

Whitaker's survey makes it clear that there was a class divide between the supporters and opponents of Ham and Eggs. He sorted those interviewed into four income classes: upper class, upper middle class, lower middle class, and lower class. Within Los Angeles city, 50.7 percent of those in the lowest income class supported Ham and Eggs. The surveys showed that the highest income group opposed the proposition by 83.6 percent. A majority of the lowest economic class supported the measure: 50.7 percent in September and 46.3 percent in October. The same pattern held in the county outside Los Angeles city limits. In the most affluent areas, in September, only 5 percent of county residents supported the measure, whereas 86.7 percent opposed it.

In October, Whitaker polled potential voters in six districts outside of the city of Los Angeles. The results also show the class nature of the Ham and Eggs vote. The movement's main strength was in the southeast towns—that stretch of land that reached from the southern industrial section of the city of Los Angeles to Long Beach. It included such towns as Maywood, Huntington Park, South Gate, Lynwood, and Compton, whose residents worked in the giant plants of Chrysler, Willy-Overland, General Motors, and Firestone Tire Company. The Depression had hit those who lived in this area hard. Economically sound or not, $30 a week seemed a good idea for people living on the edge.

Those who supported Ham and Eggs gave a variety of reasons for doing so. The largest number felt that the measure would "help old people who need it." A large percentage believed that it might "create jobs for young people." Others said that it was just "worth a try." The majority of those opposed to the plan thought that it was "unsound" and that it would "ruin or bankrupt" the state. A smaller but significant percentage believed that the plan could not work unless it was "national."[38]

On November 8, Proposition 1 went down to defeat by nearly a two-to-one margin. The statewide vote was 1,933,557 to 993,204. In Los Angeles County, voter turnout was unusually high, a remarkable 80 percent of registered voters. The results in the county were equally lopsided against the measure: 790,473 against, 444,751 in favor. Only a handful of Los Angeles County towns voted for it—Baldwin Park, Bell, Hawthorne, and Downey. These were all working-class suburbs.[39]

• • • •

The election was the end of any realistic chance that the voters would approve a Ham and Eggs amendment, but for the Allen brothers defeat was only a pause in the game. Their next move was to launch a recall election against Governor Olson. In radio broadcasts, Roy G. Owens and Lawrence Allen said that we "are never going to have Ham and Eggs in California . . . until we have a Governor in the Governor's seat that is for us." Olson is "as good as out right now." The recall attempt went nowhere. In May 1940 the Allens attempted to place another initiative on the ballot but failed to collect the necessary number of signatures. In December they filed articles of incorporation for a new organization, Pay Roll Guarantee Association. Exactly what the new organization was supposed to do is not clear. Its stated purpose was to "initiate a study of and develop an interest in social, economic and financial questions thereby plans for improvement in our social, financial and economic structure may be formulated, proposed and enacted into law." In March 1941 the Allen brothers came up with a new plan that provided $29 a month in warrants to all citizens who did not have an income of $2,400 a year. In addition, "junior citizens," between the ages of twenty-one to fifty, if not making at least $40 a week could receive seven dollars every Thursday. The measure failed to qualify for the ballot. Willis and Roy Owens tried again with a similar measure in 1946; it also never made it onto the ballot. In January 1948, Willis Allen and Roy Owens received authorization to collect signatures for yet another initiative. This one was called the California Bill of Rights and asked for a monthly pension of $100 a month (to be increased to $130 a month in 1952). It also asked for a bizarre list of other things such as a 2 percent gross tax on all business income, abolition of all other taxes, legalization of gambling, legalization of the sale of colored oleomargarine, and pensions for teachers. The initiative failed to qualify for the ballot. Reluctant to give up on an easy way to make money, in 1949 Willis, Lawrence, and Owens formed the Pension and Taxpayers Union and sought signatures for an initiative called the Pension and Welfare Funding Act. This measure proposed paying for old-age pensions by "licensing, taxing, regulating and rigidly controlling off-track bookmaking and gambling." The initiative created a five-person commission (with salaries set at $10,000 each) that included Allen and Owens, which would regulate the gambling industry. It qualified for the ballot as Proposition 6 in the November 1950 election. In connection with this initiative, Lawrence was accused of selling gambling franchises in exchange for $3,000 contributions to the campaign fund. The initiative went down to defeat by a three-to-one margin.[40]

After a short stay in Washington, D.C., Bainbridge returned to the West Coast, where he became editor of Townsend's newspaper, the *Weekly*. In the 1944 fall elections in California, he directed an initiative campaign for an unsuccessful proposition that Townsend sponsored, called "$60 at 60," that provided for $60 a month for all citizens sixty years or older. In later years he lived in La Crescenta and worked as a freelance writer and advertising executive. He died in 1950.[41]

Robert Noble faded slowly from the pension movement but reemerged as a founder of the Friends of Progress, a pro-fascist group opposed to American participation in World War II. Noble believed that Jews were at the center of a conspiracy to bring the United States into the conflict. "I have quit my Jewish doctor and Jew lawyer, and I now declare myself anti-Semitic," he announced. Only a few days before Pearl Harbor, he helped organize a mock impeachment trial of Franklin Roosevelt. Even after the United States entered the war, Noble continued his opposition. The State of California convicted him of failing to register as a subversive under the state's Subversive Organization Registration Act. A federal jury found him guilty of violating a 1917 sedition law that prohibited disloyal acts or statements during time of war. The court found Noble's assertion that General MacArthur should receive a medal from the Japanese for abandoning his troops in the Philippines especially alarming. A state appeals court reversed the state conviction, but the federal charge stood. In the "Great Sedition Trial of 1944," he was one of thirty-three defendants accused of being propaganda agents of the Nazis. Those proceedings ended in a mistrial, but not before the judge admonished Noble for disrupting the trial with unruly behavior.[42]

CONCLUSION

The Politics of Fear

> The early mass political movements in Southern California, characterized by marked social inventiveness, were healthy manifestations of a people's impulse to do something for themselves.
>
> Carey McWilliams, *Southern California: An Island on the Land*

Writers of all kinds have tried to explain why tens of thousands of Southern Californians in the 1930s became devoted followers of such radical movements as the Utopian Society, Townsend's Old Age Revolving Pension plan, Sinclair's End Poverty in California, and Retirement Life Payments—otherwise known as Ham and Eggs, or $30 Every Thursday. These movements advocated programs that would change the very nature of the capitalist system. Why an aging, churchgoing, largely conservative population of midwestern origins supported these movements left the writers confused and perplexed. They chose to look for explanations not in economic conditions but in the character of the population. They believed that Southern Californians lived empty and unhappy lives devoid of meaning. For these writers, ignorance, naïveté, and greed explained their support for these radical movements.

If Southern Californians really lived empty, aimless lives and had no sense of community, how could the remarkable phenomenon of the self-help cooperatives come about? The sociologist Constantine Panunzio captured the nature of this movement in few words: "A small proportion of the 10,000,000 or more unemployed in the nation shrank from relief and banded themselves together to form loosely constructed organizations, known as self-help cooperatives. These organizations arose simply and spontaneously. Small groups of men and women of comparatively advanced age united under the leadership of an enterprising member, and went about in the cities and the countryside offering to work for food, clothing, shelter, utilities, and other goods, or services." A sense of community and sense of purpose seem minimal qualifications for neighbors coming together spontaneously to help one another. They asked for no government help or guidance. Carey McWilliams pointed out that, by December 1934, Los Angeles County alone had nearly 45 percent of all the self-help cooperatives in the United States. This was no small accomplishment for a region that was supposed to have been mired in aimlessness, emptiness, and lacking a basic sense of community.[1]

The view that Southern Californians of midwestern origins were supposed to be conservative, dull-witted, and incapable of independent thought or action is simply wrong. Any historian should know that there is a danger in making sweeping generalizations about any large population. Although generally churchgoing and conservative, midwesterners have a long history of independent and sometimes radical political action. In Iowa, farmers hit hard by the Great Depression formed the Farmers Holiday Association and demanded relief. In one county, an angry mob dragged a judge from his bench and threatened to hang him if he didn't immediately stop foreclosures. In Minnesota, voters elected Floyd B. Olson governor. Olson openly called himself a radical and talked of taking over factories and putting the unemployed to work. Some midwestern transplants in Southern California were old enough to remember, or even to have participated in, the Populist revolt, the North Dakota Non-Partisan League, or the Green Corn rebellion in Oklahoma. In the early twentieth century, hundreds of communities scattered across the Midwest elected Socialist Party officials to public office. In the 1920s, John Lewis, the former Socialist mayor of Elwood, Indiana, settled in Burbank. Others like him may have chosen to spend their retirement years in Southern California. Los Angeles had its own experience with radicalism in 1910 when unionists bombed the *Los Angeles Times* building and the city nearly elected a Socialist mayor.

The real reason why Southern Californians came out in large numbers for these radical movements can be summarized in a single word: fear. This was not the "nameless, unreasoning, unjustified terror" of Roosevelt's first inaugural address, but, in the words of the *Whittier News*, "a panicky, unreasoning fear that hunger and want are likely to overtake a person in spite of the best he can do."[2] The possibility of homelessness, hunger, and even starvation was all too real for Southern Californians who had no chance of finding work. Few economic safety nets existed. Pensions were rare. The federal social security act did not become law until 1935 and did not begin providing small monthly benefits until 1940. Mutual aid societies provided limited support to those fortunate enough to belong to one. Unemployment compensation did not exist. The elderly, and this included anyone forty years or older and unemployed, depended on savings, help from relatives, or the generosity of their neighbors, churches, and other charitable organizations. Eligibility requirements for county relief were strict and excluded many of those in need or who had not lived in the county or state long enough. A California old-age assistance law passed in 1929 was very restrictive and, in any case, provided paltry benefits. In the winter of 1933–34, the Great Depression was entering its fifth year, and the older unemployed had reached the limit of their resources.

Politicians and county officials were more interested in restricting the number of people receiving relief than in expanding benefits. Both liberal and conservative members of the Los Angeles County board of supervisors advocated the repatriation of foreigners, mostly Mexicans, to lighten the burden. In 1936 police chief James E. Davis assigned LAPD officers to checkpoints on the state's borders to intercept indigents headed for the Los Angeles County welfare paradise.

Rex Thomson, the superintendent of charities for the county of Los Angeles, warned that "Southern California may well become the Poor Farm of the United States." Thomson made applying for relief very difficult. At the beginning of 1937, a committee of the Democratic Central Committee reported that some applicants had to wait in the county welfare offices for an entire day; sometimes they were required to return the next day. Such long waits for older people, some with disabilities, were difficult. Even if their applications were approved, it was not uncommon for six months or a year to elapse before relief payments began. In June 1938, Thomson proudly informed the board of supervisors that "it will be possible on June 30th to return to your Board for disposition many thousands of dollars in unexpended appropriations." This bonanza was possible because $400,000 was not used for aid to aged persons. Thomson offered bureaucratic reasons for this failure: it "was not possible to clear the Aged Aid applications in accordance with the schedule established at the time the budget was adopted due to several factors, one of which was the fact that the Department was not provided sufficient personnel, because of legal technicalities, early enough in the year to facilitate the clearance of the cases within an average of ninety days." County supervisor Ford, for one, was not persuaded. In a note scribbled at the bottom of his copy of Thomson's memo, Ford wrote, "I have long felt that we were 'making' money at the expense of these old people."[3]

Southern Californians did not rush to support novel movements because they were naïve, greedy, or bored with life. Nor is it likely that many of these reputedly dull-witted voters did not understand how unworkable, even dangerous, these plans were. They simply did not care. By voting for them, they had everything to gain and nothing to lose. It "may be a racket," one Ham and Eggs supporter said, "and maybe it won't work for more than a couple of weeks, but that will be $60 more than I ever got before for one vote."[4] If the movements proved a disaster as predicted, the politicians and business interests would sort it out. In the meantime, those desperately in need would get some help. Thousands of Southern Californians rushed to support these movements because there were no alternatives and it was in their interest to do so. In retrospect, it is clear that they were not pursuing utopia, just trying to survive.

NOTES

ABBREVIATIONS

Cleland Papers	Robert G. Cleland Papers, Huntington Library, Art Museum, and Botanical Gardens, San Marino, Calif.
Fifteenth Census	U.S. Census Bureau, *Fifteenth Census of the United States*, 1930, Microfilm Roll M1932, Record Group 41, National Archives and Records Administration
Ford Papers	John Anson Ford Papers, Huntington Library, Art Museum, and Botanical Gardens, San Marino, Calif.
Kelley Collection	John R. Kelley Collection, UCLA Special Collections, University of California, Los Angeles
LACC Archive	Los Angeles Area Chamber of Commerce Archive, Regional History Center, University of Southern California, Los Angeles
Sinclair Papers	Upton Sinclair Papers, Lilly Library, Indiana University, Bloomington
Social Welfare Archives	California Social Welfare Archives, Special Collections, USC Libraries, University of Southern California, Los Angeles

INTRODUCTION

1. Carey McWilliams, *Southern California: An Island on the Land.* (Santa Barbara, Calif.: Peregrine Smith, 1973), 273–74; Carey McWilliams, *The Education of Carey McWilliams* (New York: Simon and Schuster, 1978), 67.

2. H. L. Mencken, "Sister Aimée," in *Writing Los Angeles: A Literary Anthology,* ed. David L. Ulin (New York: Library of America, 2002), 65; Edmund Wilson, "The City of Our Lady the Queen of the Angels," in Ulin, *Writing Los Angeles,* 92.

3. Morrow Mayo, *Los Angeles* (New York: A. A. Knopf, 1933), 270.

4. Nathanael West, *The Day of the Locust* (New York: Penguin Books, 1983), 192–93.

5. Arthur M. Schlesinger Jr., *The Age of Roosevelt: The Politics of Upheaval* (Boston: Houghton Mifflin, 1960), 110.

6. David M. Kennedy, *Freedom from Fear: The American People in Depression and War, 1929–1945* (New York: Oxford University Press, 1999), 225.

7. Jackson K. Putnam, *Old Age Politics in California: From Richardson to Reagan* (Stanford, Calif.: Stanford University Press, 1970), 32–33.

8. Robert M. Fogelson, *The Fragmented Metropolis: Los Angeles, 1850–1930* (Cambridge, Mass.: Harvard University Press, 1967), 194, 197.

9. McWilliams, *Southern California,* 294; Leonard Leader, *Los Angeles and the Great Depression* (New York: Garland, 1991), 112–13, 159.

10. *Fifteenth Census,* Population, Vol. 2, 160; McWilliams, *Southern California,* 167; Buford E. Pierce, comp., *Illustrated Annual of the Federation of State Societies, 1914,* Federation of State Societies of Southern California (Los Angeles: Kruckeberg Press, [1914]), 29.

11. Willard Huntington Wright, "Los Angeles—the Chemically Pure," in Burton Rascoe and Groff Conklin, eds., *The Smart Set Anthology* (New York: Reynal and Hitchcock, 1934), 90.

12. Freeman Tilden, "Los Angeles: The Tenth Tourist Never Goes Home," World's Work 60 (Sept. 1931): 56; *Fifteenth Census,* Population, Vol. 3, Part 1, 243, 248–50, 279, 609, 671, 1131.

13. Tilden, "Los Angeles," 243, 245, 248–49, 621.

14. *National Vital Statistics Reports,* Vol. 66, No. 4, 3, 46, www.cdc.gov/nchs/data/nvsr/nvsr66/nvsr66_04.pdf; *Fifteenth Census,* Population, Vol. 3, Part 1, 243, 248.

CHAPTER 1

1. Louis Adamic, *Laughing in the Jungle* (New York: Harper and Brothers, 1932), 15–16, 194–204.

2. Adamic, *Laughing,* 206; Louis Adamic, *The Truth about Los Angeles* (Girard, Kan.: Haldeman-Julius, [c 1927]), 17–18.

3. *Los Angeles Times,* May 26, 1929.

4. *Upton Sinclair's EPIC News*, Oct. 8, 1934.

5. *Los Angeles Times*, May 26, 1929, Feb. 28, 1932.

6. Stanley Rogers, "Attempted Recall of the Mayor of Los Angeles," *National Municipal Review* 21 (Jun. 1932), 416; Mark S. Still, "'Fighting Bob' Shuler: Fundamentalist and Reformer" (Ph.D. dissertation, Claremont Graduate School, 1988), 147; John Bentzien, "James Whitcomb Brougher, D.D.," sdrc.lib.uiowa.edu/traveling-culture/chau1/pdf/Brougher/1/brochure.pdf; "Presbyterians' Moderator," *Time Magazine*, Jun. 2, 1941 [page unk].

7. Still, "'Fighting Bob' Shuler," 27–28, 37–42, 139, 141–43, 158, 248–51.

8. Edmund Wilson, "The City of Our Lady the Queen of the Angels," in Ulin, *Writing Los Angeles*, 95; Still, "'Fighting Bob' Shuler," 154–55, 172–73.

9. Matthew Avery Sutton, *Aimee Semple McPherson and the Resurrection of Christian America* (Cambridge, Mass.: Harvard University Press, 2007), 21.

10. Sutton, *Aimee Semple McPherson*, 32, 44–45, 49, 79–80.

11. Sutton, *Aimee Semple McPherson*, 36.

12. In the 1930 census only, there was a separate race category for Mexican. *Historical Census Statistics on Population Totals by Race, 1790 to 1990, and by Hispanic Origin, 1970 to 1990, for Large Cities and other Urban Places in the United States, Fifteenth Census*, Population, Color or Race, Nativity, and Parentage, Vol. 2, 69.

13. Walter Nugent, *Into the West: The Story of Its People* (New York: Vintage Books, 2001), 218, 220; Fogelson, *Fragmented Metropolis*, 78–79; *Fifteenth Census*, Population, Vol. 1, Number and Distribution of Inhabitants, 128–29, 134, 196.

14. Becky M. Nicolaides, *My Blue Heaven: Life and Politics in the Working-Class Suburbs of Los Angeles, 1920–1965* (Chicago: University of Chicago Press, 2002), 11–13.

15. James C. Findley, "The Economic Boom of the Twenties in Los Angeles" (Ph.D. dissertation, Claremont Graduate School, 1958), 175; Dennis McDougal, *Privileged Son: Otis Chandler and the Rise and Fall of the L.A. Times Dynasty* (Cambridge, Mass.: Perseus, 2001), 98.

16. W. W. Robinson, "The Southern California Real Estate Boom of the Twenties," *Southern California Quarterly* 24 (Mar. 1942): 27; James Thomas Keane, *Fritz B. Burns and the Development of Los Angeles: The Biography of a Community Developer and Philanthropist* (Los Angeles: Loyola Marymount University and the Historical Society of Southern California, 2001), 41–43; "Summary of Building Restrictions" for Windsor Hills, Fritz Burns Papers, CSLA-2, series 3, box 10v, Department of Archives and Special Collections, Loyola Marymount University, Los Angeles.

17. Findley, "Economic Boom," 342; Jules Tygiel, *The Great Los Angeles Swindle: Oil, Stocks, and Scandal during the Roaring Twenties* (Berkeley: University of California Press, 1994), 14, 21, 25–27.

18. Tygiel, *Great Los Angeles Swindle*, 30; Findley, "Economic Boom," 119, 351; Sarah S. Elkind, "Oil in the City: The Fall and Rise of Oil Drilling in Los Angeles," *Journal of American History* 99 (Jun. 2012): 82–90.

19. Tygiel, *Great Los Angeles Swindle*, 37, 40.

20. Tygiel, *Great Los Angeles Swindle*, 39, 60–61, 121–22.

21. Findley, "Economic Boom," 248–49, 255; Greg Hise, "Industry and Imaginative Geographies," in *Metropolis in the Making: Los Angeles in the 1920s*, ed. Tom Sitton and William Deverell (Berkeley: University of California Press, 2001), 19.

22. Findley, "Economic Boom," 262, 264–65, 275–76, 259.

23. Robert Moats Miller, *Bishop G. Bromley Oxnam: Paladin of Liberal Protestantism* (Nashville, Tenn.: Abingdon Press, 1990), 34.

24. Miller, *Bishop G. Bromley Oxnam*, 91.

25. Miller, *Bishop G. Bromley Oxnam*, 25–91.

26. John Kenneth Galbraith, *The Great Crash, 1929* (Boston: Houghton Mifflin, 1954), 8.

CHAPTER 2

1. *Los Angeles Times*, Oct. 22, 1929, Jan. 5, 1931.

2. *Los Angeles Times*, Oct. 25, 1929.

3. Robert C. McElvaine, *The Great Depression: America, 1929–1941* (New York: Random House, 1984), 47; *Los Angeles Times*, Oct. 25, 1929.

4. *Los Angeles Times*, Jun. 12, 1928.

5. McElvaine, *Great Depression*, 48; *Los Angeles Times*, Oct. 30, 1929.

6. *Los Angeles Times*, Oct. 31, 1929.

7. McElvaine, *Great Depression*, 48, 66; William H. Mullins, *The Depression and the Urban West Coast, 1929–1933: Los Angeles, San Francisco, Seattle, and Portland* (Bloomington: Indiana University Press, 1991), 14; Broadus Mitchell, *The Depression Decade from New Era through New Deal, 1929–1941* (New York: Rinehart, 1947), 85; *Los Angeles Times*, Nov. 28, 1929.

8. Community Welfare Federation, Social Welfare Committee minutes, Jan. 9, 1930, box 1, folder 4.3, 2, folder 5.1–5.2, Council of Social Agencies of Los Angeles Records, Collection no. 0480, Social Welfare Archives; Leonard Leader, *Los Angeles and the Great Depression* (New York: Garland, 1991), 3–4.

9. *Los Angeles Times*, Jan. 7, 1930; *St. Petersburg Evening Independent*, Jun. 27, 1928; "R. M. Schindler: 1925 James Eads How House," *Michael LaFetra*, Nov. 4, 2012, http://michaellafetra.com/schindler-2422-silver-ridge-ave-neutra-designed garden.

10. *Los Angeles Times*, Jan. 7, 18, 23, 28, 30, Feb. 4, Mar. 6, 1930.

11. *Los Angeles Times*, Apr. 28, Jun. 27, 1930.

12. *Los Angeles Times*, Jun. 25, 27, 1930.

13. *Los Angeles Times*, Jun. 27, 1930; *Fifteenth Census*, Unemployment, Vol. 1, 142; Mitchell, *Depression Decade*, 91–92.

14. *Los Angeles Times*, Jan. 25, 1931; *Fifteenth Census* Unemployment, Vol. 2, General Report, Chapter 5, the Special Census of Unemployment, Jan. 1931, 365, 373.

15. Citizens Committee on Coordination of Unemployment Relief, Speakers Bureau, n.p., n.d., Council of Social Agencies of Los Angeles Records, Collection no. 0480, Social Welfare Archives.

16. *Los Angeles Record*, Mar. 14, 1930.

17. *Los Angeles Record*, Mar. 30, 1931.

18. Outline of History of Development of Social Welfare, box 5, folder 6.11 and 6.13, Council of Social Agencies of Los Angeles Records, Collection no. 0480, Social Welfare Archives; Putnam, *Old Age Politics*, 22-23.

19. Richard David Lester, "Building the New Deal State on the Local Level: Unemployment Relief in Los Angeles County during the 1930s" (Ph.D. dissertation, University of California, Los Angeles, 2001), 50-53; *Los Angeles Times*, Feb. 2, 1931; Mullins, *Depression and the Urban West Coast*, 70.

20. Council of Social Agencies, Executive Committee minutes, Oct. 2, 1930; and Council of Social Agencies, Executive Committee minutes, extract from the speech of Mr. C. A. Lyman, Jan. 22, 1931, box 1, folder 6.5, p. 1, Council of Social Agencies of Los Angeles Records, Collection no. 0480, Social Welfare Archives.

21. Council of Social Agencies Executive Committee, Extract from Speech of Mr. C. A. Lyman, Jan. 22, 1931, box 1, folder 6.6, p. 2; and Outline of History of Development of Social Welfare and Related Events in Los Angeles Until the Organization of the Community Chest, 1850-1925, box 5, folder 6.17, p. 17, Council of Social Agencies of Los Angeles Records, Collection no. 0480, Social Welfare Archives.

22. *Los Angeles Times*, Oct. 7, 1930.

23. *Los Angeles Times*, Oct. 7, 1934.

CHAPTER 3

1. John Robertson Quinn, "Memoirs of John Robertson Quinn" (University of California, Los Angeles, Oral History Program, 1966), 90. Thanks to Tom Sitton for this quote. The voters elected Shaw mayor in 1933, but his political career ended abruptly in 1938 when in a special election the voters recalled him from office.

2. *Los Angeles Times*, Nov. 18, 19, 20, Dec. 3, 1930, Jan. 1, 31, 1932.

3. *Los Angeles Times*, Nov. 18, Dec. 5, 1930; Lester, "Building the New Deal State," 59-60.

4. *Los Angeles Times*, Jan. 9, Feb. 5, 24, Mar. 13, Apr. 15, Jun. 16, Oct. 10, 1931.

5. *Los Angeles Times*, Nov. 25, 27, Dec. 5, 6, 1930, Jan. 7, 28, 1931; Mullins, *Depression and the Urban West Coast*, 66; Leader, *Los Angeles*, 52-55.

6. Irving Bernstein, *The Lean Years: A History of the American Worker, 1920–1933* (Boston: Houghton Mifflin, 1960), 294; *Los Angeles Times*, Feb. 2, 4, 11, 20, Mar. 12, 28, Apr. 16, 1931.

7. *Los Angeles Times*, Feb. 5, 10, 11, Mar. 1, 14, Apr. 5, 1931; Leader, Los Angeles, 59–60.

8. Leader, *Los Angeles*, 61–63; Mullins, *Depression and the Urban West Coast*, 63–66.

9. *Los Angeles Times*, Dec. 15, 1930, Apr. 7, May 5, 1931.

10. *Los Angeles Times*, Feb. 13, Apr. 23, May 23, 1931; Mullins, *Depression and the Urban West Coast*, 67.

11. *Los Angeles Times*, Apr. 15, 1931.

12. *Los Angeles Times*, May 28, Jun. 4, 1931.

13. *Los Angeles Times*, Jun. 5, 14, 1931; Mullins, *Depression and the Urban West Coast*, 67; Lester, "Building the New Deal State," 69.

14. *Los Angeles Times*, Oct. 21, 1931; William R. Harriman, Superintendent of Charities, to Board of Supervisors, Aug. 7, 1933, box 64/B III 14 c bb aaa (1), Ford Papers.

15. "Report on the Expenditures of the County Welfare Department for Public Relief, August 17, 1931," box 63/B III 14, Ford Papers. The four members of the committee were Elmer Nelson, Hazel Henderson, Watson H. Watters, and George A. Green; Lester, "Building the New Deal State," 69–70.

16. "Report on the Expenditures," Ford Papers.

17. "Report on the Expenditures," Ford Papers; *Los Angeles Times*, Aug. 18, 1931.

18. California State Relief Administration, Division of Special Surveys and Studies, *Transients in California* (San Francisco, 1936), 4, 7; Council of Social Agencies, Executive Committee Minutes, Oct. 2, 1930, box 1, folder 3.5, p. 3, Council of Social Agencies of Los Angeles Records, Collection no. 0480, Social Welfare Archives.

19. *Los Angeles Times*, Aug. 25, 1931.

20. *Los Angeles Times*, Mar. 10, Oct. 7, Nov. 1, 1931.

21. Abraham Hoffman, *Unwanted Mexican Americans in the Great Depression: Repatriation Pressures, 1929–1939* (Tucson: University of Arizona Press, 1977), 39–66.

22. *Los Angeles Times*, Jan. 26, 1931. Hoffman reproduces the text of Visel's release in Hoffman, *Unwanted Mexican Americans*, 170–71.

23. Quoted in Hoffman, *Unwanted Mexican Americans*, 47.

24. *Los Angeles Times*, Feb. 15, 1931; Venegas Family Papers, Feb. 17, 1931, LMU, box 1, folder 5, collection 099, Department of Archives and Special Collections, Loyola Marymount University, Los Angeles.

25. Hoffman, *Unwanted Mexican Americans*, 59–64.

26. Hoffman, *Unwanted Mexican Americans*, 65.

27. Hoffman, *Unwanted Mexican Americans*, 88.

28. Hoffman, *Unwanted Mexican Americans*, 95.

29. Earl E. Jensen, Superintendent of Charities, to Board of Supervisors, Feb. 15, 1934, box 75/B IV 5 idd (2), Ford Papers.

30. John Anson Ford to Wayne R. Allen, Nov. 21, 1941; John Anson Ford (by Edward Stickney, Field Secretary) to Culbert L. Olson, Dec. 31, 1941; and John Anson Ford to Culbert L. Olson, Mar. 31, 1942, box 75/B IV 5 I dd (7–8), Ford Papers.

31. Clark Kerr, "Productive Enterprises of the Unemployed, 1931–1938" (Ph.D. dissertation, University of California, Berkeley, 1938), 86–87.

32. Lester, "Building the New Deal State," 71–72; *Los Angeles Times*, Apr. 26, 1932.

CHAPTER 4

1. Fifteenth Census, *Population*, Vol. 1, 134; Emily E. Straus, *Death of a Suburban Dream: Race and Schools in Compton, California* (Philadelphia: University of Pennsylvania Press, 2014), 26–30.

2. Kerr, "Productive Enterprises," 83–84, 99.

3. Kerr, "Productive Enterprises," 86–87, 92–93, 102, 104.

4. Constantine Panunzio, *Self-Help Cooperatives in Los Angeles* (Berkeley: University of California Press, 1939), 7–8, 11.

5. Panunzio, *Self-Help Cooperatives*, 14.

6. Panunzio, *Self-Help Cooperatives*, 16–17, 25; Kerr, "Productive Enterprises," 95–96; Winslow Carlton, "Semi-Annual Report Self Help Cooperative Service Emergency Relief Administration, State of California, Dec. 31, 1934," Workman Family Papers, CSLA-9, Series 2, box 4, folder 7, 19, Loyola Marymount University Library, Los Angeles.

7. Kerr, "Productive Enterprises," 85, 93, 99–100.

8. Kerr, "Productive Enterprises," 95.

9. Kerr, "Productive Enterprises," 94; United States Bureau of Labor Statistics, "Cooperative Self-Help Activities among the Unemployed," *Monthly Labor Review* 36 (May 1933): 723–25.

10. Kerr, "Productive Enterprises," 192, 198, 200–202.

11. *Los Angeles Times*, Sept. 25, 1932.

12. Kerr, "Productive Enterprises," 97–99, 177–76; *Los Angeles Times*, Nov. 17, 1932.

13. Kerr, "Productive Enterprises," 114, 119, 123; Clark Kerr and Paul S. Taylor, "The Self-Help Cooperatives in California," in *Essays in Social Economics in Honor of Jessica Blanche Peixotto*, ed. E. T. Grether (Berkeley: University of California Press, 1935), 196.

14. Carlton, "Semi-Annual Report," 7; Kerr, "Productive Enterprises," 104, 107; Panunzio, *Self-Help Cooperatives*, 11.

15. Kerr, "Productive Enterprises," 107.

16. Kerr, "Productive Enterprises," 108, 145.

17. Kerr, "Productive Enterprises," 106, 141–43.

18. Kerr, "Productive Enterprises," 93, 144.

19. Kerr, "Productive Enterprises," 126–27, 144; *Los Angeles Times*, Dec. 22, 1932.

20. Kerr, "Productive Enterprises," 157–61, 170.

21. Kerr, "Productive Enterprises," 212.

22. Kerr, "Productive Enterprises," 206–11, 229, 238.

23. Kerr, "Productive Enterprises," 213, 236.

24. Kerr, "Productive Enterprises," 247–51.

25. Carlton, "Semi-Annual Report," 27.

26. Tom Sitton, *The Courthouse Crowd: Los Angeles County and Its Government, 1850–1950* (Los Angeles: Historical Society of Southern California, 2013), 214; Telegram, Ford to Robert A. Ridell, Vice Chairman Young Democratic Club, Los Angeles, Jan. 8, 1936, box 46/B III 11 e aa (3), Ford Papers.

27. *Illustrated Daily News*, Dec. 18, 1934; *Upton Sinclair's EPIC News*, Dec. 24, 1934, Feb. 25, 1935; *United Progressive News*, Jun. 28, Aug. 9, 1935; Weekly newsletter, Jun. 25 1935; box 52/B III 12 d cc; Oct. 27, 1936, box 52/B III 12 ddd; Weekly newsletter, Jan. 14, 1936, May 4, 1936, box 52/B III 12 ddd; and Rex Thomson to Ford, Oct. 25, 1938, box 64/B III 14 c bb aaa (6), Ford Papers.

28. Carlton, "Semi-Annual Report," 10.

29. Kerr, "Productive Enterprises," 269, 272, 275, 279.

30. Kerr, "Productive Enterprises," 398–403, 412–13, 433.

31. Kerr, "Productive Enterprises," 380.

32. Carlton, "Semi-Annual Report," 31–32, 38; Kerr, "Productive Enterprises," 394–95, 428–48.

33. Kerr, "Productive Enterprises," 485–88.

34. Frank T. McLaughlin and C. I. Schottland, "Self-Help Cooperatives," Oct. 10, 1935, Workman Family Papers, SLA-9, Series 2, box 6, folder 4, Loyola Marymount University, Los Angeles.

35. Kerr, "Productive Enterprises," 499–502, 509–10.

36. Kerr, "Productive Enterprises," 502, 519, 526, 530, 559.

37. Kerr, "Productive Enterprises," 565, 575.

38. *Los Angeles Times*, Jul. 1, 1934, Jan. 3, 1940, Feb. 26, 1941.

39. *Los Angeles Times*, Jul. 16, Oct. 14, 1941.

CHAPTER 5

1. *Los Angeles Times*, Oct. 2, 1929.

2. Steno Reports, box 20, Jun. 29, 1933, 9–10, LACC Archive.

3. United States, Commission on Industrial Relations, *Final Report and Testimony Submitted to Congress by the Commission on Industrial Relations Created by the Act of August 23, 1912*, Vol. 6 (Washington, D.C.: U.S. Government Printing Office, 1916), 5501.

4. Errol Wayne Stevens, *Radical L.A.: From Coxey's Army to the Watts Riots, 1894–1965* (Norman: University of Oklahoma Press, 2009), xvi.

5. Dennis McDougal, *Privileged Son: Otis Chandler and the Rise and Fall of the L.A. Times Dynasty* (Cambridge, Mass.: Perseus, 2001), 45; Robert Gottlieb and Irene Wolt, *Thinking Big: The Story of the Los Angeles Times, Its Publishers, and Their Influence on Southern California* (New York: Putnam, 1977), 18–23.

6. Grace Heilman Stimson, *Rise of the Labor Movement in Los Angeles* (Berkeley: University of California Press, 1955), 104.

7. United States, Commission on Industrial Relations, *Final Report*, 5489.

8. Stimson, *Rise of the Labor Movement*, 366; *Los Angeles Times*, Oct. 1, 1929.

9. *Los Angeles Times*, Oct. 1, 1929. The series ran Oct. 1–Nov. 2, 1929.

10. *Los Angeles Times*, Nov. 2, 1929.

11. *Los Angeles Times*, Aug. 2, 1917; Letter, Otis to Dear Daughter, Dec. 2, 1898, copy in the Otis Collection, Seaver Center for Western History Research, Natural History Museum of Los Angeles County; Gottlieb and Wolt, *Thinking Big*, 21; William G. Bonelli, *Billion Dollar Blackjack* (Beverly Hills, Calif.: Civic Research Press, 1954), 32.

12. Gottlieb and Wolt, *Thinking Big*, 121–26; McDougal, *Privileged Son*, 20–34.

13. Gottlieb and Wolt, *Thinking Big*, 86, 89–90, 151.

14. *Annual Report of Officers and Membership List of The Merchants and Manufacturers Association of Los Angeles, California, 1908–1909* (Los Angeles: author, 1909).

15. Marco R. Newmark, "A Short History of the Los Angeles Chamber of Commerce," *Southern California Quarterly* 27 (Jun.–Sept. 1945): 56–79; Tom Zimmerman, "Paradise Promoted: Boosterism and the Los Angeles Chamber of Commerce," *California History* 64 (Winter 1985): 22–33.

16. Newmark, "Short History," 73; Steno report, box 20, Feb. 23, 1933, 3, LACC Archive.

17. Stevens, *Radical L.A.*, 183–84; Steno reports, box 2, Jun. 7, 1934, 1, box 20, Jun. 7, 1934, 8, LACC Archive.

18. McDougal, *Privileged Son*, 115; *Los Angeles Times*, Mar. 11, 12, 1930; *Los Angeles Record*, Mar. 10, 1930. Haldeman was the grandfather of President Nixon's chief of staff, H. R. Haldeman. U.S. Congress, *Investigation of Communist Propaganda, Hearings Before a Special Committee to Investigate Communist Activities in the United States of the House of Representatives, Seventy-first Congress, Second Session*, Part 5, Vol. 3 (Washington, D.C.: U.S. Government Printing Office, 1930–31), 2, 11, 79; Better America Federation of California, "A Brief Outline of Arguments against the Programme for Industrial Reforms Which Is Being Submitted to Various Social and Industrial Organizations" (Los Angeles: Better America Federation of California, 1920); Edward Layton, "The Better America Federation: A Case Study of Superpatriotism," *Pacific Historical Review* 30 (May 1961): 137–47.

19. Mitchell, *Depression Decade*, 82–85.

20. *Los Angeles Times*, Nov. 19, 20, 1930.

21. Board of Directors meeting, box 19, Nov. 20, 1930, Jan. 28, 1932, Mar. 10, 1932, 15, Jun. 2, 1932, 11, box 19, LACC Archive.

22. *Los Angeles Times*, Aug. 6, 1933; Steno Reports, Board of Directors, Los Angeles Chamber of Commerce, box 20, Sept. 7, 1933, LACC Archive.

23. *Los Angeles Times*, Dec. 20, 1949; Scope and Content Notes, W. C. Mullendore Papers, Herbert Hoover Presidential Library, West Branch, Iowa.

24. *Los Angeles Times*, Nov. 8, 1923, Jan. 13, 1929. Read's meeting with Mullendore is recounted in Kim Phillips-Fein, *Invisible Hands: The Businessmen's Crusade against the New Deal* (New York: W. W. Norton, 2009), 16–17.

25. *Los Angeles Times*, Apr. 4, Jun. 11, 1931; Arthur M. Schlesinger Jr., *The Crisis of the Old Order, 1919–1933* (Boston: Houghton Mifflin, 1957), 118–24.

26. *Los Angeles Times*, Nov. 28, 1935; William Clinton Mullendore, "The American Way Is Not the Easy Way," address delivered before the Institute of Industrial Relations at Los Angeles, Mar. 14, 1944, 3, Research Files, box 388, folder 23, Southern California Edison Records, Huntington Library, San Marino, Calif.

27. W. C. Mullendore, Executive Vice President, Southern California Edison Company, "The Bewildered American," address before the thirty-third annual banquet of the Los Angeles Chapter, American Institute of Banking, Biltmore Hotel, May 26, 1936, 4–6, 12, Research Files, box 388, folder 24, Southern California Edison Records, Huntington Library, San Marino, Calif.

28. *Los Angeles Times*, Mar. 15, 1945.

29. *Los Angeles Times*, Mar. 8, Oct. 15, 1931; Sutton, *Aimee Semple McPherson*, 190–93; Darren Dochuk, *From Bible Belt to Sunbelt: Plain-Folk Religion, Grassroots Politics, and the Rise of Evangelical Conservatism* (New York: W. W. Norton, 2011), 21.

30. *Los Angeles Times*, Dec. 8, 1930.

31. *Los Angeles Times*, Dec. 14, 1934; James W. Fifield Jr., *The Tall Preacher: Autobiography of Dr. James W. Fifield, Jr.* (Los Angeles: Pepperdine University Press, 1977), vii.

32. Fifield, *Tall Preacher*, 103.

33. James W. Fifield Jr., *The Single Path* (New York: Prentice-Hall, 1957), 87–88.

34. Fifield, *Tall Preacher*, 112–18.

35. Fifield, *Tall Preacher*, 109–10, 118.

36. Fifield, *Tall Preacher*, 123–24.

37. Fifield, *Tall Preacher*, 122; Kevin M. Kruse, *One Nation under God: How Corporate America Invented Christian America* (New York: Basic Books, 2015), 11–12; *Los Angeles Times*, Oct. 3, 1938.

38. *New York Times*, Dec. 8, 1940; Fifield, *Tall Preacher*, 197; Kevin M. Kruse, "How Corporate America Invented Christian America," *Politico Magazine*, Apr. 16, 2015, www.politico.com/magazine/story/2015/04/corporate-america-invented-religious-right-conservative-roosevelt-princeton-117030.

39. *Los Angeles Times*, Jan. 3, 11, 15, 1943; Kruse, *One Nation under God*, 15–16, 18; Fifield, *Tall Preacher*, 124–25; Phillips-Fein, *Invisible Hands*, 70–76.

CHAPTER 6

1. *Los Angeles Times*, May 16, 1931.
2. U.S. Congress, *Investigation of Communist Propaganda, Hearings Before a Special Committee to Investigate Communist Activities in the United States House of Representatives, Seventy-first Congress, Second Session*, Part 5, Vol. 3 (Washington, D.C.: U.S. Government Printing Office, 1930–31), 5; "Resolutions and Proposals adopted at Los Angeles County Convention," Mar. 27, 28, 1937, 3, Jerry Voorhis Collection, box 1, folder 17A, Special Collections, Claremont Colleges Library, Claremont, Calif.; Harvey Klehr, *The Heyday of American Communism: The Depression Decade* (New York: Basic Books, 1984), 6–7.
3. Peggy Dennis, *The Autobiography of an American Communist: A Personal View of a Political Life* (Westport, Conn.: L. Hill, 1977), 20; U.S. Congress, *Investigation of Communist Propaganda*, 139.
4. *Los Angeles Times*, Oct. 6, 1927, Oct. 10, 1928, Aug. 4, 23, 1929, Mar. 9, 1930; Dennis, *Autobiography*, 21.
5. Meyer Baylin, "Meyer Baylin's Oral History" (Regional Oral History Office, Bancroft Library, University of California, Berkeley, 1993), 28–29.
6. American Civil Liberties Union, *The California Red Flag Case: The Facts of the Conviction of Five Young Women for Displaying a Red Flag at a Children's Summer Camp* (New York: American Civil Liberties Union, 1930); Zechariah Chafee Jr., *Free Speech in the United States* (Cambridge, Mass.: Harvard University Press, 1942), 363–66; Terry Eastland, *Freedom of Expression in the Supreme Court: The Defining Cases* (Lanham, Md.: Rowman and Littlefield, 2000), 24–25.
7. Dennis, *Autobiography*, 86.
8. *Los Angeles Times*, Jan. 3, 1920.
9. Edward J. Escobar, *Race, Police, and the Making of Political Identity, 1900–1945* (Berkeley, University of California Press, 1999), 80–81; *Los Angeles Times*, Dec. 10, 1931.
10. *Los Angeles Times*, Nov. 26, 1931; Joseph Gerald Woods, *The Police in Los Angeles: Reform and Professionalization* (New York: Garland, 1993), 244–47; Stephen J. Ross, *Hitler in Los Angeles: How Jews Foiled Nazi Plots against Hollywood and America* (New York: Bloomsbury, 2017), 32.
11. Ross, *Hitler in Los Angeles*, 29; Joe Domanick, *To Protect and to Serve: The LAPD's Century of War in the City of Dreams* (New York: Pocket Books, 1994), 63.
12. U.S. Congress, *Investigation of Communist Propaganda*, 308.

13. Edward P. Johanningsmeier, *Forging American Communism: The Life of William Z. Foster* (Princeton, N.J.: Princeton University Press, 1994), 214–15; *Los Angeles Times*, Mar. 4, 1924.

14. William Schneiderman, *Dissent on Trial: The Story of a Political Life* (Minneapolis: MEP, 1983), 21–22.

15. Klehr, *Heyday of American Communism*, 11–14.

16. Baylin, "Meyer Baylin's Oral History, 44–46.

17. *Western Worker*, Sept. 1, 1932, Mar. 13, 1933; *Los Angeles Times*, Aug. 9, 1932.

18. Dorothy Ray Healey and Maurice Isserman, *California Red: A Life in the American Communist Party* (Urbana: University of Illinois Press, 1993), 40; *Los Angeles Times*, Jan. 19, 1933.

19. Klehr, *Heyday of American Communism*, 31.

20. *Los Angeles Daily News*, Feb. 27, 1930; *Los Angeles Times*, Feb. 27, 1930; *Los Angeles Herald*, Feb. 27, 1930.

21. *Illustrated Daily News*, Feb. 27, 1930; *Los Angeles Times*, Feb. 27, 28, 1930.

22. *Los Angeles Times*, Feb. 28, 1930.

23. *Los Angeles Times*, Mar. 6, 1930; *Illustrated Daily News*, Mar. 6, 1930.

24. Klehr, *Heyday of American Communism*, 33–34.

25. *Los Angeles Record*, Mar. 6, 1930; *Los Angeles Times*, Mar. 7, 1930; *Illustrated Daily News*, Mar. 7, 1930.

26. United States Congress, Senate, Committee on Education and Labor, *Violations of Free Speech and Rights of Labor, Hearings Before a Subcommittee of the Committee on Education and Labor, United States Senate, Seventy-Fourth Congress, Second Session* (Washington, D.C., U.S. Government Printing Office, 1936–41), 23507–31, 23612–29.

27. Loren Miller, "Judge Taney in Uniform," n.d., folder 3, box 3, Loren Miller Papers, Huntington Library, San Marino, Calif.

28. *Los Angeles Times*, Aug. 15, 16, 1932.

29. *Los Angeles Times*, Aug. 15, 16, Sept. 2, 1932.

30. *Western Worker*, Feb. 20, 1933; *Los Angeles Times*, Feb. 13, 1933; *Los Angeles Daily News*, Feb. 17, 1933.

31. Woods, *Police in Los Angeles*, 297; *Los Angeles Daily News*, Feb. 16, 1933.

32. Quoted in Mullins, *Depression and the Urban West Coast*, 26–27; *Los Angeles Times*, Feb. 4, 1931; *Los Angeles Herald*, Mar. 11, 1930.

33. Healey, *California Red*, 40; *Los Angeles Times*, Oct. 15, Dec. 3, 1931; Woods, *Police in Los Angeles*, 295–96.

34. United States National Commission on Law Observance and Enforcement, *Report on Lawlessness in Law Enforcement* (Washington, D.C.: United States Government Printing Office, 1931), 143–47.

35. In the Municipal Court, City of Los Angeles, County of Los Angeles, State of California, Case No. 305052, Leo Gallagher Collection, box 1, folder 30e, Southern California Library for Social Studies and Research, Los Angeles.

36. *Open Forum*, Apr. 8, 1933.

37. Thomas Joseph Sitton, "Urban Politics and Reform in New Deal Los Angeles: The Recall of Mayor Frank L. Shaw" (Ph.D. dissertation, University of California, Riverside, 1983), 53, 74–75, 96–97, 223.

38. Stevens, *Radical L.A.*, 234–36.

39. "Resolutions and Proposals adopted at Los Angeles County Convention," Mar. 27, 28, 1937, 6, Jerry Voorhis Collection, box 1, folder 17A, Special Collections, Claremont Colleges Library, Claremont, Calif.

CHAPTER 7

1. James Winston to Upton Sinclair, Aug. 3, 1934, box 27, folder 1934: Aug. 3, Upton Sinclair Papers; *Los Angeles Times*, Jul. 25, 26, 1934; *Weekly Bulletin*, Apr. 1, 1935 (vol. 2, no. 20), box 4 folder 7, Kelley Collection.

2. *Illustrated Daily News*, Dec. 2, 5, 1932; Luther Whiteman and Samuel L. Lewis, *Glory Roads: The Psychological State of California* (New York: Thomas Y. Crowell, 1936), 8–9.

3. Wayne Parrish, "Technocracy's Question?" *New Outlook*, Dec. 1932, 14.

4. Harold Loeb, *Life in a Technocracy: What It Might Be Like* (New York: Viking Press, 1933), 41.

5. Newton Van Dalsem, *The History of the Utopian Society in America: An Authentic Account of Its Origins and Developments Up to 1942* (Los Angeles: Utopian Society, 1942), 17; *Weekly Bulletin*, Apr. 1, 1935 (vol. 2, no. 20), box 4, folder 7, Kelley Collection; James B. Hollis to Upton Sinclair, Jul. 22, 1934, box 27, folder 1934: Jul. 21–11, Sinclair Papers; *Los Angeles Times*, Aug. 26, 1934; James Winston to Upton Sinclair, Apr. 3, 1934, box 27, folder 1934: Aug. 3, Sinclair Papers.

6. Hollis to Sinclair, box 27, folder 1934: Aug. 8, Sinclair Papers; *Los Angeles Times*, Aug. 26, 1934.

7. *Los Angeles Times*, Aug. 29, 1934; Donald W. Whisenhunt, *Utopian Movements and Ideas of the Great Depression: Dreamers, Believers, and Madmen* (Lanham, Md.: Lexington, 2013), 14.

8. *Los Angeles Times*, Aug. 26, 1934; Van Dalsem, *History of the Utopian Society*, 18.

9. Van Dalsem, *History of the Utopian Society*, 18–21.

10. Van Dalsem, *History of the Utopian Society*, 22–25, 36; McWilliams, *Southern California*, 295.

11. Van Dalsem, *History of the Utopian Society*, 18–21, 36.

12. Van Dalsem, *History of the Utopian Society*, 27; *Weekly Bulletin*, Apr. 1, 1935, vol. 2, no. 20, folder 7, Kelley Collection.

13. Van Dalsem, *History of the Utopian Society*, 27–28.

14. Van Dalsem, *History of the Utopian Society*, 28–29.

15. Van Dalsem, *History of the Utopian Society*, 32.

16. Van Dalsem, *History of the Utopian Society*, 35.

17. *New York Times*, Nov. 14, 1934.
18. Van Dalsem, *History of the Utopian Society*, 37; Stanley Moffat to Upton Sinclair, Jun. 23, 1934, box 26, folder 1934: Jun. 23–24, Sinclair Papers.
19. Van Dalsem, *History of the Utopian Society*, 37; *Los Angeles Times*, Aug. 27, 1934; McWilliams, *Southern California*, 295; Program of the Hollywood Bowl meeting, box 25, 1934, Jun. 23–24, MS 20f, Sinclair Collection; *Los Angeles Times*, Aug. 24, 1934, Mar. 19, 1937.
20. Van Dalsem, *History of the Utopian Society*, 39–55.
21. Van Dalsem, *History of the Utopian Society*, 39–55.
22. Van Dalsem, *History of the Utopian Society*, 9.
23. *Los Angeles Times*, Aug. 27, 29, 1934.
24. *Los Angeles Times*, Aug. 24, 30–31, 1934.
25. *Los Angeles Times*, Aug. 24, 30, Sept. 4, 1934, Mar. 9, 1937; *Los Angeles Examiner*, Aug. 22–23, Sept. 6, 1934.
26. Van Dalsem, *History of the Utopian Society*, 57; *Los Angeles Times*, Aug. 31, 1934.
27. *Utopian News*, Oct. 11, 1934; Sinclair to Rube Borough, Jul. 3, 1934, box 27, folder 1934: Jul. 3–4, Sinclair Papers.
28. Van Dalsem, *History of the Utopian Society*, 66.
29. Van Dalsem, *History of the Utopian Society*, 61–62.
30. Van Dalsem, *History of the Utopian Society*, 56; *Los Angeles Times*, Aug. 29, 1934.
31. *New York Times*, Nov. 14, 15, 1934.
32. Van Dalsem, *History of the Utopian Society*, 63; *Bulletin*, Feb. 25, 1935, box 4, folder 14; *Official Field Bulletin*, Jan. 30, 1935, box 4, folder 8; and Statement of Cash Receipts and Disbursements, for the month of January, 1935, box 4, folder 7, Kelley Collection.
33. Van Dalsem, *History of the Utopian Society*, 9.
34. There is a nearly complete set of the forty-four *Revelations* in the Kelley Collection.
35. *Weekly Bulletin* (1935), box 4, folder 7, Kelley Collection.
36. *Field Bulletin* (1935), box 4, folder 6, Kelley Collection.
37. Robert M. Carriker, *Urban Farming in the West: A New Deal Experiment in Subsistence Homesteads* (Tucson: University of Arizona Press, 2010), 87.
38. *Bulletin*, Feb. 25, 1935, box 4, folder 14, Kelley Collection; *Los Angeles Times*, Feb. 12, 1935; *New York Times*, Feb. 15, 1935.
39. John G. Wenk to John [n.d.], box 4, folder 13; and *Weekly Bulletin*, Mar. 11, 1935, box 4, folder 7, Kelley Collection.
40. *Utopian Revelations*, 34th Revelation, Educational Department, Utopian Society of America, box 4, folder 12, Kelley Collection.
41. McWilliams, *Southern California*, 295–96; *Los Angeles Times*, Mar. 30, 1931.

CHAPTER 8

1. J. D. Gaydowski, "Eight Letters to the Editor: The Genesis of the Townsend National Recovery Plan," *Southern California Quarterly* 52 (1970): 365–82; Richard Neuberger and Kelley Loe, *An Army of the Aged: A History and Analysis of the Townsend Old-Age Pension Plan* (Caldwell, Idaho: Caxton, 1936), 52.

2. Gaydowski, "Eight Letters," 370–71; Abraham Holtzman, *The Townsend Movement: A Political Study* (New York: Octagon Books, 1975), 37; *New York Times*, Dec. 29, 1935.

3. Gaydowski, "Eight Letters," 375; *New York Times*, Dec. 29, 1935.

4. Neuberger and Loe, *Army of the Aged*, 34, 77; Dr. Francis E. Townsend, *New Horizons* (An Autobiography), ed. Jesse George Murray (Chicago: J. L. Stewart, 1943), 136.

5. Irving Fisher, *Stamp Scrip* (New York: Adelphi, 1933); Luther Whiteman and Samuel L. Lewis, *Glory Roads: The Psychological State of California* (New York: Thomas Y. Crowell, 1936), 66; Holtzman, *Townsend Movement*, 34. McCord's essay is preserved in U.S. Congress, *Hearings Before the Select Committee Investigating Old-Age Pension Organizations*, House of Representatives, Seventy-Fourth Congress, Second Session, two volumes (Washington, D.C.: U.S. Government Printing Office, 1936), 758–64; Neuberger and Loe, *Army of the Aged*, 36.

6. Neuberger and Loe, *Army of the Aged*, 50–52.

7. Fifteenth Census, Population, Vol. 3, Part 1; Secretary [?] to Elliott Kelly, Oct. 3, 1934, box 63/B III 14 b cc (1), Ford Papers; Putnam, *Old Age Politics*, 22–23.

8. U.S. Congress, *Hearings Before the Select Committee* (1936), 480; *New York Times*, Mar. 17, Dec. 29, 1935.

9. Neuberger and Loe, *Army of the Aged*, 33, 56.

10. *New York Times*, Mar. 17, Jul. 28, Oct. 28, Nov. 24, 1935, Mar. 29, May 23, 1936; *Los Angeles Times*, Oct. 28, 1935; Townsend, *New Horizons*, 145.

11. Townsend, *New Horizons*, 52, 78, 95.

12. Whiteman, *Glory Roads*, 64–65; Neuberger and Loe, *Army of the Aged*, 33; Townsend, *New Horizons*, 132, 136.

13. U.S. Congress, *Hearings Before the Select Committee* (1936), 3–8; *New York Times*, Nov. 3, 1935.

14. U.S. Congress, *Hearings Before the Select Committee* (1936), 92, 122–34, 161–62, 604; Edwin Amenta, *When Movements Matter: The Townsend Plan and the Rise of Social Security* (Princeton, N.J.: Princeton University Press, 2006), 40–41.

15. Amenta, *When Movements Matter*, 40, 118–19.

16. Amenta, *When Movements Matter*, 52, 54; U.S. Congress, *Hearings Before the Select Committee* (1936), 475, 480.

17. Amenta, *When Movements Matter*, 475–76, 483.
18. *Covina Argus*, Sept. 28, 1934; U.S. Congress, *Hearings Before the Select Committee* (1936), 484.
19. U.S. Congress, *Hearings Before the Select Committee* (1936), 585; Amenta, *When Movements Matter*, 41, 52, 57.
20. U.S. Congress, *Hearings Before the Select Committee* (1936), 26, 27, 128–29; Holtzman, *Townsend Movement*, 67, 68.
21. U.S. Congress, *Hearings Before the Select Committee* (1936), 43, 44–49; Townsend, *New Horizons*, 58–59; Amenta, *When Movements Matter*, 53.
22. U.S. Congress, *Hearings Before the Select Committee* (1936), 54–55; Holtzman, *Townsend Movement*, 48; *Covina Argus*, Nov. 23, 1934.
23. *Los Angeles Sentinel*, Apr. 30, 1936.
24. *Los Angeles Times*, Nov. 4, 1934.
25. *New York Times*, Nov. 18, 1934.
26. *New York Times*, Mar. 19 1935; *Los Angeles Times*, Nov. 9, 1934.
27. *Los Angeles Times*, Jan. 17, 1935; *New York Times*, Jan. 17, 1935; Holtzman, *Townsend Movement*, 39–40.
28. Amenta, *When Movements Matter*, 81: *Los Angeles Times*, Jan. 17, 1935; *New York Times*, Jan. 18, 1935.
29. *Los Angeles Times*, Jan. 17, 1935; U.S. Congress, *Hearings Before the Select Committee* (1936), part 2, 460.
30. U.S. Congress, *Economic Security Act*, Hearings before the Committee on Ways and Means, House of Representatives, Seventy-fourth Congress (Washington, D.C.: U.S. Government Printing Office, 1935), 920; Neuberger and Loe, *Army of the Aged*, 83–84; *Los Angeles Times*, Jan. 20, 1935.
31. U.S. Congress, *Economic Security Act* (1935), 453.
32. U.S. Congress, *Economic Security Act* (1935), 795, 1065; *Los Angeles Times*, Jan. 25, 1935.
33. U.S. Congress, *Economic Security Act* (1935), 851.
34. U.S. Congress, *Economic Security Act* (1935), 452, 454, 457.
35. Holtzman, *Townsend Movement*, 96–100; *New York Times*, Apr. 14, 1935.
36. Amenta, *When Movements Matter*, 111–12; *Los Angeles Times*, Oct. 22, 25, 28, 1935; *New York Times*, Oct. 25, 1935.
37. *Los Angeles Times*, Oct. 25, 27, Nov. 24, 1935.
38. Amenta, *When Movements Matter*, 107–8, 110–11; *New York Times*, Oct. 27, 1935.
39. *New York Times*, Mar. 26, Jul. 5, 1935; *Los Angeles Times*, Mar. 28, 1935; U.S. Congress, *Hearings Before the Select Committee* (1936); Amenta, *When Movements Matter*, 136.
40. U.S. Congress, *Hearings Before the Select Committee* (1936), 329, 466; Amenta, *When Movements Matter*, 125–26; *Los Angeles Times*, Jan. 18, Feb. 4, 1936.
41. *New York Times*, Nov. 25, 1935, Apr. 1, 1936; *Los Angeles Times*, Feb. 15, Mar. 29, 1936.

42. Amenta, *When Movements Matter,* 137, 139; *Los Angeles Times,* May 4, Dec. 21, 1936, Jun. 15, 1937; *San Bernardino Sun,* Apr. 8, 1936.

43. *Los Angeles Times,* May 4, 1936; *New York Times,* May 6, 18, Jun. 19, 1936.

44. *New York Times,* Apr. 4, 11, 14, 1936; U.S. Congress, *Hearings Before the Select Committee* (1936), 82, 84–85.

45. U.S. Congress, *Hearings Before the Select Committee* (1936), 600–608.

46. U.S. Congress, *Hearings Before the Select Committee* (1936), 614–15, 769–70; Holtzman, *Townsend Movement,* 166–67.

47. Amenta, *When Movements Matter,* 141; *New York Times,* Apr. 5, 12, 1936.

48. *New York Times,* Jun. 1, 17, 1936.

49. *New York Times,* Jul. 15, 1936; Amenta, *When Movements Matter,* 145.

50. Amenta, *When Movements Matter,* 146; *Los Angeles Sentinel,* Jul. 23, 1936.

51. Holtzman, *Townsend Movement,* 65, 67, 220; Amenta, *When Movements Matter,* 146–47.

52. *Los Angeles Times,* Jun. 4, 1939.

CHAPTER 9

1. Anthony Arthur, *Radical Innocent: Upton Sinclair* (New York: Random House, 2006), 162; Upton Sinclair, "What Life Means to Me," *Cosmopolitan Magazine,* Oct. 1906, 41.

2. Correspondence, box 27, folder 1934: Jul. 17–18, Sinclair Papers; Arthur, *Radical Innocent,* 87; Upton Sinclair, *American Outpost: A Book of Reminiscences* (New York: Farrar and Rinehart, 1932), 177–80.

3. Correspondence, box 27, folder 1934: Jul. 17–18, Sinclair Papers.

4. Webb Waldron, "Can Sinclair Win?" *Today,* Oct. 6, 1934, 6–7, 20, 23; Upton Sinclair, *Letters to Judd: An American Workingman* (Pasadena, Calif.: Upton Sinclair, 1932), 1–2; Arthur, *Radical Innocent,* 162–63.

5. Sinclair to editor, *Neue Welt,* Jan. 25, 1933, box 21, folder 1933: Jan. 25, Sinclair Papers; Arthur, *Radical Innocent,* 171; Clarence F. McIntosh, "Upton Sinclair and the Epic Movement, 1933–1936" (Ph.D. dissertation, Stanford University, 1955), 30–32.

6. Arthur, *Radical Innocent,* 173; Kevin Mattson, *Upton Sinclair and the Other American Century* (New York: Wiley, 2006), 119; Sinclair, *I, Governor of California, and How I Ended Poverty: A True Story of the Future* (Los Angeles: Upton Sinclair, 1933), 3.

7. Stevens, *Radical L.A.,* 151.

8. Stevens, *Radical L.A.,* 146–55.

9. Sinclair to Al Wirin, Jan. 27, 1933, box 21, folder 1933: Jan. 27; George R. Barker to Sinclair, Feb. 23, 1944, box 21, folder 1933: Feb. 22–23; and Warren E. Libby to Sinclair, Mar. 1, 1933, box 21, folder 1933: Mar. 1, Sinclair Papers.

10. Upton Sinclair, *The Way Out: What Lies Ahead for America* (New York: Farrar and Rinehart, [c 1933]), 65.

11. Sinclair, *Way Out*, 8.

12. Sinclair, *Way Out*, 36.

13. Sinclair, *Way Out*, 53–54, 10.

14. Sinclair, *I, Governor of California*, 4–5.

15. Gilbert Stevenson to Sinclair, Aug. 19, 1933, box 23, folder 1933: Aug. 19–21; Aug. 28, 1933, box 23, folder 1933: Aug. 28–31; and Nov. 1, 1933, folder 1933: Nov. 1, Sinclair Papers; Upton Sinclair, *I, Candidate for Governor, and How I Got Licked* (Pasadena, Calif.: Author, 1935), 6–7, 11, 17.

16. Sinclair to David Sinclair, Nov. 13, 1933, box 24, folder 1933: Nov. 11–13; Myra Becks to Sinclair, Sept. 23, 1933, box 24, folder, 1933: Sept. 23–6; and Sinclair to David Sinclair, Sept. 16, 1933, box 24, folder 1933: Sept. 13–15, Sinclair Papers; McIntosh, "Upton Sinclair and the Epic Movement," 38–39.

17. Fulton Oursler to Sinclair, Apr. 30, 1933, Sinclair ms., box 23, folder 1933: Aug. 28–31; and Sinclair to Oursler, Sinclair ms., Sept. 9, 1933, box 24, folder 1933: Sept. 9–12, Sinclair Papers; Sinclair, *I, Candidate*, 18.

18. Memorandum of Remarks of Mr. Jerome Politzer, Feb. 7, 1934, box 25, folder 1934: Feb. 7–9, Sinclair Papers.

19. Sinclair, *I, Governor*, 7, 14–15, 21–27.

20. Sinclair, *I, Governor*, 15–16, 21–22.

21. Sinclair, *I, Governor*, 16–17, 22–23; James Worthen, *Governor James Rolph and the Great Depression in California* (Jefferson, N.C.: McFarland, 2006), 167–68; Mimeographed EPIC flyer, Precinct No. 32, Oct. 18, 1934, Ephemera Collection, Huntington Library, San Marino, Calif.

22. Poem, box 27, folder, 1934: Jul. 3–4, Sinclair Papers.

23. Sinclair to George Pratt, Mar. 22, 1934, box 25, folder 1934: Mar. 22–23; Sinclair to Ernest Greene, Nov. 22, 1933, box 24, folder 1933: Nov. 21–22; Richard S. Otto to Sinclair, Sept. 1, 1933, Sinclair to Otto, Sept. 5, 1933, box 24, folder, 1933: Sept. 1–5; and Sinclair to Edward Roberts, Nov. 24, 1933, box 24, folder 1933: Nov. 23–24, Sinclair Papers; Joan Sullivan, "All about Baywood Park," *Baywood News*, 1994, 14; Sinclair, *I, Candidate*, 6, 18, 20; McIntosh, "Upton Sinclair," 90–91.

24. Sinclair to P. B. Montgomery, May 19, 1934, box 26, folder 1934: May 18–19; and Sinclair to Eleanor Roosevelt, Feb. 3, 1934, box 25, folder 1934: Feb. 1–3, Sinclair Papers.

25. Sinclair to Carr, Jul. 16, 1934, box 17, folder 1934: Jul. 17, 18, Sinclair Papers; Sinclair, *I, Candidate*, 21; Greg Mitchell, *The Campaign of the Century: Upton Sinclair's Race for Governor and the Birth of Media Politics* (New York: Random House, 1992), 104; McIntosh, "Upton Sinclair," 87; *EPIC News*, Feb. 1934; Royce D. Delmatier, Clarence F. McIntosh, and Earl G. Waters, *The Rumble of California Politics, 1848–1970* (New York: John Wiley and Sons, 1970), 267, 274; Sinclair to Oursler, Apr. 12, 1934, box 26, folder 1934: Apr. 10–12, Sinclair Papers.

26. McIntosh, "Upton Sinclair," 113; EPIC Merchandise Auction Sales, box 31, folder 1934, EPIC Plan, Misc., Sinclair Papers.

27. Sinclair to editor, *Illustrated Daily News*, Jun. 15, 1934, box 26, folder 1934: Jun. 15–16, Sinclair Papers.

28. Walter Davenport, "Sinclair Gets the Glory Vote," *Collier's*, Oct. 27, 1934, 32; Sam Ringquist to Sinclair, Jun. 19, 1934, box 26, folder 1934: Jun. 19, Sinclair Papers.

29. Webb Waldron, "Can Sinclair Win?" *Today*, Oct. 6, 1934, 6–7, 20.

30. Davenport, "Sinclair Gets the Glory Vote," 12, 32.

31. *EPIC News*, May 1934.

32. McIntosh, "Upton Sinclair," 139–41, 157; George Creel, *Rebel at Large: Recollections of Fifty Crowded Years* (New York: G. P. Putnam's Sons, 1947), 282–86.

33. Sinclair to Eleanor Roosevelt, Aug. 19, 1934, box 27, folder 1934: Aug. 18–19; and Telegram, Executive Office to Sinclair, Aug. 29, 1934, box 28, folder 1934: Aug. 29, Sinclair Papers.

34. McIntosh, "Upton Sinclair," 158–59; Delmatier, McIntosh, and Waters, *Rumble of California Politics*, 275–76.

35. *Illustrated Daily News*, Aug. 31, 1934; Sinclair, *I, Candidate*, 70, 76–77.

36. Sinclair, *I, Candidate*, 183; McIntosh, "Upton Sinclair," 273–74.

37. *New York Times*, Oct. 6, 1934; *Los Angeles Times*, Sept. 21, 1934.

38. McIntosh, "Upton Sinclair," 187–89, 196; *Los Angeles Times*, Sept. 28–29, 1934; "The Platform of the Democratic Party as Officially Adopted at the State Convention Los Angeles: End Poverty League, Inc. [1934], Voorhis Collection, box 83B, folder 1, Special Collections, Claremont Colleges Library, Claremont, Calif. ; Putnam, *Old Age Politics*, 39–41.

39. *Los Angeles Times*, Sept. 26–27, 1934; Mitchell, *Campaign of the Century*, 200–201, 337.

40. Arthur M. Schlesinger Jr., *The Politics of Upheaval* (Boston: Houghton Mifflin, 1960), 118; Mitchell, *Campaign of the Century*, 83–85, 128–30; *Los Angeles Times*, Oct. 10, 1934.

41. *Los Angeles Times*, Oct. 24, 1934.

42. Mitchell, *Campaign of the Century*, 71, 340, 424; *New York Times*, Oct. 6, Nov. 4, 1934.

43. McIntosh, "Upton Sinclair," 254; *Los Angeles Times*, Sept. 29, 30, Oct. 24, 1934.

44. *Los Angeles Times*, Oct. 27, 1934; George Creel to Sinclair, Nov. 27, 1934, box 30, folder 1934: Nov. 26–27; and William McAdoo to Sinclair, Sept. 27, 1934, box 28, folder 1934: Sept. 7, Sinclair Papers.

45. McIntosh, "Upton Sinclair," 311–13; Delmatier, McIntosh, and Waters, *Rumble of California Politics*, 280; *Los Angeles Times*, Nov. 9, 1934; James N. Gregory, "Upton Sinclair's 1934 EPIC Campaign: Anatomy of a Political Movement," *Labor Studies in Working-Class History of the Americas* 12 (Dec. 2015): 61, 78–79.

46. Jerry Voorhis to Sinclair, Nov. 7, 1934, box 29, folder, 1934: Nov. 7, A-Z, Sinclair Papers; Constitution of the End Poverty League, Jerry Voorhis Collection, box 83B, folder 8, Special Collections, Claremont Colleges Library, Claremont, Calif.; McIntosh, "Upton Sinclair," 328–29.

47. McIntosh, "Upton Sinclair," 330.

48. Sinclair to Horace A. Davis, Nov. 21, 1934, box 30, folder 1934: Nov. 20–21; and copy of telegram, Nov. 19, 1934, box 30, folder 1934: Nov. 19, Sinclair Papers.

49. McIntosh, "Upton Sinclair," 334–35; Olson to Sinclair, Nov. 12, 1934, box 30, folder 1934: Nov. 24–25; Ed Wolcott to Sinclair, Jan. 22, 1935, box 31, folder 1935: Jan. 22–23; Sinclair to Sessions, Nov. 22, 1934, box 30, folder 1934: Nov. 22; and Sinclair to Olson, Dec. 19, 1934, box 30, folder 1934: Dec. 19–20, Sinclair Papers; *Upton Sinclair's EPIC News*, Dec. 17, 1934; *Illustrated Daily News*, Dec. 18, 1934.

50. Sinclair to Irene Douglas, Dec. 22, 1934, box 30, folder 1934: Dec. 21–22; and Sinclair to End Poverty League Board of Directors, Jan. 2, 1935, box 31, folder 1935: Jan. 1–2, Sinclair Papers.

51. Sinclair to Kate Richards O'Hare, Aug. 5, 1935, box 33, folder 1935: Aug. 5–6; and O'Hare to End Poverty League Board of Directors, Apr. 23, 1935, box 32, folder 1935: Apr. 23–24, Sinclair Papers.

CHAPTER 10

1. Creel, *Rebel at Large*, 281; Welfare Statistics, Oct. 5, 1934, III 14 c bb aaa (2), box 64/b, Ford Papers.

2. Putnam, *Old Age Politics*, 89; McWilliams, *Southern California*, 304.

3. Putnam, *Old Age Politics*, 94–95.

4. Colin S. Hoffman, "Conspiratorial Politics: The Friends of Progress and California Radicals of the Right in California during World War Two" (M.A. thesis, California State University, Sacramento, 2011), 14; Winston and Marian Moore, *Out of the Frying Pan* (Los Angeles: DeVorss, 1939), 15–18.

5. Moore, *Out of the Frying Pan*, 16–17, 19, 23; Mrs. C. Garshwiler to Upton Sinclair, Mar. 19, 1935; and Olive Cushing Dwinell to Sinclair, Apr. 3, 1935, folder Apr. 1–2, box 32, 1935, Sinclair Papers; Putnam, *Old Age Politics*, 91.

6. Moore, *Out of the Frying Pan*, 31, 33–35; *Los Angeles Examiner*, Aug. 22, 1934; *Los Angeles Times*, Jun. 26, 1939.

7. *Los Angeles Times*, Oct. 6, 1938; Moore, *Out of the Frying Pan*, 40–42; *Los Angeles Examiner*, Apr. 16, 1939.

8. *Los Angeles Times*, Nov. 4, 6, 7, 17, 1937, Oct. 19, 1939.

9. *Los Angeles Times*, Oct. 19, Nov. 4, 10, 1937.

10. Sitton, *Courthouse Crowd*, 281–86.

11. "Sherman Bainbridge," *BFI*, www.bfi.org.uk/films-tv-people/4ce2bafc01dc3; California Secretary of State, *Statement of Vote, Primary Election Held on August 29, 1916* (California State Printing Office, 1916), 6; Putnam, *Old Age Politics*, 45–46; Moore, *Out of the Frying Pan*, 62.

12. *Beverly Hills Citizen*, Oct. 7, 1938; *Crisis* 1, no. 1, [1939]; Index of American Design, folder 11, box 14, Ephemera Collection, Huntington Library, San Marino, Calif.; Charles F. Wright, "Origin and Menace of 30 Thursday" (n.d.), 37, Index of American Design, folder 3, box 8, folder 3, box 14; *Los Angeles Times*, Aug. 29, Sept. 5, 1934; Moore, *Out of the Frying Pan*, 51–55.

13. *Crisis* 1, no. 1, [1939]; Index of American Design, in folder 11, box 14, Ephemera Collection, Huntington Library, San Marino, Calif.; *New York Times*, Oct. 2, 1938.

14. Putnam, *Old Age Politics*, 97; *Ham and Eggs for Californians*, Oct. 22, 1938; Moore, *Out of the Frying Pan*, 63–64; McWilliams, *Southern California*, 306.

15. Moore, *Out of the Frying Pan*, 76.

16. *Beverly Hills Citizen*, Oct 7, 1938; Moore, *Out of the Frying Pan*, 71, 73.

17. Moore, *Out of the Frying Pan*, 68, 72–74; *New York Times*, Oct. 1-2, 1938; *Beverly Hills Citizen*, Oct 7, 1938.

18. Moore, *Out of the Frying Pan*, 44; *Beverly Hills Citizen*, Oct. 7, 1938.

19. Moore, *Out of the Frying Pan*, 67–71; *Los Angeles Times*, Jun. 4, 1939.

20. *Beverly Hills Citizen*, Oct. 7, 1938; Moore, *Out of the Frying Pan*, 77, 81–82; Robert E. Burke, *Olson's New Deal for California* (Berkeley: University of California Press, 1953), 16–17.

21. *New York Times*, Oct. 1, 1938;

22. *Culver City Citizen*, Oct. 7, 1938.

23. California Politics, EPH F43, box 3, Ephemera Collection, Huntington Library, San Marino, Calif.

24. *New York Times*, Oct. 4, 1938; *Los Angeles Times*, Oct. 11, 12, 13, 17, 21, 1938.

25. *Los Angeles Times*, Oct. 2–15, 1938.

26. *Los Angeles Examiner*, Sept. 19, 1938; *Inglewood News*, Oct. 14, 1938; Fletcher Bowron speech on Ham and Eggs, Nov. 3, 1938, box 33, Fletcher Bowron Papers, Huntington Library, San Marino, Calif.; Burke, *Olson's New Deal*, 21; *Los Angeles Herald Express*, Oct. 5, 1938.

27. *Los Angeles Daily Journal*, Sept. 29, 1938; *Liberty*, Oct. 22, 1938, 11–12; *Los Angeles Daily News*, Sept. 21, 1938; *Los Angeles Times*, Oct. 10, 1938.

28. *Ham and Eggs for Californians*, Oct. 8, Nov. 1, 1938; *East Los Angeles Tribune*, Oct 14, 1938.

29. Putnam, *Old Age Politics*, 99–101.

30. *Los Angeles Times*, Oct. 6, Nov. 4, 1938, Feb. 2, Mar. 24, Apr. 11, Oct. 29, 1939; Burke, *Olson's New Deal*, 107–8.

31. *Los Angeles Examiner*, Apr. 16, 28, 1939.

32. *Los Angeles Times*, Dec. 7, 1938, Jan. 3, 18, 1939; Putnam, *Old Age Politics*, 105.

33. Burke, *Olson's New Deal*, 108–9; *Los Angeles Times*, May 18, 20, 26, 1939; Putnam, *Old Age Politics*, 106, 108; Transcript of Willis Allen Radio Broadcast, Jul. 3, 1939, folder 1, box 25, Cleland Papers.

34. *Los Angeles Examiner*, Jul. 5, 1939; Burke, *Olson's New Deal*,109–10; Putnam, *Old Age Politics*, 103; Index to American Design Records, box 8, folder 3, Huntington Library, San Marino, Calif.

35. Putnam, *Old Age Politics*, 106–7; Index of American Design Records, box 14, folder 7; and Report of Precinct Organization Division City and County of Los Angeles, Southern California Citizens Against 30 Thursday, Index of American Design, box 8, folder 5, Huntington Library, San Marino, Calif.

36. Charles F. Wright, "Origin and Menace of 30 Thursday," 42, Index of American Design, box 8, folder 3; Transcripts of Lawrence Allen radio broadcasts, KMTR, Jul. 5, 1939, folder 1, box 25, Aug. 29, 1939, folder 8, box 25, Cleland Papers; *Los Angeles Times*, Jul. 5, 23, 1939; Putnam, *Old Age Politics*, 110; Editorial reprint from the *Santa Ana Register*, "One Dollar for Ten Cents Scheme" (n.d.), Southern California Citizens Against 30 Thursday [press release], folder 12, box 25, Cleland Papers.

37. California Research Committee, Bulletin 11, "30 Thursday" postcard ballot, California Citizens Against 30 Thursday correspondence, folder 11, box 25; and Survey of Public Opinion Regarding California Retirement Life Payments Act and Second Survey of Public Opinion Regarding California Retirement Life Payments Act, Southern California Citizens Against 30 Thursday, Correspondence, folder 5, box 26, Cleland Papers.

38. Survey of Public Opinion Regarding California Retirement Life Payments Act, 36, 38, Cleland Papers.

39. Putnam, *Old Age Politics*,110–11.

40. Transcript of Roy G. Owens or Lawrence W. Allen radio broadcast, KMTR and KFWB, Nov. 10, 1939 and KYUA, Nov. 11, 1939, folder 10, box 25, Cleland Papers; Putnam, *Old Age Politics*, 112; *Los Angeles Times*, Jan. 30, May 25, Jul. 2, Dec. 27, 1940, Mar. 14, 1941, Apr. 18, 1942, Feb. 15, 1946, Jan. 3, 21, Jun. 4, 1948, Oct. 3, Nov. 4, Dec. 4, 1949, Feb. 3, Mar. 26, Aug. 4, Oct. 3, 5, Nov. 1, 8, 1950.

41. *Los Angeles Times*, Jun. 11, 1943, Nov. 2, 1944, Jan. 17, 1950; Holtzman, *Townsend Movement*, 194–95.

42. Holtzman, *Townsend Movement*, 2, 49–51, 58, 86–87; *New York Times*, Apr. 1, 1942, Jul. 12, 14, 1944; District Court of Appeal, Third District, California, People v. Noble et al Cr. 1816, Decided: Apr. 24, 1945.

CONCLUSION

1. Panunzio, *Self-Help Cooperatives*, 1; McWilliams, *Southern California*, 302.
2. *Whittier News*, Oct. 2, 1938.
3. Rex Thomson to John Anson Ford, Jan. 27, 1936, box 64/B III 14 c bb aaa (4); Report of Investigating Committee to the Democratic County Central Committee, Jan. 12, 1937, box 45/B III 11a (5); and Rex Thomson, Superintendent of Charities to Board of Supervisors, Jun. 17, 1938, box 64/B III 14 c bb aaa (6), Ford Papers.
4. *Los Angeles Times*, Oct. 7, 1939.

Suggested Readings

Adamic, Louis. *Laughing in the Jungle.* New York: Harper & Brothers, 1932.
Akin, William E. *Technocracy and the American Dream: The Technocrat Movement, 1900–1941.* Berkeley: University of California Press, 1977.
Amenta, Edwin. *When Movements Matter: The Townsend Plan and the Rise of Social Security.* Princeton, N.J.: Princeton University Press, 2006.
American Civil Liberties Union. *The California Red Flag Case: The Facts of the Conviction of Five Young Women for Displaying a Red Flag at a Children's Summer Camp.* New York: American Civil Liberties Union, 1930.
Appleby, Joyce. *The Relentless Revolution: A History of Capitalism.* New York: W. W. Norton, 2010.
Arthur, Anthony. *Radical Innocent: Upton Sinclair.* New York: Random House, 2006.
Balderrama, Francisco, and Raymond Rodríguez. *Decade of Betrayal: Mexican Repatriation in the 1930s.* Albuquerque: University of New Mexico Press, 1995.
Bernstein, Irving. *The Lean Years: A History of the American Worker, 1920–1933.* Boston: Houghton Mifflin, 1960.
Bonelli, William G. *Billion Dollar Blackjack.* Beverly Hills, Calif.: Civic Research Press, 1954.
Brinkley, Alan. *The End of Reform: New Deal Liberalism in Depression and War.* New York: Knopf, 1995.
———. *Voices of Protest: Huey Long, Father Coughlin, and the Great Depression.* New York: Knopf, 1982.

Bullock, Paul. *Jerry Voorhis, the Idealist as Politician.* New York: Vantage Press, 1978.
Burke, Robert E. *Olson's New Deal for California.* Berkeley: University of California Press, 1953.
Chafee, Zechariah, Jr. *Free Speech in the United States.* Cambridge, Mass.: Harvard University Press, 1942.
Coodley, Lauren. *Upton Sinclair: California Socialist, Celebrity Intellectual.* Lincoln: University of Nebraska Press, 2013.
Delmatier, Royce D., Clarence F. McIntosh, and Earl G. Waters. *The Rumble of California Politics, 1848–1970.* New York: John Wiley and Sons, 1970.
Dennis, Peggy. *The Autobiography of an American Communist: A Personal View of a Political Life.* Westport, Conn.: L. Hill, 1977.
Domanick, Joe. *To Protect and to Serve: The LAPD's Century of War in the City of Dreams.* New York: Pocket Books, 1994.
Elsner, Henry, Jr. *The Technocrats: Prophets of Automation.* Syracuse: Syracuse University Press, 1967.
Epstein, Daniel Mark. *Sister Aimee: The Life of Aimee Semple McPherson.* New York, 1993.
Fifield, James W., Jr. *The Tall Preacher: Autobiography of Dr. James W. Fifield, Jr.* Los Angeles: Pepperdine University Press, 1977.
Flamming, Douglas. *Bound for Freedom: Black Los Angeles in Jim Crow America.* Berkeley: University of California Press, 2005.
Fogelson, Robert M. *The Fragmented Metropolis: Los Angeles, 1850–1930.* Cambridge, Mass.: Harvard University Press, 1967.
Gottlieb, Robert, and Irene Wolt. *Thinking Big: The Story of the Los Angeles Times, Its Publishers, and Their Influence on Southern California.* New York: Putnam, 1977.
Ham and Eggs for Californians: Life Begins at Fifty. $30 a Week for Life. Questions and Answers. California State Retirement Life Payments Act. Hollywood: Petition Campaign Committee, 1938.
Hassan, Amina. *Loren Miller: Civil Rights Attorney and Journalist.* Norman: University of Oklahoma Press, 2015.
Healey, Dorothy Ray, and Maurice Isserman. *California Red: A Life in the American Communist Party.* Urbana: University of Illinois Press, 1993.
Hoffman, Abraham. *Unwanted Mexican Americans in the Great Depression: Repatriation Pressures, 1929–1939.* Tucson: University of Arizona Press, 1977.
Holtzman, Abraham. *The Townsend Movement: A Political Study.* New York: Octagon Books, 1975.
Katz, Michael. *In the Shadow of the Poorhouse: A Social History of Welfare in America.* New York: Basic Books, 1986.
Kennedy, David M. *Freedom from Fear: The American People in Depression and War, 1929–1945.* New York: Oxford University Press, 1999.

Kerr, Clark, and Paul S. Taylor. "The Self-Help Cooperatives in California." In E. T. Grether, ed. *Essays in Social Economics in Honor of Jessica Blanche Peixotto*. Berkeley: University of California Press, 1935.

Klehr, Harvey. *The Heyday of American Communism: The Depression Decade*. New York: Basic Books, 1984.

Leader, Leonard. *Los Angeles and the Great Depression*. New York: Garland, 1991.

Leuchtenburg, William E. *Franklin D. Roosevelt and the New Deal, 1932–1940*. New York: Harper & Row, 1963.

Mayo, Morrow. *Los Angeles*. New York: A. A. Knopf, 1933.

McDougal, Dennis. *Privileged Son: Otis Chandler and the Rise and Fall of the L.A. Times Dynasty*. Cambridge, Mass.: Perseus, 2001.

McElvaine, Robert C. *The Great Depression: America, 1929–1941*. New York: Random House, 1984.

McWilliams, Carey. *Southern California: An Island on the Land*. Santa Barbara, Calif.: Peregrine Smith, 1973.

Mitchell, Daniel J. B. *Pensions, Politics and the Elderly: Historic Social Movements and Their Lessons for Our Aging Society*. New York: M. E. Sharpe, 2000.

Mitchell, Greg. *The Campaign of the Century: Upton Sinclair's Race for Governor and the Birth of Media Politics*. New York: Random House, 1992.

Panunzio, Constantine. *Self-Help Cooperatives in Los Angeles*. Berkeley: University of California Press, 1939.

Phillips-Fein, Kim. *Invisible Hands: The Businessmen's Crusade against the New Deal*. New York: W. W. Norton, 2009.

Putnam, Jackson K. *Old Age Politics in California: From Richardson to Reagan*. Stanford, Calif.: Stanford University Press, 1970.

Schlesinger, Arthur M., Jr. *The Coming of the New Deal, 1933–1935*. Boston: Houghton Mifflin, 1958.

———. *The Crisis of the Old Order, 1919–1933*. Boston: Houghton Mifflin, 1957.

Sinclair, Upton. *I, Candidate for Governor, and How I Got Licked*. Pasadena, Calif.: Author, 1935.

Sitton, Tom. *The Courthouse Crowd: Los Angeles County and Its Government, 1850–1950*. Los Angeles: Historical Society of Southern California, 2013.

Sutton, Matthew Avery. *Aimee Semple McPherson and the Resurrection of Christian America*. Cambridge, Mass.: Harvard University Press, 2007

INDEX

References to illustrations appear in italic type.

ACLU. *See* American Civil Liberties Union
Adamic, Louis, 8–9, 14–15, 21
AFL. *See* American Federation of Labor
African Americans: and Communist Party, 100, 110; and neighborhoods, 93; and OARP, 149; and population, 14; and Sinclair, 171; and unemployed councils, 100–101; and Utopian Society, 115
Alameda Street, *52*
Alexander, N. P., 41
Alhambra, Calif., 6, 15
Allen, Lawrence, 177–79, 181–85, 190–93, 195–96
Allen, Willis, 177–79, 181–85, 190–93, 195
Alliance of Social Agencies, 36
American Civil Liberties Union (ACLU), 81, 96–98, 104, 106–7, 155
American Federation of Labor (AFL), 74, 77, 99–100, 108–9

American Legion, 41–42, 95, 97–98, 104, 106, 115, 119
American Manufacturers Export Association, 181
American Newspaper Guild, 109
American Relief Administration, 84
Angelus Temple, *13*, 87, 89
Appleby, Joyce, 25
Area Conference (of cooperatives), 63–64
Arnoll, Arthur, 83
Arts and Professions Cooperative, 58
Associated City Employees Unemployment Relief Association, 41
Associated Produce Dealers and Brokers, 187
Austin, John, 74

BAF. *See* Better America Federation
Bainbridge, Sherman J., 181–83, 190–91, 196
Baldwin Park, Calif., 195
Barbashano, M. P., 177–78

Barton, Bruce, 130–31
Baxter, Leone, 169
Baylin, Meyer, 95, 101
Baylin, Vera, 95
Beccali, Luigi, 105
Bell, Alphonzo, 18
Bell, Calif., 60, 170, 195
Bell, C. Jasper, 145–47
Bellamy, Edward, 114, 120
Bellflower, Calif., 55
Belvedere Township, Calif., 170
Benjamin, Walter, 73
Berger, George W., 177–78
Berkowitz, Isadore, 95–96
Bernstein, Irving, 41
Better America Federation (BAF), 21, 23, 81–82, 95, 115
Better Government League, 90
Beverly Hills, Calif., 21, 40, 155, 170, 182
Black Thursday, Monday, and Tuesday, 26–27
Bloor, Ella Reeve, 99
Boddy, Manchester, 112
Bogardus, Emory, 22
Bogue, Minnie, 134
Bonelli, William G., 78
Bonus March on Washington (1932), 146
Borough, Reuben, 162
Boudreau, John T., 118, 121
Bowron, Fletcher, 109
Boyle Heights neighborhood, 21, 93–94, 97–98
Briegleb, Gustav A., 11
Bright, William J., 49
Brougher, James Whitcomb, 11
Brown, Bill, 189
Budd, James, 158
Bullocks department store, 122
Burbank, Calif., 20, 198
Burchfield, "Shorty," 54–56
Bureau of Immigration, 47–48, 50
Burns, Fritz B., 17

California Authority for Money (CAM), 160
California Authority for Production (CAP), 159
California Bill of Rights, 195
California Citizens Against 30 Thursday, 192–93
California Club, 89
California Cooperative Units, 69
California Corporations Department, 19
California Criminal Syndicalism Act, 79, 97
California Department of Industrial Relations, 191
California Fair Employment Commission, 91
California Intelligence Service Bureau, 122
California Manufacturers Association, 187
California Pension Plan, 177, 179, 182; promotion of, *178*
California Retailers Association, 187
Call, Asa, 168
Camacho, Manual Avila, 51
Campaigns, Inc., 169
Carlton, Winslow, 65–66, 69
Carnahan, H. L., 25
Carr, W. E., 48
Carson, Reggie, 93
Carter, James S., 47
Catholics, 6, 10, 12, 23, 88, 159
Catholic Welfare Bureau, 34, 42, 87
Cecil, George H., 47
Chamber of Commerce. *See* Los Angeles Chamber of Commerce
Chandler, Harry, 16, 20–21, 78–79, 82–83, 122
Chase, Ezra F., 101
Chesebro, Ray L., 188
churches, 10–14, 21–24, 28, 87–90
Church of All Nations, 21, 23–24, 29, 34

Church of the Blessed Sacrament, 87
Church of the Open Door, 87
Cinema Advertising Agency, 177–79, 185, 191
CIO. *See* Congress of Industrial Organizations
Citizens' Committee on Unemployment Relief, 40, 47, 62
Civilian Conservation Corps, 69, 156
Clark, Eli P., 81
Clements, George P., 50
Clements, Robert Earl, 132–35, 137, 140, 143–48
Cleveland, Ohio, 31, 149
Coker, Robert L., 176
Comintern, 93, 99–100, 102, 109–10
Commerce, Calif., 20
Commission on Industrial Relations, 75
Committee on Economic Security, 142
Committee on Technocracy, 113–14
Commonwealth Party, 166, 180
Communist International. *See* Comintern
Communist Needle Trades Workers Industrial Union, 100
Communist Party, 55, 92–110; demonstrations, *105*
Community Chest, 32, 35–36, 42, 87
Compton, Calif., 15, 21, 54–58, 60, 62, 72, 170, 194
Congress of Industrial Organizations (CIO), 109–10
Connelly, Philip M. "Slim," 109
Continental Committee on Technocracy, 113
Cooney, Patrick J., 165
Coughlin, Charles E., 145, 148–49
Council of Social Agencies, 34
Covell, Mary, 42
Covina, Calif., 136, 138
Creel, George, 164–67, 170, 174

Criminal Syndicalism Act, 79, 125
Cryer, George E., 12, 38, 97

Daley, Marcus, 139
Dalton Auto Loan, 191
Davenport, Walter, 163–64
Davis, James E., 12, 47, 80, 97–98, 108–9, 122, 199
Debs, Eugene V., 153
De Donato, Florian, 122
Dee, Maggie, 180
Democratic Party, 157–59, 162, 164, 166–67, 170–72, 190
Dennis, Peggy, 92–93
department of charities, Los Angeles County, 32–33, 45, 51, 66, 174
Department of Self Help, 70. *See also* Self Help Cooperative Service
Department of Social Service, 22
Dickinson & Gillespie real estate, 17
dining halls, charity, *35*, 58–59
Disabled American War Veterans Association, 54
Doak, William N., 47–48, 50
Doane, Robert R., 142
Dockweiler, Isidore E., 159, 164, 167, 186
Dockweiler, John, 186
Doheny, Edward L., 17
Douglas, C. H., 130
Douglas, Donald, 20
Downey, Calif., 195
Downey, Sheridan, 51, 146, 165–67, 183, 186
Downing, Bill, 55, 57–58
Downtown Business Men's Association, 41
Dubin, Maxwell, 88
Durant, Will, 88
Dwinell, Olive Cushing, 176

East Los Angeles, 49, 137, 170, 189
Echo Park, 12

Einstein, Albert, 152
El Cerrito, Calif., 170
Elliot, John B., 175
Ellis, Mr. (of Utopian Society), 113–14
El Monte, Calif., 49, 60, 125, 189
El Segundo, Calif., 20
End Poverty in California (EPIC), 5, 65, 71, 146, 151, 159–73, 176, 181, 197; promotion of, *160*, *163*
End Poverty League, 171–73
EPIC. *See* End Poverty in California
EPIC News, 162, 164, 171–72
Epstein, Edward, 141
Evans, William E., 139

Fair Employment Commission, 91
Farmers Holiday Association, 198
Federal Emergency Relief Administration (FERA), 63–65, 67–68, 70
Federal Radio and Television Corporation, 177–78
Federal Resettlement Administration, 125
Federal Surplus Relief Corporation, 69
Federal Transient Service, 69
Federal Writers Project, 181–82
Fenton, Stanley, 62
Fielder, Charles N., 118
Fifield, James W., Jr., 88–91
Firestone Boulevard, 52
Firestone Tire and Rubber Company, 20, 83, 109, 194
Fisher, Irving, 130, 176–77
Fitts, Buron, 92
Fogelson, Robert M., 4, 72
Food Administration, Los Angeles County, 63
Ford, Henry, 88
Ford, John Anson, 51, 65, 200
Fremming, Harvey, 39–40
Friends of Progress, 196
Friends of the Soviet Union, 104, 108

Frisbie, James, 189
Fritz, Raymond D., 185

Galalian, Vratian, 103
Galbraith, John Kenneth, 24
Gallagher, Leo, 104, 106
Garland, Arthur H., 25
Gartz, Kate Crane, 154
Gast, Ross, 126
General Motors, 109
Giannini, A. P., 27
Gillette, King, 152
Glendale, Calif., 15, 65–66, 71
Glendon, Jonathan F., 118–19, 121, 127
Golos, M. J., 93
Gould, Arthur, 94
Great Sedition Trial of 1944, 196
Griffith, D. W., 20

Hadfield, H. R., 113
Haight, Raymond, 166, 168
Haldeman, Harry M., 81, 209n18
Haldeman, H. R., 209n18
Hama, Karl, 106
Ham and Eggs movement, 5, 121, 174, 180, 182–95, 197, 200
Hanna, Byron Calvin, 84
Harding, Warren G., 84
Harriman, William R., 45, 53
Hartley, Forrest, 114
Hawthorne, Calif., 170, 195
Healey, Dorothy Ray, 101, 107
Helicon Hall, 152, 169
Highley, George, 138, 146
Hill, Ricardo, 49
Holizer, Harry, 108
Holland, William H., 32, 42–45, 53
Hollis, James B., 113–14
Hollywood, 16–17, 20, 106, 177, 184–85
Hollywood Assistance League, 58
Hollywood Bowl, 19, 118, 120, 127, 164, 168

Hollywood Hills, 16
Hoover, Herbert, 26, 28, 30, 53, 82, 84, 159
Hoovervilles (squatter settlements), 52, 53, 58
Hopkins, Harry, 142
How, Ingeborg, 30
How, James Eads, 29–30
Hughes, Charles Evans, 96
Hughes, W. B., 70
Hunt, John W., 182
Huntington Beach, Calif., 17
Huntington Park, Calif., 21, 55, 60, 62, 137, 194
Hynes, William "Red," 80, 98–99, 101, 103–4, 106, 108

I, Candidate for Governor: And How I Got Licked (Sinclair), 171
I, Governor of California and How I Ended Poverty: A True Story of the Future (Sinclair), 157–58, 160, 162
Illustrated Daily News, 112
Industrial Workers of the World (IWW), 62, 79, 97–98, 153–54
Inglewood, Calif., 15, 176, 188
Ingram, E. Snapper, 30
Insull, Samuel, 85
Intelligence Bureau (LAPD), 97–98
International Association of Bridge and Structural Iron Workers, 77
International Brotherhood Welfare Association, 29–30
International Labor Defense, 103
International Ladies Garment Workers Union, 100
International Typographical Union, 75–76
International Unemployed Conference, 29
International Unemployment Day, 102
IWW. *See* Industrial Workers of the World

Japanese Americans, 21, 55, 93
Jewish Social Service Bureau, 34, 42, 87
Jews, 23, 87–88, 94; anti-Semitic attitudes toward, 10, 12, 94, 97–98, 114, 185, 196; and neighborhoods, 21, 93
John Reed Club, 106
Johnson, George H., 95
Jones, Harry L., 63–65
Julian, C. C., 18–19

Karasick, Berta, 93–94
Karasick, Meyer, 93–94
Karasick, Regina "Reggie," 93–94, 96
Kennedy, Aimée Elizabeth, 12
Kennedy, David M., 3
Kennedy, Merritt T., 111–14, 116, 121–23
Kerr, Clark, 55–58, 60, 64, 67
Kindig, William, 165, 175, 192
KMTR radio, 179, 191
Kraft, F. H., 27
Ku Klux Klan, 10, 12, 14, 158
Kynette, Earle, 178–81, 190–91

Lamont, Thomas W., 26–27
Leader, Leonard, 4
League of Homeless Youth, 101
League of Women Voters, 85
Legg, Herbert C., 65
Lemke, William, 133, 148–49
Lewis, Evan, 30
Lewis, John (of Elwood, Ind.), 198
Lewis, John L. (head of CIO), 109
Lewis, Samuel L., 112
Lieberman, E. Louis, 97
Ling, Benjamin, 97
Llewellyn, John, 76
Llewellyn, Reese, 81
Llewellyn Iron Works, 76, 81
Lockheed Aircraft, 20
Long, Huey, 148, 176

Long Beach, Calif., 5, 17, 20, 131–32, 134–36, 166, 194; and population, 5–6, 15, 131, 135
Los Angeles Bar Association, 107
Los Angeles Chamber of Commerce, 19–21, 35, 43, 50, 76–77, 79–83, 87, 97–98, 109
Los Angeles City Council, 29–30, 38, 40–41, 47, 62, 106, 124, 193
Los Angeles County, map of, 16
Los Angeles Credit Men's Association, 187
Los Angeles Harbor, 8, 18, 98, 153
Los Angeles Herald, 78–79
Los Angeles Ministerial Association, 107
Los Angeles Nationalist Club, 120
Los Angeles Oil Exchange, 19
Los Angeles Plaza, 8–9, 49, 102, 108
Los Angeles Police Department, 47, 49, 80, 95, 97–99, 103, 106–8, 115, 154, 199
Los Angeles River, 4, 29, 52–53, 93
Los Angeles Stock Exchange, 19, 25, 27
Los Angeles Times: bombing of, 76–77; and Chandler, 78–79; and communism, 102–3, 106; and Great Depression, 36, 82, 106; and Ham and Eggs movement, 187–88, 190; and McGroarty, 139–41; and open shop, 74, 77–78; and Otis, 75; and self-help, 59; and Sinclair, 168–70; and stock market collapse, 26–28, 30; and unemployment, 30–33; and Utopian Society, 115, 120–21
Los Angeles Tribune, 79
Lyman, C. A., 35
Lynwood, Calif., 60, 170, 194

MacArthur, Douglas, 88, 196
Macbeth, Hugh, 115, 125–26
Malthus, Thomas, 155
Man-a-Block program, 39
Mangold, George, 34
Margett, Ed J., 147–48
Marine Transport Workers Industrial Union, 153
Martin, Glenn, 20
May, Pat, 62–63, 65
Mayer, Louis B., 169
Mayo, Morrow, 2–3
Maywood, Calif., 60, 170, 194
McAdoo, William Gibbs, 158–59, 167, 170, 186, 188
McCord, Stewart, 130
McDonough, Gordon, 65
McGroarty, John S., 37, 139–46
McKibben, Robert A., 24
McNamara, James, 77
McNamara, John J., 77
McPherson, Aimee Semple, 3, 11–12, *13*, 14, 19, 21, 35, 87
McPherson, Harold, 12
McWilliams, Carey, 1, 4, 7, 115, 126, 175, 197–98
Mencken, H. L., 2, 19, 21, 72
Men's Club of Beverly Hills, 155
Merchants and Manufacturers Association (M&M), 21, 75–77, 79, 154
Merriam, Frank F., 69, 71, 141, 166, 168–70, 190
Methodist Ministers Association, 107
Metropolitan Life Insurance Company, 31
Mexican Americans: and census, 203n12; and deportation, 48–51, 199; and neighborhoods, 21–22, 49, 93
Miami, Fla., 15
Midnight Mission, 23, 34, 42, 46–47
Miller, Loren, 104
Mission Playhouse, 139
M&M. *See* Merchants and Manufacturers Association
Moffat, Stanley, 118

INDEX

Monrovia, Calif., 6
Montebello, Calif., 17
Mooney, Tom, 105
Moore, Marian, 176, 181, 185
Moore, Viola, 179–80
Moore, Winston, 176, 181, 185
Morgenthau, Henry, 188
Morrison, Frank, 99
Mullendore, William Clinton, 84–86
Municipal League, 38, 107
Murphy, Foghorn, 191
Murphy, Thomas J., 168
Mussolini, Benito, 64, 88

National Association of Manufacturers, 90
National Foundation of the Utopian Society of the United States, 114–15, 121
National Recovery Administration, 85, 165
Nazis, 98, 185, 196
Needle Trades Workers Industrial Union, 100, 103
New Deal, 53, 83; and Fifield, 89–90; and Glendon, 119; and Mullendore, 85; and Sinclair, 155–56, 163; and Townsend, 129, 145, 148
Newman Methodist Episcopal Church, 22–23
Nicolaides, Becky M., 16
Noble, Robert, 176–79, *180*, 182–84, 190–92, 196
Noble News, 177, 180
Norris, George W., 85

Oaks, Louis D., 154
OARP. *See* Old Age Revolving Pensions, Ltd.
O'Hare, Kate Richards, 173
Olachea, Augustín, 51
Old Age Revolving Pensions, Ltd. (OARP), 135, 137–40, 143, 145–47, 149, 197

Olson, Culbert L., 71, 167, 171–72, 183, 186, 190–92, 195
Olson, Floyd B., 198
Olympic Auditorium, *136*, 145
Olympics, 104–5, 118
open shop, 21, 74–77, 79, 84
Otis, Harrison Gray, 75–79, 139
Otto, Richard S., 161–62, 171–73
Oursler, Fulton, 158, 171
Owen, Russell, 132
Owens, Roy G., 118, 121, 175, 181–84, 190–92, 195–96
Oxnam, G. Bromley, 21–24
Oxnam, Thomas Henry, 21–22

Palmer, A. Mitchell, 96
Palmer, Kyle D., 9
Panunzio, Constantine, 56–57, 198
Parrot, Kent, 12, 38
Pasadena, Calif., 6, 45, 151–52, 164
Patterson, Ellis, 186
Patton, Carl Safford, 88
Pauper Act, 33, 46
Pay Roll Guarantee Association, 195
Penney, J. C., 88, 90
Pension and Taxpayers Union, 195
Pension and Welfare Funding Act, 196
Pepperdine, George, 88
Peterson, Frank, 142
Pew, J. Howard, Jr., 91
Phelan, James D., 159
Pierce, Mark, 106
Pinchot, Gifford, 85
Pomeroy, Harold, 70
Pomona, Calif., 6
Popular Front, 109–10
Porter, John Clinton, 9–10, 25, 28, 40, 47, 62–63, 97, 102–3, 107
Porter, Lee, 103
Portland, Ore., 6
Price, Archie, 183–84
Prohibition, 10, 25, 158–59
Proposition 1 (1939), 192, 194
Proposition 6 (1950), 196

Proposition 25 (1938), 175–76, 183–84, 187, 190
Protestants, 6, 9, 11, 13, 23, 87–89, 158
Public Utility Holding Company Act, 124
Putnam, Jackson K., 4, 168, 175, 190

Quinn, John Robertson, 39, 43–44, 48

Rauschenbusch, Walter, 22
Raymond, Harry, 181
Read, Leonard, 85
Reausaw, Walter, 111–14, 121, 123
Red Cross, 42, 59
Red Scare, 96–97
Red Squad, 80, 95, 97–98, 101, 104, 106–9
Reed, Eugene J., 111–12, 114, 116, 121–23
Reed, John, 106
Retirement Life Payments Act, 175, 182, 185, 187, 189, 192, 197
Revelations (Utopian Society publication), 116, 124, 126
Ricardo, David, 82, 155
Riggs, Alonzo J., 121
Righteous Government Act of 1936, 182
Riley, James Whitcomb, 94
Roberts, Horace D., 101
Rogers, Stanley, 10–11
Rogers, Will, 40
Rolph, James, 161, 166
Roosevelt, Eleanor, 165
Roosevelt, Franklin D.: election of, 53, 112, 158–59; and first hundred days, 63, 83–85; and Ham and Eggs, 188; and Sinclair, 163, 166–68; and Townsend, 140–41, 144–45, 148–49; and Utopian Society, 125
Ryan, Reggie, 93
Ryland, E. P., 22

Salazar, Rodolfo, 51
Salvation Army, 34, 42, 47, 62, 101
Samson Tire and Rubber Company, 20
San Diego, Calif., 6, 135, 183
San Fernando, Calif., 125
San Francisco, Calif., 15, 19, 105, 114, 164, 166
San Gabriel, Calif., 139
San Marino, Calif., 21, 170
San Pedro, Calif., 8, 15, 21, 23, 103
San Quentin Penitentiary, 95, 105, 125, 181
Santa Fe Springs, Calif., 17–18
Santa Monica, Calif., 6, 14
Schenck, Joseph M., 169
Schiller, Bob, 189
Schindler, Rudolph M., 29
Schlesinger, Arthur M., Jr., 3, 168
Schneiderman, William, 94, 99–100
Scott, Howard, 112
Scott, Joseph, 42, 89
Seattle Labor College, 56
Seattle Unemployed Citizens' League, 56
Security First National Bank, 88
self-help cooperatives, 54–60, *61*, 62–67, 71–72, 157
Self Help Cooperative Service, 65, 67, 69–71
Selig, William N., 20
Sellers, Horace B., 87
Semple, Robert, 12
Senate Finance Committee, 141, 145
SERA. *See* State Emergency Relief Administration
Shaw, Frank Leslie, 38–40, 42–45, 50, 63, 82, 108–9, 179, 181, 205n1
Sheinman, B. J., 108
Shell Oil Company, 17
Shrine Auditorium, 118, 123, 190
Shuler, Robert P., 10–14, 19, 21
Signal Hill, 17–18

Sinclair, Craig, 151–52, 157–58
Sinclair, David, 157
Sinclair, Upton, 3, 23, 65, 151–59, *160*, 161–76, 189
Sklar, Carl, 102
Smith, Adam, 152
Smith, Al, 12
Smith, C. C., 71
Smith, Clyde E., 135–37
Smith, Gerald L. K., 133, 148–49
Smith, Gomer, 149
Smith, Herbert Booth, 11
Smith, Leroy F., 23, 81
Smith, Maxwell P., 113–14, 122
Socialist Party, 41, 92–93, 153, 157–59, 198–99
Social Security Act, 7, 191
Southern California Restaurant Association, 187
Southern California Retail Council, 187
Southern California Wholesale Grocery Distributors Association, 187
South Gate, Calif., 21, 55, 60, 70, 118, 164, 170, 194
South Pasadena, Calif., 21, 170
Sparks, Fred, 125
Sparks Plan, 125
Spiritual Mobilization, 90–91
SRA. *See* State Relief Administration
Standard Oil Company, 17, 20
State Emergency Relief Administration (SERA), 63, 65
State Relief Administration (SRA), 46, 63, 69–71
Steckel, Roy E., 47–48, 98, 102
Steele, C. K., 41
Stevens, W. Bernard, 88
Stevenson, Gilbert, 157
Stimson, Grace Heilman, 76
stock market, 18–19; and crash of 1929, 24–28, 92

St. Petersburg, Fla., 15
Stromberg, Yetta, 95–96
Subversive Organization Registration Act, 196
Swing, Ralph E., 170
Sykes, James, 78

Taft, Clinton J., 98, 106
Technocracy movement, 112–14, 116–17, 119, 121, 127–30
Thalberg, Irving, 169
Third Period, 100, 102, 104, 109–10
$30 Every Thursday, 183, 188, 197
Thomas, Martin Luther, 10
Thompson, James Carlile, 41
Thomson, Rex, 51, 66, 199–200
Tilden, Freeman, 6
Tilden, Samuel, 159
Tomlinson, Pierre, 135–37
Toplitzky, Joe, 26
Townsend, Francis E., 128–35, *136*, 137–50, 168, 196
Townsend, Robert, 149
Townsend, Walter, 135
Townsend clubs, 137–39, 141, 143–44, 146
Townsend National Legion, 144
Townsend National Recovery Plan, Inc., 149
Townsend Plan, 5, 128–50, 168, 174, 176, 185
Townsend Weekly, 144, 148, 196
Trade Union Educational League (TUEL), 99
Trade Union Unity League (TUUL), 100, 103, 109
Traeger, William I., 48
Trinity Methodist Church, 10–11, 13
Twenty-Five Dollars Every Monday Morning, 177, 182; promotion of, *178*
Tygiel, Jules, 19

Unemployed Aid Society, 55
Unemployed Cooperative Distribution Association (UCDA), 64–65
Unemployed Cooperative Relief Association (UCRA), 60–62, 64
Unemployed Council of America, 101
Union Party, 148–49
Union Rescue Mission, 34, 87
University of California, Los Angeles (UCLA), 56, 80, 189
University of Southern California (USC), 22, 184
Utopian National Dated Money, 121, 182
Utopian News, 122
Utopian Society, 5, 111–27, 135, 165, 182, 185, 197

Van Dalsem, Newton, 117–21
Vandenburg, Arthur H., 88
Venegas, Miguel, 49
Vermillion, Inez, 25
Visel, Charles P., 40, 47–50
Voorhis, Jerry, 157, 171

Waldron, Frank, 96, 102
Waldron, Webb, 164
Ward, Harry F., 22
Wardell, Justus, 158–59, 167

Warmbold, Walter, 147
Watkins, William F., 48–49
Watson, Emmet H., 108
The Way Out (Sinclair), 155–56
Wenk, John G., 123–26
West, Nathanael, 2–3, 72
Whitaker, Clem, 169, 193–94
Whiteman, Luther, 112
Wickersham Commission, 107
Willys-Overland, 20
Wilshire, H. Gaylord, 120
Wilson, Edmund, 2, 11–12, 21, 72
Wilson, Woodrow, 153, 158
Wirin, A. L., 155
Witte, Edwin, 142–43
Woll, Matthew, 99
Woman-a-Block program, 39
Workers Ex-Service Men's League, 106
Workers Party of America, 99
Works Progress Administration, 70
Wright, Charles F., 193
Wright, Willard Huntington, 6
Wunder, Clinton, 144

Yoneda, Karl, 106
Young Communist League (YCL), 94–95

Zeehandelaar, Felix J., 75–76, 79

www.ingramcontent.com/pod-product-compliance
Lightning Source LLC
Chambersburg PA
CBHW020835160426
43192CB00007B/660